How to Do *Everything* with Your

Sony VAIO

C000300964

How to Do *Everything* with Your

Sony VAIO®

Tom Dunlap

McGraw-Hill/Osborne

New York Chicago San Francisco Lisbon
London Madrid Mexico City Milan New Delhi
San Juan Seoul Singapore Sydney Toronto

McGraw-Hill/Osborne
2100 Powell Street, 10th Floor
Emeryville, California 94608
U.S.A.

To arrange bulk purchase discounts for sales promotions, premiums, or fund-raisers, please contact **McGraw-Hill**/Osborne at the above address. For information on translations or book distributors outside the U.S.A., please see the International Contact Information page immediately following the index of this book.

How to Do Everything with Your Sony VAIO®

1234567890 FGR FGR 01987654

ISBN 0-07-223137-8

Publisher	Brandon A. Nordin
Vice President &	
Associate Publisher	Scott Rogers
Acquisitions Editor	Marjorie McAneny
Senior Project Editor	LeeAnn Pickrell
Acquisitions Coordinator	Agatha Kim
Contributor	Stephanie Bruzzese
Technical Editors	Stephanie Bruzzese, Brian Nadel
Photographer	Jody Gianni
Copy Editor	Mike McGee
Proofreaders	Susie Elkind, LeeAnn Pickrell
Indexer	Valerie Haynes Perry
Composition	International Typesetting and Composition
Illustrator	International Typesetting and Composition
Cover Series Design	Dodie Shoemaker

VAIO images courtesy of Sony Electronics, Inc.

This book was composed with Corel VENTURA™ Publisher.

Dedication

For Charlotte and Paul

About the Author

Tom Dunlap has been a journalist for the past 15 years in the San Francisco Bay Area. After stints at the *Oakland Tribune* and other daily newspapers, his wife coaxed him into the world of technology and computers, where he's been for more than a decade. Tom is now a senior editor at CNET Networks, specializing in notebook computers and mobile technology. His writing, editing, and online product videos appear regularly on CNET.com and ZDNet.com, with his writing and editing also showing up in *Computer Shopper,* the *San Francisco Chronicle,* MSN.com, and elsewhere. He's a notebook guru of sorts, often quoted in other publications such as CBSMarketwatch.com. Tom holds a degree in journalism and lives in California with his wife and son.

About the Contributing Writer and Technical Editor

Stephanie Bruzzese has reviewed hundreds of laptops and PCs since 1997—first as a CNET senior editor, and then as a freelance writer and editor. Her work has also appeared in *PC World* and *Fortune,* among other publications. She currently lives in the San Francisco Bay Area and spends her free time with her horse.

About the Technical Editor

Brian Nadel is a freelance writer specializing in technology. He is the former Editor-in-Chief of *Mobile Computing Magazine,* and his work can be seen on CNET.com and in *Computer Shopper, PC Magazine,* and *Laptop Magazine.* Brian is based in suburban New York City.

Contents at a Glance

Contents

Acknowledgments

Thanks mostly to Stephanie Bruzzese, my contributing writer and technical editor, for her stamina and pluck. Many thanks to the pros at Osborne, including Margie McAneny, LeeAnn Pickrell, Agatha Kim, and Mike McGee.

Thanks to CNET's photographer, Jody Gianni, who contributed many shots to this book including the cover, and to my other contributing writers and editors Brian Nadel and Jon L. Jacobi. Finally, I owe a big thanks to the contributors of the "Voices from the Community" sidebars, including Steve Alimonti, Annalee Newitz, Darrell Whitworth, and Victor Chen.

Introduction

Any book dedicated to the proposition that Sony VAIO laptops and PCs are unique, brilliant, versatile machines naturally runs the risk of sounding like a brochure. But the fact is the first purplish VAIO notebooks sparked a huge reaction in the tech world, and the latest models are even far more advanced, cutting-edge, sleek-looking, sought-after (choose your adjective) than the first generation VAIOs. So a VAIO book is warranted, nay, demanded by the circumstances.

This book is meant to guide you through the new breeds of Sony VAIO and be your guide to the things that you'll need to know to set up, use, travel with, and maintain your new machine. Beyond that, I introduce many of Sony's excellent multimedia applications and cover a wide variety of topics, ranging from how to fight spam and set up a home network to how to record live TV, make your own movies, and copy a DVD.

I divided the book into four parts. In Part I, "Getting Started," you'll do exactly that. We first examine the different VAIO models, including Sony's latest. Then I give you a taste of all the different cool things you can do with your VAIO and give you some tips on setting up your system for the first time. In Chapter 1, I also introduce the first of the "Voices from the Community" sidebars, this one from VAIO-toting San Francisco journalist Annalee Newitz. Once you have the bare basics down, we get to work with a tour of the hardware and unique benefits of Sony VAIOs.

In Part II, "Everyday Stuff with Your VAIO," you'll learn how to configure and tweak your system to your liking, transfer files from your old computer, install and remove hardware, and more. You'll learn how to get connected to the Internet, send e-mail, beef up your defenses against spam, and how to interact with hundreds of online forums in the untamed world of newsgroups. This part of the book includes a "Voices from the Community Sidebar" from a managing editor in Budapest, Hungary.

The pace picks up in Part III, "Cool Things to Do with Your VAIO." In that section, you'll be introduced to some of the most cutting-edge things you can do with your VAIO, including hooking up your camcorder, editing your own movies, and burning them to a blank DVD. You'll learn how to use the little camera that's built into the VAIO TR Series notebook. You'll be introduced to Sony programs like DVGate Plus, Click to DVD, and Giga Pocket, which allow you to do a myriad of things, including watching, recording, and editing live TV shows on your computer. If you want to play games on your VAIO, I've got the basics covered in Chapter 14. If you're curious about copying a DVD, consult the color spotlight section on that topic. This part of the book includes a "Voices from the Community Sidebar" from the gentleman who created and runs the Sony TR World online forum.

In Part IV, "Upgrading, Maintaining, and Troubleshooting Your VAIO," we look at performing preventative maintenance on your new toy, as well as examining Sony's many warranty options. We also cover keeping your data safe, preventing data loss, and where to find help in the unlikely event of a water landing.

This book is written in a casual, easy-to-read style. It's designed so that you can read the whole thing cover to cover, or use it as a reference to learn how to do specific tasks. To make this book easy and quick, you'll find the following features:

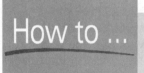

Check out these boxes for fast and easy information about certain tasks.

These boxes give you extra information about a variety of topics. Check these out as you read each chapter.

Get a fresh perspective on the VAIO universe with these tales from Sony users.

 *These icons point out quick, helpful information.*

 These icons provide additional information you might need.

 *These icons flag things that you need to be aware of to avoid potential problems.*

Can't get enough of me (and who could blame you)? Go to CNET.com or ZDNET.com for my stories and online product videos. You can also send questions to tomd@cnet.com.

Part I

Getting Started

Chapter 1

Meet Your Sony VAIO

How to...

- Examine your VAIO hardware
- Learn the different VAIO models
- Decide between a laptop or PC
- Find out which models I like and why

Watch, pause, or record live TV on your PC or notebook. Turn heads with a drop-dead gorgeous, 2-pound laptop. Convert your camcorder movies to DVD. Wirelessly log on to the Internet and crank for seven hours on a battery. Store and play thousands of songs. Easily convert your old VHS tapes to DVD. Create a wired or wireless home network. Snap, and then e-mail pictures with a small digital camera that's built in to the top of a 3-pound notebook, or use that camera as a *web cam*. Master some of the best multimedia software anywhere.

In other words, welcome to the world of Sony VAIO notebooks and PCs. Thanks to many remarkable advancements in computing, every item in the preceding list (and much more) can be accomplished with either a VAIO notebook or PC (although not all Sony laptops and desktops will include every one of those skills). Since you're reading this book, you've probably bought yourself a VAIO, or you're thinking about buying one, or your company provided you with one. Whichever the case may be, you obviously want to get the most out of your new toy (or tool) that you can.

NOTE *Besides being a catchy word, VAIO is also an acronym, meaning Video Audio Integrated Operation.*

In the pages and chapters to come, you'll learn the differences between the models in the VAIO universe, and, of course, learn everything you need to know about using them. To do that, you'll need a basic understanding of your shiny new machine, the Windows XP Home or Pro operating system that runs on it, and other software like Sony's robust multimedia applications. So let's start at the beginning, by exploring that new machine.

Examine Your VAIO Hardware

When you take your Sony VAIO out of the box, spend some time looking it over. Depending on what you bought, you may be fondling a sleek, 2-pound notebook, a big, powerful desktop computer, or something in between. You might have the three-pound TR Series portable (Figure 1-1), which early in 2004 added a built-in

FIGURE 1-1   The VAIO TR Series is a 3-pound notebook with a built-in camera above the screen.

DVD-burner to its arsenal. Or you might have snapped up the popular, curvy Z1 Series laptop (Figure 1-2) or the new A Series notebook, which features a 17-inch screen. Or you might have bought the all-in-one V Series PC (Figure 1-3) or the powerhouse RZ Series PC (Figure 1-4). Laptops take minimal setup, but PCs are another ball of wax; all those hunks of metal, components, cords, pamphlets, manuals, and whatnot can seem daunting at first. How do you hook it all up? Here's some basic advice:

- Don't be in a rush. Expect to spend at least an hour setting everything up, depending on how many extras you have.

- Remove all the wrappings and save them in the box. You'll need that box in case you need to return your VAIO for repair.

- You might need a small screwdriver, usually a standard head type, for securing connectors at the end of cables.

- You need a good place to sit your VAIO, preferably with plenty of room to work.

- Place it near an AC wall outlet, or find an extension cord, or better yet a power strip that reaches the outlet.

- Consider a *surge protector,* also called a power strip, if you live in an area that has unreliable electricity or is vulnerable to spikes (big increases in line voltage that happen very quickly, such as from lightning strikes). If your friend Serge is bothering you, however, get a *Serge protector.*

FIGURE 1-3   The unique curve design of the VAIO Z1 Series includes room on the side for ports.

FIGURE 1-2   The V Series is Sony's latest all-in-one PC—the guts of the system are behind the screen, not in a separate tower. It includes a wireless mouse, keyboard, and remote control.

Voices from the Community The Journalist

I'm a journalist, so most of my time is spent writing articles or doing research on the go. I often travel to interview people and do a lot of my work on wireless networks in cafés or hotels. So I need a light laptop that I can fit in my backpack— and it has to have enough battery power to allow me to spend hours writing in places with no outlets.

I've had a Sony VAIO Z505 since 2001, and my little purple ultralight laptop has survived many adventures unscathed. It's traveled to England, the U.S., Canada, and Cuba. Although it came to me running Windows, I knew I couldn't endure that for long, so I took the whole thing apart, removed the hard drive to format it with Red Hat Linux, and then reflashed the BIOS. I also added 128MB of memory. My trusty VAIO made it through its OS upgrade without any problems, and now I can run Open Office, as well as many lovely UNIX utilities. With my VAIO, I can surf the Web, write, and use Nmap all at the same time. I never go anywhere without it.

—Annalee Newitz is a writer living in San Francisco. Her column appears in the SF Bay Guardian *and in* Metro, *Silicon Valley's weekly newspaper. Her web site is www.techsploitation.com.*

FIGURE 1-4 The RZ Series is one of Sony's fastest, most-versatile PCs. It includes Windows Media Center Edition 2004 and Sony's own Giga Pocket DVR software for recording and pausing live TV. (Learn about that software in Chapter 13.)

 *The first time you turn on your VAIO, Windows will walk you through some setup procedures. Just follow the onscreen instructions and answer the questions and you should be done with that process shortly. If you're required to enter a new username and password, make sure you write down this information so you can log back on.*

 *You shouldn't turn off your VAIO by hitting the power switch, unplugging the machine from the wall, or anything like that. If you don't want to risk losing data and playing havoc with your computer, you need to follow the proper steps for shutting down. See "Turn Off Your VAIO" in Chapter 3.*

An Overview of the Different VAIO Models

When it comes to naming notebooks, PCs, and other devices like the Sony Clie handhelds, Sony can be a tad alphabet-soup crazy. (To be fair, most computer makers have this affliction.) Here's how it works: If you're interested in the TR Series notebook, you'll actually be buying the VAIO PCG-TR3AP1, or something similar. If you want the V505 Series notebook, you'll actually get the VAIO PCG-V505EC, or something close to that. If you bought a slightly different version of those notebooks in 2003, or if you bought them in Japan, it may be called something else. Unfortunately, that name will likely change shortly, too, even if the notebook only gets a slight internal upgrade. It can be confusing, but just try to focus on the series name. Further complicating matters, Sony updates its notebook and PC lines several times a year, and sometimes it kills or adds an entire series. For instance, the VAIO GRT Series notebook—for years Sony's biggest and one of its most popular portables—is in the process of being phased out and replaced by the new, even larger A Series.

VAIO Notebooks

Not every Sony notebook over the past seven years has been a roaring success, but the notebooks have maintained an incredible cachet in the portable world and are very popular. Walk into a crowded Internet café and you're bound to see a distinct-looking, purplish VAIO fired up and wirelessly logged onto the Internet. Or just whisper "VAIO" to a young computer user and gauge his or her reaction. Or do what I did: write a story on the VAIO X505 (a tiny, 1.7-pound laptop nicknamed Extreme, sold only in Japan at the time) at the January 2004 Consumer Electronics Show in Las Vegas, post the story online, and watch the clicks skyrocket and the e-mail pour in. Who am I? I've been a journalist for 15 years, the last 6 as a Senior Editor at CNET Networks (www.cnet.com), covering notebooks, tablet PCs, software, accessories, and other topics. My work appears across the CNET Network: on CNET.com, ZDNET.com, in *Computer Shopper Magazine*, and on web sites or in newspapers where CNET has a content deal (for instance, *The San Francisco Chronicle* and MSN.com).

But enough about me. My point is VAIO notebooks are very in-demand items, and they helped the industry cross an important threshold in 2003: Sales of laptop computers in U.S. stores outpaced those of desktop computers for the first time in May 2003, according to a survey by market research firm The NPD Group. Laptops accounted for more than 54 percent of the nearly $500 million in retail computer sales in May of last year, the company said. Check the table for a few key specs of these distinct portables.

Notebook	Weight (.lbs)	Screen Size (inches, diagonal)	Processor
X505 Series	Under 2 (Exact weight not confirmed at press time)	10.4	Intel Pentium M Ultra Low Voltage
U101 Series*	1.9	7.1	Intel Celeron 600A
TR Series	3.1	10.6	Intel Pentium M Ultra Low Voltage
Z1 Series	4.7	14.1	Intel Pentium M
V505 Series	4.3	12.1	Intel Pentium M
K Series	7.3	15	Intel Pentium 4 or Mobile Pentium 4
A Series	7.9	17	Intel Pentium M
FRV Series**	7.7	15	Intel Pentium 4
GRT Series**	7.7	15 or 16.1	Intel Pentium 4, Mobile Pentium 4, or Celeron

*At the time of this writing, Sony sold this notebook only in Japan, although, you can buy it from small companies that import Japanese products. See the sidebar "Did you know? Where to Buy Rare Japanese Notebooks" later in this chapter.

**Sony is phasing out this series.

VAIO Desktops

Sony has five lines of multimedia-friendly PCs. Three are the traditional tower-and-separate-monitor setups, while two are *all-in-ones,* where the guts of the PC are connected to the back of the screen and there's no separate tower. The following are just a few of the basics of the five PC lines.

Desktop Model	Processor	Hard Drive	Memory
RA Series	Intel Pentium 4	250GB	512MB to 2GB
RZ Series*	Intel Pentium 4	80 to 250GB	512MB to 2GB
RS Series	Intel Pentium 4	80 to 250GB	256MB to 2GB
V Series	Intel Pentium 4	120GB	512MB to 1GB
W Series	Intel Pentium 4	160GB	512MB to 1GB

*Sony is phasing out this series.

Laptop vs. Desktop PC: Which Is Better?

For many, the convenience and ease of using a notebook computer far outweighs the need for the expansion options and power a desktop computer offers. It's a lot easier to set up a notebook, too. Just plug it in and go. You don't need to mess with all those cables, *and* you can take it on the road. For me, the notebook-or-PC question is an easy one. I've been using a portable computer since the early 1990s, and I wrote this book on a few different portables. We're an all-notebook household: my wife and son only use portables. If you haven't decided which world to enter, here's a quick snapshot of the differences between notebooks and PCs. I explore them more fully in Chapter 2.

Laptops

You may be concerned about the small size of the display or the keyboard, but those really are not a concern. A full-sized VAIO GRT Series notebook has a 16-inch screen, the new A Series has a 17-inch display, and both sport a full-sized keyboard

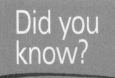

Did you know?

Where to Buy
Rare Japanese Notebooks

Whether made by Sony, Panasonic, Toshiba, Fujitsu, or others, consumer electronics in Japan are the most innovative and advanced in the world, like the aforementioned VAIO X505 or U101 laptop. Products that might never come to market in the U.S. because they're too niche-oriented or pricey, regularly appear on Japanese shelves. Luckily, a few U.S. companies resell the products in this country, often bundling things like lifetime toll-free technical support. Among this cadre of resellers are Dynamism.com and MobilePlanet.com.

Did you know?

My Favorite VAIOs

When I wrote this book, I hadn't been lucky enough to spend quality time with Sony's new stable of VAIOs, announced in May 2004. I'm most interested in the desktop replacement VAIO A Series, which looked stunning in demos. But among the VAIO notebooks I *do* know well, the Z1 Series and GRT Series are my two favorites. Why? Well, for traveling, my favorite class of notebooks are sometimes called *thin-and-lights,* and the Z1 is one of the best. They're a little bigger than one of Sony's smallest notebooks, the popular TR Series, and so have a bigger 14.1-inch screen and bigger keyboard. I also like the 3-pound TR Series for travel and for its cool built-in camera, but I need a bigger keyboard for serious typing.

The GRT Series, until recently Sony's biggest notebook, kicks butt on multimedia applications and is great for watching or burning CDs or DVDs, or for recording TV shows with Sony's Giga Pocket application. It's a perfect desktop replacement for the den or kitchen. I'll explore those multimedia and disc-burning features more in later chapters. When it comes to VAIO PCs, I'm partial to the power and options you get with the souped-up RZ Series and new RA Series. I also like the all-in-one V Series. In my book, Sony's V Series is a better all-in-one than its sister, the W Series, because the W Series includes an attached keyboard, while the V Series' keyboard roams free, wirelessly.

(although it doesn't have the dedicated number pad over on the right side—number crunchers like those). And you can always plug in an external keyboard, mouse, and monitor. Laptops also produce less radiation than desktops, and they save energy. Laptops are perfect for watching DVDs on the commuter train or plane, an increasingly popular pastime, judging by how many of my fellow train commuters are watching movies on their notebooks as we chug toward San Francisco. On the other hand, some of the huge 9-pound desktop replacement notebooks should probably stay on your desk or kitchen counter as much as possible.

Desktops

If you need serious expansion, specialized video cards or sound cards, a bigger hard drive or display than a typical laptop's, or plan to use your computer as a network server or media server, then get a desktop machine. Also, if you want the fastest

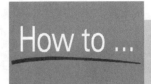

How to ... Decide Which Model to Buy

Sorry... I can't get too specific on this one. So many great VAIOs, so little time. Every model has it merits. Do you need a 3-pound notebook with a built-in camera and DVD burner, or a curvy, 4.7-pound notebook with a few more features, or a huge notebook with a 17-inch screen that will mostly squat on your desk? Do you crave an affordable work PC with just the basics, or a tricked-out PC with all the bells and whistles for playing games? Only you can decide. My basic advice is: First decide if you're a laptop or PC person. Then decide which four or five features are most important to you. With those in mind, you can focus on other aspects you might find important: price, portability, screen size, multimedia features, processor, software needs, and so on.

machine possible, note that laptops usually lag behind desktops in speed. Generally speaking, however, most of the power of a desktop PC can be packed into a notebook, and notebooks offer a lot more convenience. Lugging your desktop on your vacation or onto the commuter train is only for the criminally insane.

Where to Find the Best Prices

Are you still shopping for your VAIO or looking to upgrade? Everyone likes a bargain, and with a little research on the Internet or at your neighborhood brick-and-mortar store, you can do just that.

There are numerous sites in the expanding online shopping and price comparison universe, not to mention a plethora of computer stores in your city, so I won't go into them here.

Also remember to check Sony's web site (www.sonystyle.com) for special offers and rebates. The site's clearance area usually offers some great deals that you won't find anywhere else.

Web auctions are another excellent destination. eBay is a rich source of new, used, and refurbished Sony devices. Just keep your wits about you on auction sites: Don't get caught up in a bidding battle and end up paying more for a used model than you should.

Chapter 2

A Guided Tour of the VAIO

How to...

- Get to know the desktop PC hardware
- Delve into the VAIO laptop hardware
- Understand software fundamentals
- Learn about Sony's multimedia software

Now that I've introduced you to each of the VAIO PC and notebook models, I'll dig a little deeper into what these systems offer in the way of hardware and software. But first—is your VAIO all set up and ready to go? If not, follow the quick-start guide that came with your system to get up and running. Then you'll be able to follow along as I walk you through a whole world of things you can do with your VAIO throughout the rest of this book.

Get to Know the Hardware

Desktop PCs and notebooks include many hardware components that are based on similar technologies. Those components come in different shapes and sizes in order to accommodate the tiniest laptops to the roomiest desktops. While desktops and laptops offer some of the same core technologies, their roads diverge at other specific parts, like batteries and pointer controls. First, let's talk about the main components that keep both laptops and notebooks running. Then we'll dive into the eccentricities that are specific to the two types.

The Big Four Hardware Components

No matter whether your VAIO is a desktop or a notebook, the same four basic parts power all of its operations: CPU, hard drive, RAM, and graphics card.

CPU

CPU stands for *Central Processing Unit*. You might also hear the CPU referred to as a *processor*. Simply stated, it's the brain of your VAIO, and it works just like the one inside your head. Whenever you instruct your computer to do something by typing on your keyboard, clicking with your mouse buttons, or manipulating another one of its parts, that instruction travels to the CPU. The CPU then instantly interprets the instruction and doles it out to the appropriate computer part that handles the execution of the command. When all of the stars are aligned, this whole process

2

happens as quickly and seamlessly as the process that occurs when your brain tells your hand to take a glass out of the cupboard.

Desktop CPUs have traditionally run faster than laptop processors, although the fastest notebook CPUs have now reached desktop speeds of 3 GHz (gigahertz) and higher. Some desktop CPUs, like the Intel Pentium 4, still have the one-up on notebook processors due to desktop-CPU-only technologies, such as *Hyper-Threading,* which helps the processor execute several different tasks at once (for more on Hyper-Threading, head to www.intel.com/technology/hyperthread/).

NOTE	*Putting desktop CPUs into laptops is a fairly new trend among notebook manufacturers. Sony has taken this tack with the VAIO FRV Series laptop. The advantages to this approach are fast desktop performance in a portable case and saving you some bucks. Notebooks including desktop CPUs can also cost less than those with laptop CPUs, since the former processor type often sells for hundreds less than the latter. But unless your laptop is plugged into a power outlet almost all the time, you can count on getting only about two short hours of battery life. Compared to the three- and four-hour times of many notebooks running laptop-specific CPUs, that's a considerable difference.*

The Hard Drive

The hard drive is your VAIO's long-term storage space. It contains circular disks that look like an average-sized CD, only smaller. All of your computer's programs and files are stored on those disks.

Did you know?

Some Laptop CPUs Alter Speed and Power Automatically

CPUs that run at lightning-quick speeds require a lot of power to back them up. For a desktop that's constantly attached to a power outlet, that doesn't pose a problem. But for a notebook that runs on a limited supply of battery power, a lot of speed equals less battery life. In an effort to minimize this battery impact, processor manufacturers like Intel, AMD, and Transmeta make laptop CPUs, such as the Pentium M, mobile Athlon, and Crusoe (or Transmeta's new Efficeon), that can automatically pinpoint the appropriate speed and power output needed for a certain task and then expend just the right amount to get the job done.

Imagine the hard drive as the cupboard from which you removed that glass a minute ago. Your VAIO's cupboard literally holds everything from your spreadsheets to your vacation photos. And like the flexible space inside a cupboard, you can fill and refill the hard drive's space with whatever programs or files you choose.

Notebook hard drives are comparatively puny next to desktop drives, with the former maxing out at 80GB (gigabytes). Still, 80GB is nothing to sneeze at when you consider that the typical spreadsheet is only a couple hundred kilobytes and the average song measures a few megabytes.

Hard drives also run at different speeds, which are measured in *revolutions per minute,* or rpm, of the disks inside the drive. Typical desktop drives run at 5,400 or even 7,200rpm, while most notebook drives run at a slower 4,200rpm in order to conserve battery life.

TIP

An internal hard drive is not made to be removed and carried with you, which can make you nervous if you're using it to store sensitive info. To keep private data under wraps, consider getting a removable or external hard drive. These drives either slip into the swappable bay inside your system or plug into the outside of your computer, making them easy to remove and reconnect whenever you need them.

RAM

RAM is short for *random access memory*. Most of the time, you'll probably hear RAM called simply *memory.* This is a different type of short-term memory than the long-term memory in your hard drive. Remember that glass in your hand? RAM is the hand your computer uses to hold on to whatever document, spreadsheet, or other file you're currently using. When you're done using a file, you tell your computer to close it, which signals the CPU to tell the RAM to drop the file back in the hard drive (unless you've chosen to delete it instead)—just like when your brain tells your hand to put the glass back in the cupboard. Your hand is then free to take something else out of the cupboard, use it, put it back again…you get the picture.

TIP

Desktops and notebooks come with only a limited amount of slots for memory modules—usually one or two for notebooks, and one or two more for desktops. If all of the slots are full of modules when you buy your system, and you want to add more RAM later, you'll have to trash one of your existing modules. To avoid wasting money on modules, try to get all of your RAM on one module when you order your VAIO. It's a tad more expensive, but it could save you cash in the long run.

Where RAM is concerned, the old saying "two hands are better than one" definitely applies. The more RAM you have, the more programs and files your VAIO can hold open at once. RAM modules for notebooks come in increments up to 1GB. Desktop modules have that beat at 2GB. But the nice thing about RAM is that if you find you need more, you can add it pretty easily on your own.

Like the processor and hard drive, RAM also comes in various speeds measured in megahertz (MHz). Most notebook RAM runs at 266 MHz or 333 MHz, while cutting-edge desktop memory sports speeds of 400 MHz or faster.

CAUTION   *Adding memory may be fairly easy to do yourself, but memory modules are not a one-size-fits-all proposition. Rather, the modules come in plenty of different shapes and sizes. The best way to know whether a module you want to add will work with your VAIO is to either buy it straight from Sony, or at least place a call to tech support to get the scoop on whatever module you're considering.*

Graphics Cards

Rendering graphics is some of the hardest work your VAIO will do. Unlike something as simple as a typewritten word, a picture or image contains colors, curves, and plenty of other details that translate into a ton of information your computer must interpret before it can accurately display your image on the screen. This can bog your CPU and RAM down considerably, preventing them from doing much of anything else while working on reproducing the image.

Most desktops and notebooks have a secret weapon for dealing with these cumbersome images and pictures: the graphics card. The card is a microcosm of the system's main CPU and RAM. Graphics cards contain their own mini-CPUs, often called *graphics accelerators,* and dedicated VRAM, or *video RAM,* which handle graphics-related tasks. That way, your primary CPU and RAM can spend more of their time on other stuff. This lets multitaskers do several things at once, like watch a movie out of the corner of one eye while catching up on e-mail.

TIP   *Cheaper VAIO computers, like the FRV notebook and RS desktop, contain* integrated graphics *systems that don't include dedicated video RAM. Rather, these graphics systems borrow VRAM from main RAM to carry out graphics tasks. This arrangement helps keep the cost of the computer down, but the decrease in the total amount of RAM also results in slower overall performance. If you plan to play games or do a lot of image-related work with your VAIO, get a graphics card with dedicated VRAM. You can add a new graphics card to a desktop at any time, but remember—you can't open your notebook's case to change its internal components, so you're stuck with the graphics card that shipped with your laptop.*

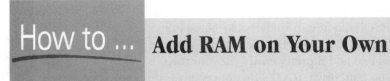

How to ... Add RAM on Your Own

Installing more memory in your VAIO desktop or notebook isn't as scary as it sounds. Your user manual should outline the brief process in detail, which will most likely include the following steps:

1. Check the manual to find out the exact location of your memory slots. For desktops, the slots will be located inside the case; for notebooks, the slots will likely be found underneath a removable memory-slot cover on the bottom of the system.

2. Shut down your VAIO and unplug it from any power outlet it may be connected to.

3. Look at the screws that hold your desktop's case together or your notebook's memory-slot cover closed. Determine whether those screws require the use of a screwdriver (most likely a Philips head) to remove them, and if they do, get your hands on one.

4. Remove your desktop's case cover or your laptop's memory-slot cover and locate the memory module. While laptop modules will always lie in a horizontal position, desktop modules may sit vertically in their slots.

5. As shown next, grasp the two metal or plastic prongs on either side of the module and *gently* pull them away from the center of the module, until it pops out of the slot on its own. Do not begin by pulling on the module itself. If the prongs don't easily pull away from the module, use a small screwdriver to gently pry them free. And if the module doesn't pop out automatically, try wiggling it lightly until it dislodges.

6. Insert the new module in the slot and apply very light pressure until it pops into the slot. If the prongs don't return to their original positions, put them back into place by pushing them toward the center of the module.

7. Replace the cover and screws…and you're done!

You can check to see whether your VAIO is recognizing the new addition by turning on the system, and then using your mouse to move the arrow on your screen over the tiny image, or *icon,* that looks like a desktop and monitor, called My Computer. Rest the arrow on top of the My Computer icon, and then press once on the right mouse button. A gray menu box will appear; move your arrow over the last item in the menu, Properties, and press your left mouse button once. A new box will appear on the screen, like the one shown next, and will say System Properties at the top. Underneath that title, there will be several tabs; the General tab should appear in the foreground. Look at the last line of information in that tab for the total amount of RAM in your system. The amount you see may be a few megabytes off from the total amount listed in the system's feature set, due to slight variations in the way different memory modules report their capacity to the computer. If that happens, don't worry—all of your RAM is still there.

If the total is more than a few megabytes off from what you know it should be, retrace the steps you took to install the RAM in the first place. Still no luck? Call tech support! After all, support is part of what you paid for when you bought your VAIO.

Other Important Hardware Players

Aside from the big four essential components, you should familiarize yourself with several additional parts that will play an everyday role in your computing routine.

The Monitor

You undoubtedly know function of your VAIO desktop or notebook screen, also called a *monitor* or *display*. But you may not know about the two main types of monitor technology: CRT and LCD.

■ CRT, or cathode-ray tube, is similar to the technology in your TV. It enables images to appear on the screen by lighting up dot patterns inside of a long, cylindrical tube that sits horizontally inside the monitor—which is why CRT monitors are so bulky.

■ LCD, or liquid-crystal display, is a technology involving two thin pieces of polarized glass that sandwich a liquid concoction containing crystals. To render images, the display sends electrical currents through the liquid, which cause the liquid to swirl around and either block light or allow it through. The resulting pattern creates an image. Since an LCD monitor doesn't need the long tube, it's much flatter than a CRT, earning it the nickname *flat panel*. Check out the difference in width between the two in Figure 2-1. And width isn't their only difference: The schmancy liquid-crystal technology inside LCDs causes them to cost hundreds more than CRTs.

FIGURE 2-1   Due to the long, horizontal tubes they hold inside, CRT monitors are super bulky compared to LCDs.

2

The screens of CRTs and LCDs are measured diagonally to determine their size. Both monitor types are currently available in excess of 20 inches.

While desktops can handle either a CRT or LCD monitor, notebooks are obviously too small to support CRT technology. Therefore, all laptops include LCDs, contributing to the overall higher price of notebooks to desktops.

Optical Disc Drives

I'm not going to spend much time on optical disc drives here, since I cover them in detail in Chapter 12. But for now, I'll tell you that these drives are devices which store data. They differ from hard drives in the way they record that data. While a hard drive acts as a magnet to hold data on its disks, an optical drive uses a laser to burn data on a disc. Hence the term "burning a CD," which you've probably heard tossed around. Types of optical disc drives include CD (compact disc), DVD (digital video disc or digital versatile disc), CD-RW (CD-rewriteable), DVD-RW (DVD-rewriteable), and more.

Another difference between optical and hard drives is that the disks inside of a hard drive are *fixed*—that is, you can't take them out of the hard drive and put them in your briefcase like you would a CD or DVD.

Audio Cards

Each VAIO notebook and desktop includes an audio card that handles all sound-related tasks. If you've ever heard the warbling that comes out of a laptop, you already know that notebook sound is largely unimpressive. That's less a reflection of the audio card

Did you know?

Floppies Are Going the Way of the Dodo

If you're wondering where the floppy fits into this storage melee—it doesn't. Sony has largely discontinued its inclusion of this antiquated storage technology, putting it inside only the VAIO RZ and RS desktops while leaving it out of VAIO notebooks entirely (although if you really need one, you can still buy an external floppy drive and connect it to your computer).

Don't shed any tears over the floppy's departure. The biggest floppy disks offer a paltry 1.44MB (megabytes) of storage space, which is barely big enough to hold one song or picture. On the other hand, recordable CDs and DVDs hold anywhere from hundreds of megabytes to several gigabytes of data.

than the laptop's speakers, or lack thereof. Desktop sound is a different story, since most VAIO desktops come with powerful external speakers and even subwoofers. You always have the option of connecting external speakers to your VAIO notebook, too, but you'll still have to tolerate your laptop's thin strains when listening to sounds through its speakers alone.

Connection Ports

Even if you're using a VAIO laptop, you'll almost certainly need to plug a lot of external devices into your system, such as a keyboard, mouse, monitor, and printer. On top of those items, you'll probably want to connect extra toys, including digital cameras and PDAs (personal digital assistants, like the Sony Clie or PalmPilot). Your VAIO's various connection ports are there to help in this department. Here's a list of the connection ports you can expect to see in most VAIO desktops and notebooks.

NOTE   *Not all VAIO laptops and desktops will have every port in this list; each model includes its own specific mix of ports. Your system may also offer other ports that aren't in my list, since I'm just covering the biggies here. If you don't see a port listed here that you're curious about, remember—the user manual is your friend.*

USB 2.0   Short for *Universal Serial Bus,* USB is the standard connection technology that almost all new external devices are based on today. While old USB 1.1 ports offered slow data transfer speeds of only 12 Mbps (megabits per second), USB 2.0 sports a much faster maximum speed of 480 Mbps. USB-based devices have the added convenience of being *Plug-and-Play* (for more on Plug-and-Play, see Chapter 5).

iLink   iLink is Sony's own name for an IEEE-1394 port. IEEE-1394 (pronounced eye-triple-e-thirteen-ninety-four) technology was originally developed by Apple Computer, which christened the technology *FireWire.* At 400 Mbps, IEEE-1394 used to be the fastest connection port in town, until USB 2.0's 480 Mbps came on the scene. However, Sony still includes iLink ports in most of its desktops and notebooks, because many of the company's customers have already invested in other expensive Sony equipment based on iLink technology, such as its digital video recorders and cameras. Figure 2-2 shows an example of an iLink port.

Parallel and PS/2   Used to be most mice and printers were based on PS/2 and parallel technologies, respectively. However, you don't see too many of these or any other parallel and PS/2 devices anymore. But Sony has hung on to the ports in some of its VAIO desktops and laptops so you can still use any of the old devices you might have that are based on these technologies.

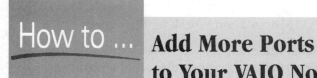

How to ... Add More Ports to Your VAIO Notebook

Notebooks typically offer only a fraction of the ports found on desktops. Common sense tells you why: Laptop cases just don't have room for excess. But there is a way to bolster your notebook's port supply. *Port replicators,* or port reps for short, are add-ons that measure about the size of a box of toothpaste. They literally replicate the most common ports on your notebook, so they usually include VGA, Ethernet, a couple of USB 2.0s, and a few additional ports. Most port reps connect to the laptop through a docking port on the notebook itself.

The best part about port reps is that you can plug all of your external devices into the port rep, and then just take your laptop in and out of the port rep whenever you want. That way you only deal with one connection between the laptop and port rep, rather than several individual connections between each device and your system.

VGA and DVI   These acronyms stand for *video graphics array* and *digital visual interface,* respectively. VGA and DVI ports allow you to connect monitors with one of these two types of connectors to your desktop or notebook.

S-video and Composite Video   S-video, or super video, and composite video ports enable you to export the picture you see on your VAIO's monitor to a television, or import a TV image to your VAIO. S-video is the newer technology of the two and generally results in a clearer overall image on your TV or computer display.

FIGURE 2-2   An iLink port—also known as IEEE-1394 or FireWire—sits on the right, sandwiched between a USB 2.0 port to its left and an external optical-drive port to its right.

Headphone Out and Microphone In These two ports speak for themselves.

S/PDIF Short for Sony/Philips Digital Interface, S/PDIF is the VAIO's optical connector for high-end audio devices, such as a cutting-edge set of speakers or a digital amplifier.

56k Modems and Ethernet 56k modem and Ethernet technologies encompass the two primary ways to get on the Web. A 56k modem port lets you plug in a standard phone cord to dial-out to the Internet, while an Ethernet port lets you connect your VAIO to a DSL or cable modem. For more on both technologies, head over to Chapter 6.

 *While there's no port for it, per se, wireless is another type of connection that's becoming a standard part in desktops, and laptops especially. I spend all of Chapter 9 describing this new technology in detail.*

Expansion Slots

Ports aren't the only means of plugging a device into your VAIO. Both desktops and notebooks include several types of expansion slots that support all sorts of add-ons, like TV tuner cards that turn your computer into a television, and mini-memory cards that are no bigger than a stick of gum. The usual suspects in the expansion slot group include PCI, PCMCIA, AGP, and flash media.

PCI PCI stands for peripheral component interconnect, which is a wordy way to say that PCI slots let you attach extra cards to your desktop. PCI slots lie inside the desktop, so you have to remove the case cover to get at them. A 3.5-inch-long standard PCI slot (shown in Figure 2-3) would take up too much room inside a notebook, so a laptop contains a smaller version of the slot that's aptly called mini-PCI. But because a notebook's insides aren't meant to be tampered with, you can't swap cards in and out of a mini-PCI slot the same way you can with a standard PCI slot. That means the card that comes in the mini-PCI slot—which is usually a wireless card—stays in the slot.

AGP Most desktops have one slot inside that's based on AGP, or accelerated graphics port, technology. AGP slots serve a single purpose: to hold a graphics card. Having a dedicated slot for these cards just makes graphics tasks run all that much faster.

PCMCIA Say this three times fast: Personal Computer Memory Card International Association. Or, just call PCMCIA slots by their shorter, more common moniker—PC card slots. Two-and-a-quarter-inch PC card slots are most commonly contained in notebooks and Sony's smallish, all-in-one desktops: the V and W series. You can access them from the edges of your system, making them a good alternative for cases

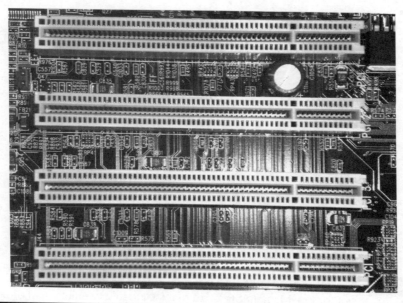

FIGURE 2-3   A standard desktop PCI slot is 3.5 inches long and holds add-on cards of about the same length.

you can't crack open. They support credit-card sized add-ons, such as modems and wireless cards, should you not have them inside your computer already.

Flash Memory   Flash memory slots are the smallest of the bunch. They accept tiny storage cards that range in size from a book of matches to a piece of chewing gum. Your computer can call up the data on these cards in a literal flash, just like it can with the data held by your VAIO's main RAM. But unlike RAM, flash memory doesn't forget that data once you turn off your system.

All VAIO notebooks include a slot for Sony's own flash memory card, which the company has coined the Memory Stick (take a gander at Figure 2-4 to see what this slot looks like). Some Sony desktops, including the RZ series, offer slots that support Memory Sticks as well as other flash memory types, such as the CompactFlash card.

Expansion Bays

Last but not least in the hardware lineup are expansion bays. Both desktops and notebooks have them, although they look and act a little differently.

Desktop bays measure between 3.5- and 5.25-inches high. An internal bay dwells entirely inside the desktop case, where you can't access it unless you remove the case cover. Most of an external bay sits inside the case as well, but the front of an external

FIGURE 2-4 The TR series notebook is just one of the VAIOs that includes a dedicated slot for tiny Memory Stick and MagicGate flash memory cards.

bay opens to the outside. Classic examples of internal and external bay devices are hard drives for the former and DVD drives for the latter. Desktops usually ship with a couple of bays already filled, as well as a few free bays that you can fill with devices you decide to add at a later date.

Laptop bays are much slimmer so they can fit inside lean laptop cases. The bays typically measure an inch or less in height.

In most VAIO laptops, the bays for optical drives are fixed *in the same fashion as the disks in the hard drives we discussed earlier. This means you can't swap out the optical drive inside the bay with another module. A bummer, since most laptops include flexible optical bays that provide the freedom to add other options like second batteries or extra modular hard drives.*

Hardware Specifics of VAIO Desktops

We've just about exhausted all of the major desktop hardware components in the preceding sections. But there are still a few particulars I wanted to chat about before wrapping up our desktop discussion.

Voices from the Community

The Seabird Biologist

With my job as a seabird biologist, I spend a considerable amount of time on boats where space is limited and the work conditions often difficult, so my notebook is indispensable. The notebook comes in handy for direct data entry when I'm doing fieldwork or for downloading data from electronic monitoring stations. When I'm not out studying the birds, I break out the notebook to do a little data entry and analysis, report research and writing, e-mailing, or word processing, or (more likely) to view a *Simpson's* DVD. And if the seas get a little rough, I stow the notebook away in a safe place to weather the storm.

I split my time between my home and office in Italy and my fieldwork in the U.S., which makes a notebook especially convenient. With a notebook I take all the data and programs I need with me wherever I go without having to worry about whether I left this data in California or that program in Italy.

—Darrell Whitworth, a nationally recognized seabird biologist, has
spent the past 14 years studying the Xantus's Murrelet and other
creatures great and small on the California Channel Islands.

The Keyboard

The keyboards that ship with VAIO W and V series desktops are nothing like the one on your mother's typewriter. These boards offer much more beyond the regular QWERTY keys, including dedicated buttons for launching your favorite software applications and controlling volume. You can use the W series' wireless keyboard without plugging it into your system, and you can fold up the V series' board when you're not using it.

The Mouse

Unless you've been living on a mouse-less planet, you've likely seen your share of these critters. These devices have traditionally connected to the computer via a PS/2 port, but many of the colorful, cutting-edge mouse designs out there today—including the one that ships with the VAIO W series—will even work wirelessly.

NOTE   *You can always plug an external keyboard or mouse into a laptop, as long*
as the notebook has a port to put it in.

Hardware Particulars of VAIO Notebooks

Despite all of the technological similarities between desktops and notebooks, these two types of computers contain some distinct differences. Here are a couple of key notebook components that you won't find in a VAIO desktop.

The Battery

Your VAIO laptop literally lives and dies by its battery. A good rule of thumb about batteries is the bigger the battery, the longer it lasts—but even the smallest batteries tend to last for at least a couple of hours. Other factors besides size also play a part in your battery's life, including the speed of your CPU and the size of your screen.

Sony sells additional, high-capacity *batteries for some VAIO laptops like the TR series. These batteries often offer double or even triple the life that a primary battery musters. But beware that these heavier high-capacity batteries can also add a pound or more on to your notebook.*

The Touchpad

The touchpad is a laptop's answer to the mouse. The pad is generally square-shaped and is always located beneath the notebook's keyboard. When you move your finger across the pad, your arrow moves across the screen just as it does when moving the arrow with a mouse. Two buttons beneath or beside the touchpad function like the two buttons that flank a mouse, letting you do left and right mouse clicks.

Pointing Sticks Do Mouse Duty, Too

While Sony favors the touchpad for its VAIO notebooks, other laptops like IBM ThinkPads rely on pointing sticks for mouse tasks. Pointing sticks look exactly like the eraser on the end of a pencil and usually sit square in the middle of the keyboard. To move your onscreen arrow, just move the pointing stick with your finger. One of the great laptop debates has been whether touchpads or pointing sticks are ultimately better, but I'm here to tell you that it's merely a matter of personal preference.

Did you know?

Giga Pocket Lets You Record TV Shows to Your VAIO

Although I discuss it in detail in Chapter 13, I'd be remiss if I didn't briefly mention Sony's Giga Pocket technology here. This combo of hardware and software makes your VAIO into a personal video recorder (PVR) like TiVo, allowing you to record television shows straight to your hard drive and then play them back on your computer's display or on your TV screen. Pretty cool, huh?

Understand Software Fundamentals

If you've skipped ahead to the end of the chapter, you already know that this section on software is pretty short. That's because we'll spend heaps of time on software throughout the remainder of the book. For the time being, I'll give you a taste of the programs you'll be learning about in the pages to come.

Windows XP: The Operating System

The operating system, or OS for short, is the mother of all software programs. It's to your software what the CPU is to your hardware, governing each of the additional programs you install on your VAIO. Sony's operating system of choice for all VAIO desktops and notebooks is Microsoft's Windows XP, which comes in three editions: Home, Professional, and Media Center.

Entire books have been written on the subject of Windows XP, including a tome just like this one called *How to Do Everything with Windows XP.* This book doesn't have space for quite the same level of detail about XP, but I'll still provide plenty of tips in subsequent chapters on using XP to do everything from setting up your system to managing your files.

Sony's Slick Multimedia Software

Sony really piles on its own multimedia applications to help you take full advantage of your VAIO's ability to make music, record video, burn discs, edit images, share data, and more. Here's a quick list of the applications we'll explore in the pages ahead:

■ **DVgate Plus**   Helps to capture images and video from your digital camera or digital video recorder, and then edit the images and send them back out to a VCR or DVD player for recording on videotape or DVD. Also helps you convert VHS tapes to DVD.

- **Click to DVD**   Burns videos, images, or other files to DVD.

- **PictureGear Studio**   Lets you import images to your VAIO, edit them, and then arrange the shots in online albums.

- **SonicStage and SonicStage Mastering Studio**   Serves to both organize your music collection and play it back. SonicStage Mastering Studio also lets you remaster music from an analog source to better-than-CD quality. It uses Sony music studio mastering tools, and music hounds who can't afford actual studio time can use it to produce professional-sounding music.

- **VAIO Media**   Helps you transfer media files, like music and pictures, to other computers or devices on your home network.

Congratulations—you made it through basic hardware and software 101. With this solid background under your belt, you can move right into Chapter 3 where we'll talk about running your programs as well as creating and organizing files in just the way you want them.

Chapter 3

Run Programs and Manage Your Files

How to...

- Choose single-click or double-click
- Run programs
- Download and install software
- Create, save, and open files
- Remove programs
- Create shortcuts
- Turn off your VAIO

Now that you've become acquainted with your VAIO hardware, it's time to fire up some programs and get to work (or to the fun). Although the Windows XP operating system is not quite as user friendly as Microsoft says, it has improved the way programs run. If you're an extreme computer newbie, you might be wondering "what's a program?" In short, it's an application that lets you do things, like writing a letter with Microsoft Word, listening to music with Windows Media Player, watching a DVD with InterVideo WinDVD 4, editing your own DVD with Sony's DVgate Plus, or accessing e-mail with Eudora Pro. You can run programs from the Start menu or the Windows desktop, switch between programs in the Taskbar, or open a document and program at the same time by double-clicking the document's icon. To take advantage of these tricks, you must learn all the nuances of running programs, saving files, downloading software, and more. This chapter provides all the basic instructions you need, plus many tips for advanced users.

Single-Click vs. Double-Click

Before delving into the depths of running programs, you should know that most Sony VAIO notebooks and PCs come with a "single-click" left-mouse-button setup as the default, rather than the more common "double-click" setup. Unless you're an Apple computer user, you're probably used to opening a program or folder by double-clicking it.

I'd Rather Switch than Fight Single-Click

When it comes to single-clicking, you'll either love the simplicity, or you'll be frustrated (like me) with time-wasting steps caused by the single-clickyness. For me,

Voices from the Community

It Takes a (VAIO) Village

I've been involved with Sony VAIO support and community network building for several years now with VAIO Village, the unofficial Sony VAIO users support forum (www.vaiovillage.com). We've had this moniker for over three years now, but in fact go back with a lot of our current team and members much longer, and many of us have come from even earlier sites that either failed or self imploded.

Ironically, all of these sites developed from Sony's own attempts to launch and maintain Club VAIO. Club VAIO was originally supposed to be a perk for VAIO owners, of which I was an early adopter (my first was a PCV150—loved that purple hue and the fact that Sony was the first manufacturer that had those ATI All in Wonders etc.). Unfortunately, Sony never maintained Club VAIO with any real consistency—no moderation and very limited administration.

Eventually a handful of us VAIO owners, wanting more support for our VAIOs than Sony could give us and knowing the many, many problems that have and do occur when you have hybrid proprietary systems, rolled up our sleeves and went to work, and created our own VAIO support site.

I personally "took over," at least in terms of ownership name, the VAIO Village site about two years ago, hoping to keep alive the wealth of knowledge and experience we had built and accumulated for our growing global community. There have been a few bumps along the way, but we have endured and continue to see our Village grow and thrive. Many have followed us through a variety of incarnations and have selflessly donated both monetarily and of their time and efforts to really support and help each other. As the saying goes, "It takes a Village," hence our name.

—Besides running the VAIO Village Forums,
Steve Alimonti of Berkeley, California, has worked for several
nonprofit agencies in the San Francisco Bay Area and for the last
several years has been the Services Co-coordinator for the Residential
Program for Bonita House, Inc. (http://www.bonitahouse.org).

double-clicking a folder or program is now part of my DNA. For instance, in single-click mode, a folder or program pops open when I'm just trying to select it, forcing me to constantly close unnecessary windows. Thankfully, if your VAIO's single-click

FIGURE 3-1   You can open items in folders and on the desktop by double-clicking them
or single-clicking them.

setup drives you crazy, you can change to the double-click method by following
these steps:

1. Open the Start menu. Choose Control Panel | Appearance and Themes |
   Folder Options | General tab. (See Figure 3-1.) You can also get there by
   selecting Start | My Computer | Tools | Folder Options | General tab.

2. In the Click Items As Follows section, select Double-Click To Open An Item
   (Single-Click To Select).

3. Click OK (or Apply).

NOTE   *If you're new to computers, the first time you hear "desktop" you might
think it refers to the actual desk on which your computer sits. It doesn't. It
means the electronic desktop on your screen, the first screen you see after
booting up. It's where icons, various types of documents and files, and the
long thin Taskbar live. The desktop works just like a regular folder (more
on that later).*

3

Adjust to Single-Click

On the other hand, if you want to stay with the single-click default, you may have to learn some new tricks:

- The entire concept of double-clicking is now gone.

- To select an icon, move the pointer over it. Don't click it.

- To open an item, click it once.

- To select multiple items, hold down CTRL or SHIFT while moving the pointer over each desired icon. (Don't click them.) CTRL selects individual icons. SHIFT selects a range of icons.

- To rename an icon, move the pointer over it, press F2, type the name, and then press ENTER. Or, right-click the icon, choose Rename, type the name, and then press ENTER.

Run Your Programs

Once you get the clicks to your liking—for most of this book I'll assume you switched to double-click—it's time to run some programs. Usually, the only hard part about running a Windows program is deciding how you want to launch it. The standard way to run a program is to open the Start menu, point to All Programs, and then click the program's name. However, in some cases, you have to follow a trail of three or four submenus to find the program you want. If you're familiar with Windows, you surely know other ways to launch a program. There are many ways to do it:

- Open a document, which launches the program. For instance, if you created a Word document on your desktop called Story.doc, double-click the document's icon. The file opens and Word starts automatically.

- Open the Start menu, click the program's icon on the left side of the menu (if it appears). The left side of the Start menu contains icons for commonly used programs.

- On the Quick Launch bar, click the program's icon (if it appears). The Quick Launch bar is a section of the Taskbar that lets you launch programs with a single click. (For more on the Taskbar, read "Customize the Taskbar" in Chapter 4.)

- Open the Start menu, then click My Computer | Local Disk (C:) | Program Files. In the program's subfolder, double-click the program's icon (or select the icon and press ENTER). See Figure 3-2.

■ Right-click the program's icon, and then choose Open.

As you'll learn later in this chapter, you can add shortcut icons to various places, such as the desktop, Start menu, and Quick Launch bar.

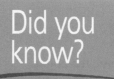

Learn Filename Extensions

The file that runs a program is called an executable file; its name ends in .exe, .com, or .bat. (The number of filename extensions keeps growing, which can lead to a lot of frustration if you don't know what they mean. Extensions include .doc, .tmp, .bmp, .gif, .avi, .pdf, and so on. See the following table.) However, Microsoft hides filename extensions by default to make Windows appear friendlier. But even beginners appreciate visible extensions, especially if you're looking for the executable file you just downloaded from the Internet. To display the extensions, choose Start | My Computer | Tools | Folder Options | View tab | Advanced Settings list | Uncheck Hide Extensions For Known File Types, as shown here.

Common File Extensions	Type of Application
.doc	Microsoft Word (or WordPad)
.exe	Program (not a document)
.avi	Windows Media Player
.mov	QuickTime
.bmp	Bitmap image
.ppt	Microsoft PowerPoint
.tmp	Temporary file
.txt	Text file (Notepad)
.xls	Microsoft Excel
.pdf	Adobe Portable Document Format
.zip	Compressed Zip file
.gif	Gif image
.jpg/.jpeg	JPEG image
.htm/.html	Web page

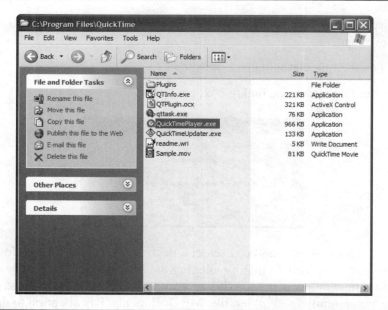

FIGURE 3-2   I've highlighted the program in the QuickTime folder, which is one way to open programs.

■ Choose Start | Run (or press the WINDOWS LOGO KEY-R), type the program's name, and then press ENTER. You may have to include the path to where the program lives.

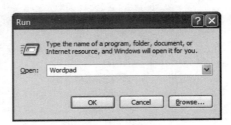

Download and Install Software

The Internet is full of software that you can *download* (copy to your computer) and use. Some of the software you have to pay for, some is free, and some you can use for a trial period, and then pay for later. In the past, you needed to mess with complicated File Transfer Protocol (FTP) programs to download software. (See Chapter 10 for more on FTP.) But now it's much easier to download files with your web browser by following these steps:

1. Use Internet Explorer to find a web page that has software you want to download.

2. Click the link that initiates a download.

3. In the File Download dialog box, click Save.

4. In the Save As dialog box, select a destination folder for the download (Figure 3-3). You do that by clicking the little down arrow to the right of the little window at the top. If you want to find programs easily, save them to a commonly used folder, like My Documents. Pay attention to the name of the program you're downloading and where it will be stored. It's no fun downloading a program, forgetting what it was called and where it was saved, and then having to hunt for it.

5. The download will almost always be an executable (.exe) file or a compressed (.zip) file.

NOTE *Compressed folders have their own, unique icon, which has a zipper on it. That identifies the folder as compressed and not a regular folder.*

6. After the download completes, go to the folder where you saved it (My Documents, for instance). Double click the file. If the download is an executable file, setup starts automatically. If it's a Zip archive, extract its files, and then double-click the installer program (usually named setup.exe) among the extracted pieces. (See "How to…Extract Compressed Files.")

TIP *CNET's popular Download.com (www.download.com) is a good place to explore the crowded world of software downloads.*

TIP *You can password-protect archives to prevent others from extracting files. To do that, select any item in a zipped folder (not the folder itself). Choose File | Add A Password, and then complete the Add Password dialog box. The password applies to every file in the archive.*

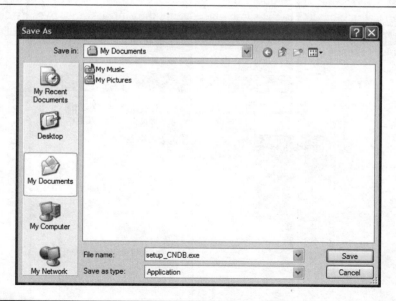

FIGURE 3-3   Choose a destination folder for the file you're about to download. My Documents is a good choice.

 **Extract Compressed Files**

You may have used the popular WinZip program to compress or extract files or folders. What's all the fuss about zipping? Because zipping certain types of files shrinks them down quite a lot, which means you can e-mail many more photos of the kids, for instance, than you could if they weren't compressed. To extract all files and folders in a compressed file, first find where you stored the file, and then right-click the zipped folder. A submenu appears, giving you a list of options, including Extract All, Extract Here, and Open With. Which option you choose depends on how comfortable you are with extracting files and which extraction program you use (there are several in addition to WinZip.) If you click Extract All, the extraction starts immediately; the uncompressed data is copied to the same folder you have open (My Documents, in this case). There are other ways to extract files, depending on how Windows Explorer is set up. For instance, if you have a zipped file in the My Documents folder, you can double-click the file, which calls up the Explorer window. On that screen, you'll likely see an Extract All Files option in the left column. Click that option to launch the Extraction Wizard. Click Next at the opening screen and you'll see the screen shown here. You can extract the data to the same place where the zipped folder lives by clicking Next, or you can save the extracted data to a new folder by clicking the Browse button and choosing a new folder.

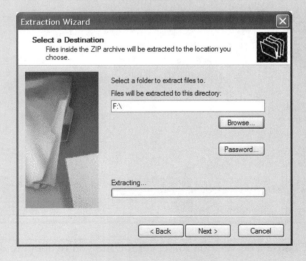

Create, Save, and Open Files

So far, we've only talked about adjusting your mouse clicks, running programs, and downloading software. As you probably know, your programs are primarily used for creating documents and other kinds of files. All the documents you create and save (and even the programs you run) are stored on your VAIO's hard drive as files.

Create New Documents

There are many ways to create new documents; most people do it from within a program. You decide which program you want to create the document with (Microsoft Word, for instance), and then you find and run that program (described earlier). Using that program, you create a new document, usually by clicking the New command in the File menu. But there are other ways to create a new document.

If you're reading a document in Microsoft Word and you want to create a new, blank document, press CTRL-N. That keyboard shortcut also works in many other programs. Or you can create a document by right-clicking a folder or using a few menus on the desktop. To do this, follow these steps:

1. Open the folder where you want the document to live, or just go to a blank area of the desktop and store it there.

2. Right-click the folder, and then slide the pointer over New. A submenu of document type choices pops up. Click the type of document you want to create.

Save Documents

Most programs let you save your work as documents, which you can open again later, print, attach to an e-mail message, delete, copy, and so on. Nearly all programs use Windows' standard Save dialog box. The first time you save a document, Windows asks you to name it and pick a folder where it will live. (Two files in the same folder can't have the same name.) To save a document:

1. Choose File | Save. Or to save a file under a different name or in a different folder, choose File | Save As. (See Figure 3-4.)

2. Find the folder where you want to store the document. There are several ways to navigate to that folder. Double-click folder icons in the folder box to drill down the folder tree. Use the left-side buttons to go to a common destination quickly. Use the top-side Save In list to pick a different drive.

3. If you want to create folders within folders, click the Create New Folder button in the dialog box's toolbar. A new folder is automatically created. Its name is highlighted, waiting for you to type in the name you want. Type the name and press ENTER to rename the folder. Double-click it to open it in the dialog box.

4. In the Save As Type section of the dialog box, you can change the file type. Under certain conditions, you may want to change this setting. For instance, suppose you wrote a letter with Microsoft Word, but your friend has a different word processing program like WordPerfect. You could opt to change the Save As Type setting to WordPerfect so that your colleague could open the file in his program.

5. Click Save.

TIP *If you're on a network and you try to open a document that somebody else already has open, the program usually warns you to open a read-only copy of the document, unless it's a multiuser document, such as a database. You can also have the program notify you when the original user closes the document. To do that, click Notify or Receive Notification When The Original Copy Is Available, indicated by the appearance of the File In Use window. When the user closes the document, a File Now Available message opens on your screen.*

FIGURE 3-4   The Save dialog box pops open the first time you save a file, or when you choose File | Save As.

Did you know?

Tips for Saving Documents

The Save dialog box can be confusing, as there are many ways to save documents and various tricks and shortcuts that experienced users rely on. Here are some tips:

- Save your work frequently! You don't want a computer crash to extinguish your Great American Novel, do you? Also, save your work in more than one place, not just to your hard disk, and *don't* make the second place your hard disk. The second place can be a recordable CD or DVD (see Chapter 12 for information on how to burn those discs), a USB thumb drive, a Zip disk, a floppy drive, and so on.

- The Save dialog box must be closed before you can use another part of the program.

- Some older programs use the old-style Save dialog box, which lacks some of the navigation features of the new dialog box.

- You can't save your work in some game and utility programs, such as Solitaire and Calculator.

- The Save dialog box acts like an Explorer window. You can right-click an item to rename or delete it. You can even drag items into and out of this box, or use the standard navigation keys.

Open Documents

Opening a file works much the same as saving it. When you use the Open command on your program's File menu, you'll see a dialog box similar to the one shown in Figure 3-4, except it's named Open. You could type in the name of the file you're looking for, but it's usually faster to just navigate to the file.

In the Open dialog box, scroll to the file you seek, and then double-click it. If the file is in a different folder, first double-click the folder to open it, and then double-click the file. If you don't see the folder you're looking for, you might need to navigate down or up the folder tree. You back up by clicking the Up One Level button. You move down a level by double-clicking a folder and looking inside for a subfolder.

Of course, you don't have to use the Open command in the File menu to open a document. As you've probably done countless times, if you want to open a Word document that lives on your desktop, just double-click it.

Remove Programs

When you download and install software, it scatters components all over your VAIO, not just in the Program Files subfolder it creates. Only the *uninstall* function of a program can wipe it out completely. Don't just delete the program's folder; you'll leave behind *readme* files, shortcuts, support documents, Registry entries, hidden folders, and more rubbish on your hard drive. To remove a program:

1. Choose Start | Control Panel | Add Or Remove Programs.

2. Find the program you want to delete (see Figure 3-5).

3. Click the Change/Remove button (or Remove button) and confirm the removal if a message box appears. Windows runs the program's uninstall utility, which varies by program. Follow any onscreen options.

FIGURE 3-5   The Add Or Remove Programs list shows a program's size, the date you last used it, and more. If you have tons of programs, use the Sort By list to select a sorting option.

Most uninstall utilities show a progress bar, explain what they're deleting or not deleting, and tell you whether you must restart your VAIO to complete the removal process.

Create Shortcuts

Shortcuts are huge time savers that let you access an original file from anywhere on a computer's disk system, but without the extra baggage needed to copy the full file in several different spots. For example, you can create a shortcut to a subfolder you created in My Documents. That way you can get to it quickly without searching for it.

To create a shortcut icon to a file or folder, first open the folder that contains the item you want to create a shortcut to. Next, click and hold the file or folder with the right mouse button to drag the file or folder from its original home to a blank space on the desktop, and then release the mouse button. From the menu that appears, choose Create Shortcuts Here.

If you want to keep your desktop free of shortcuts, you can drag an icon over the Start button and release the mouse button. A shortcut is placed in the Start menu, on the left.

CAUTION *Be careful when deleting shortcuts. Make sure you're actually deleting the shortcut and not the item it points to, like a program. The icon should say Shortcut to My Computer, for instance.*

Turn Off Your VAIO

When you're done running programs, downloading software, creating shortcuts and the like, keep in mind that shutting down your computer requires more than punching the power button. Windows needs to prepare itself for shutdown, saving system information and disconnecting external connections. If you don't let it go through this shutdown procedure, Windows may corrupt some of your files. To turn off your VAIO:

1. Choose Start | Turn Off Computer. Or click the desktop, and then press ALT-F4.

2. In the Turn Off Computer dialog box, choose one of the options listed. To see a fourth option, press SHIFT. The Stand By button then changes to Hibernate.

3. Hibernate saves everything to memory on your hard disk. If you have a lot of RAM, you need a lot of free disk space to put your VAIO into hibernation. Don't use hibernation all the time. Use Turn Off occasionally to let Windows perform backup and other tasks.

4. Always save your work before putting your computer on standby. Standby saves your session in RAM (not on hard disk), so a power interruption will delete your session.

Now that you've learned the ins and outs of running programs, downloading software, creating folders and shortcuts, let's journey into the world of system configuration.

Part II

Everyday Stuff with Your VAIO

Chapter 4

Configure Your VAIO for Your Needs

How to...

- Import your old files and settings
- Decide how to transfer files
- Use the Files and Settings Transfer window
- Configure the Windows interface
- Customize the Start menu
- Customize the taskbar
- Configure Windows Explorer

Now that you've had a chance to explore your Sony VAIO a bit, it's time to get down to business. In this chapter, you'll learn about the various ways to transfer data from your old PC to your new machine, how to configure the Start menu on your new VAIO, how to avoid some annoying "features" of the Taskbar, and how to tweak Windows Explorer.

Import Your Old Files and Settings

An important task in setting up your Sony VAIO is transferring your files and settings from your old PC onto the new machine. You devoted a lot of time to tweaking your old system to get it to fit your eccentricities, so save time and transfer as much of that work as you can.

Decide How to Transfer Files

There's more than one way to skin a cat and more than one way to copy files from your old computer to your new one. The venerable floppy drive might have just popped into your head as an option, but if that's the case, give your time machine a kick; you might be stuck in the 1990s. Besides, new Sony VAIOs don't come with floppy drives, and anyway those drives hold a miniscule amount of data, so forget floppies. But if you miss the simplicity of floppies, you might try another small storage device called a *thumb drive* or *keychain drive* (see Figure 4-1). These little drives are about the size of a pack of gum and can usually hook onto your keychain when you're done transferring data. They connect to your computer via a USB 2.0 port (see Figure 5-5 in Chapter 5) and can hold from 8MB up to 1GB of data. If you just can't give up your floppies, keep in mind that Sony sells external floppy drives that plug into your VAIO's USB port.

FIGURE 4-1   This small storage device, called a thumb drive or keychain drive, plugs into a USB 2.0 port and can store or transfer data.

If you choose to use a thumb drive, simply plug it into the USB 2.0 port. Windows XP will recognize the device and create a new drive letter for you, something like drive D or E, depending on how your system is set up. To find the new drive letter, double-click the My Computer icon. You'll see the new drive under your existing drives, like C for your hard drive.

From there, *drag* the files or folders you want to transfer to the newly created drive. (Dragging means putting your pointer on an item, pressing and holding the left mouse button, then moving the folder where you want.) To unplug the thumb drive, first tap the Safely Remove Hardware icon (look for the little green arrow) in the Taskbar. Removing hardware is discussed in more detail in Chapter 5.

Use a DirectParallel Cable

Another transfer choice is to create a direct connection between the two computers using a parallel or serial cable. This is a bit more technical in nature, but the only cost would be the special cable. A parallel cable is the better choice for Sony VAIOs, because parallel ports are much more common these days. To use this data-transfer method, first buy a DirectParallel cable, which you can get from your local computer store or from DirectParallel's web site at www.lpt.com. Windows XP contains the software it needs to use these cables, so you don't need to do any configuring.

NOTE *You must be logged on as an administrator or a member of the Administrator's group to complete the transferring of files with a DirectParallel cable. If your computer is connected to a network, network policy settings may also prevent you from using this procedure.*

To link two computers using a DirectParallel cable, follow these steps:

1. Connect the cable to the parallel ports of both computers.

2. Open the Network Connection window by choosing Start | Control Panel | Network And Internet Connections | Network Connections. (This is the procedure when the window is in Category View. If you're looking at the window in Classic View, choose Start | Control Panel | Network Connections.)

3. Under Network Tasks in the left-hand column (see Figure 4-2), click Create A New Connection, and then click Next.

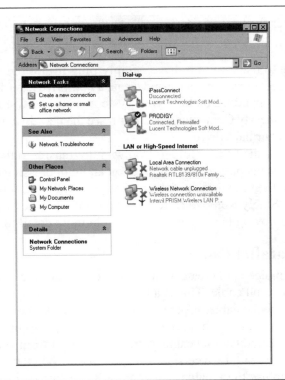

FIGURE 4-2   The Network Connection window will help you create a new connection, either to another computer or to a network.

4. Click Set Up An Advanced Connection, and then click Next. The New Connection Wizard should appear.

5. Click Connect Directly To Another Computer (Figure 4-3), click Next, and then do one of the following:

   ■ If you want your computer to act as the guest, click Guest and then Next.

   ■ If you want your computer to act as the host, click Host and then Next.

   Follow the step-by-step instructions.

Use the Files and Settings Transfer Wizard

If you can get both your old computer and your new Sony VAIO on the same network, you won't need a cable to transfer files and settings. If you're already on a network (either at home or the office), first add your new VAIO to the network. If you're at work, you might have to get your network administrator to help you do this. Once both computers are on the network, you can use the Files And Settings Transfer Wizard (Figure 4-4) to help you move settings and files from one computer to the other.

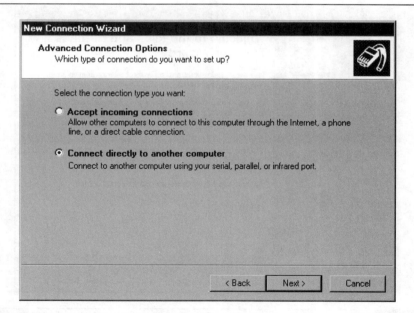

FIGURE 4-3   The New Connection Wizard can help you transfer data to another computer.

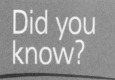

Some Settings Won't Be Transferred

Some old settings may not make it to the new computer. The wizard won't transfer old-computer settings for devices that aren't available on, or are incompatible with, Windows XP. When you're done with the transfer, the wizard lists files or folders that it couldn't restore. In particular, the wizard won't transfer third-party driver files for devices that aren't installed on the new computer or for network printers unavailable on the new system.

Once the two computers are on the same network, start the Files And Settings Transfer Wizard on the machine that has Windows XP (or either one if they are both running Windows XP). The wizard can be found by choosing Start | All Programs | Accessories | System Tools.

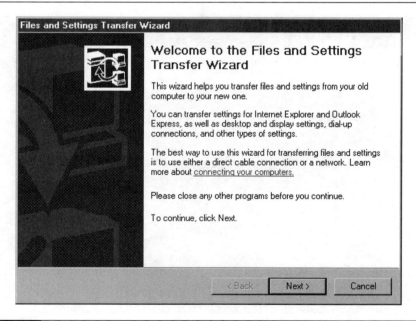

FIGURE 4-4 Use the Files And Settings Transfer Wizard to transfer files from your old computer to your new one.

Voices from the Community

Budapest Managing Editor

The Budapest Times is a 10,000 print run weekly newspaper for the English-speaking community in Hungary. The same number of German speakers read its partner paper, the *Budapester Zeitung.*

Almost half of *The Budapest Times* layout and photo prep, and the final print process and CD-burn for both papers is done on my souped-up VAIO PCG-GRX516MD (P-4M 2.66 GHz, 1GB RAM, Hitachi 60GB 7200rpm). The machine's UXGA display is the best we have in the company (and we have some nice 17-inch LCDs and 19-inch CRTs), and with all the various XP tweaks applied the VAIO outruns even a brand-new P4 2.8 GHz desktop.

Visitors and partners marvel at the fact that this notebook can do so much and to such a high standard—several have even commented that it would make a great advertisement for Sony! The machine has been in use for exactly one year now and still looks good and performs wonderfully, despite being in use 12-hours-plus every day, including weekends, and being transported about several times daily.

—Fraser S. Allan, managing editor of The Budapest Times

You'll need to run the wizard on both machines. If your other machine is not running Windows XP, no problem. You can use your Windows XP CD on your non-XP machine. The wizard is relatively easy to use. Follow the step-by-step instructions and answer the questions that appear in order to complete the transfer.

Configure the Windows Interface

Once you have your important files and settings moved to your Sony VAIO, it's time to start configuring your new system. The following sections address some of the areas where you can customize various elements of your VAIO, such as the Start menu, the taskbar, and the Explorer bar. I don't have space to cover all the ways to tweak your system, so I've focused on some major points and some of my favorite configuration tricks.

Customize the Start Menu

Begin by exploring and customizing the Start menu, which you open by tapping the Start button, usually found on the left edge of the taskbar. You can also open the Start menu by pressing CTRL-ESC, or by pressing and releasing the Windows

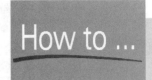 **Turn Off My Recent Documents**

The Start menu keeps a record of the documents you opened most recently, so you can access them again quickly. Depending on how your Start menu is set up, you might have a link in the right-hand column called My Recent Documents. Put your pointer on top of that link and it opens a submenu of documents you've worked on. But if you share your computer with someone and you don't want them to see the stuff you opened recently, you can clear that list and turn the record-keeping function off completely. Follow these steps:

1. Right-click the Start button.

2. Choose Properties.

3. Click Customize, which calls up the Customize Start Menu dialog box, as shown here. Select the Advanced tab.

4. Under Recent documents, uncheck List My Most Recently Opened Documents, and select Clear List.

5. Click OK twice to close the dialog boxes.

logo key, which usually resides to the left of the spacebar. To close the Start menu, press and release the Windows logo key, or press ESC, or click anywhere off the menu (on the desktop, for instance).

If you've used previous versions of Windows, you might notice that the redesigned Start menu contains two columns instead of one. The left side shows a list of programs, and the right side shows links to common Windows components and system folders.

> **NOTE** *If you're like me and you're sentimental for the old, single-column look of the Start menu, you can change it back. Right-click the Start button, select Properties, click Classic Start Menu, and click OK. Voilà! You're back to the single-column look.*

Some General (Tab) Advice

There are dozens of ways to customize your Start menu. The General tab of the Customize Start Menu dialog box (shown in the previous "How to…" sidebar), lets you control which application shortcuts appear in the menu and how large the icons are. It also allows you to specify a web browser and e-mail program that will show up in the *Pinned Item* list, as well as the number of programs that will appear in the Most Frequently Used Programs list. You can also clear the list of *shortcuts* in your Start menu, which is helpful if the menu gets too crowded. What's a shortcut? In the Start menu, icons are shortcuts, which are links to items on your computer or network, such as programs, files, folders, web pages, or devices.

Pin an Item to the Start Menu

So what's "pinning" an item to the Start menu mean? It's all about creating shortcuts to folders or programs you want to quickly access. You can add any item or object to the Start menu by dragging and dropping or pinning. You can also remove items.

> **NOTE** *Changing or deleting a shortcut doesn't affect the item to which it links. Removing a program's shortcut won't uninstall the program.*

If you want to pin your Solitaire game to the Start menu, for instance, follow these steps: Click Start, move your pointer over All Programs, and then over Games, which calls up a submenu. Scroll down to Solitaire and right-click it, and then click Pin To Start Menu. Back on the Start menu, you'll see the Solitaire icon appear in the left column (see Figure 4-5). To remove the icon, right-click it and tap Unpin From Start Menu.

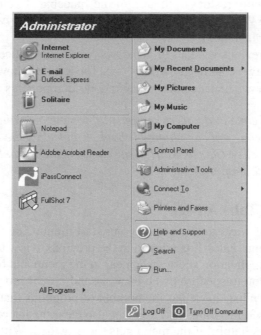

FIGURE 4-5   The Solitaire icon has been pinned to the Start menu.

TIP   *It's fine to rename any folder in the Start menu, including My Documents. But don't rename the Startup folder. If you do, Windows won't launch programs automatically when the computer boots.*

Customize the Taskbar

The taskbar is that long thin rectangle at the bottom of your screen (though at the bottom, you can move it around if you want). Proceeding from left to right, the taskbar is divided into several sections: the Start button, the Quick Launch toolbar, an area for holding buttons for each running application, and the system tray (sometimes called the systray).

TIP   *Point to any icon on the taskbar to display a helpful tool tip.*

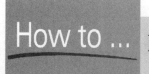

Push the Taskbar to the Edge

The taskbar doesn't have to remain at the bottom of your screen, nor is it a fixed size. It can live on any of the four edges of the screen, and it can be as wide as you want. If you want to move your taskbar, first make sure it's not "locked" in place (see this chapter's "Avoid Annoying Taskbar 'Features' " section to find out how to unlock it). Then move the taskbar with your mouse. To do this, point the mouse at any blank area on the taskbar, press and hold the left mouse button, and then drag the taskbar to any other edge of the screen. To shrink or expand the taskbar, point the mouse at the taskbar's top edge. The pointer changes to a this-way-or-that-way arrow. Drag the taskbar to whatever thickness you desire.

Avoid Annoying Taskbar "Features"

You can customize the taskbar in several ways. You can move it, add toolbars and shortcuts to it, group or ungroup programs, and change its properties. How you tweak the taskbar is very personal: it depends on how you like to work and how much clutter you like on your screen. For instance, the taskbar includes a feature that "stacks" multiple buttons for the same program in one menu; in other words, when your taskbar gets crowded, all your open web pages stack up behind just one Internet Explorer button, which displays "4 Internet Explorer," or something similar (see Figure 4-6). But I can't stand that feature. It wastes time trying to figure out which pages or documents I have open, so I always turn it off. Here's how to adjust that and other taskbar features:

1. Right-click a blank space on the taskbar, and then choose Properties, which calls up a dialog box (Figure 4-7).

2. Uncheck Group Similar Taskbar Buttons to turn off the stacking feature.

| Start | 4 Internet E... | FullShot 7.02 Pr... | 3 Microsoft W... | SONY VAIO BO... | New Bitmap Im... | chapter 4 scree... | Acrobat Reader... | « 2:06 PM |

FIGURE 4-6   A group button displays a small arrow and the number of open documents for the program. Click the button to access the document you want.

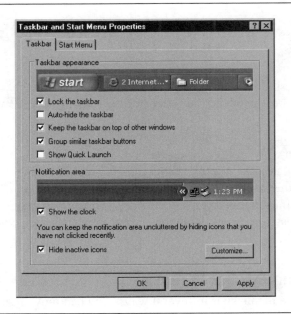

FIGURE 4-7 The Taskbar And Start Menu Properties dialog box lets you change the taskbar's appearance and functions.

3. Check Auto-Hide The Taskbar to hide the taskbar when you don't need it. The taskbar disappears until you point to the edge of the screen where it's located. (Watch out for this one. It can also be filed under annoying if you're not used to your taskbar magically disappearing while you're working.)

4. Check Keep The Taskbar On Top Of Other Windows to prevent other windows from covering the taskbar.

5. Check Lock The Taskbar to keep it at its current size and position. Uncheck this box if you want to resize or move the taskbar.

Sort Out the Systray

The system tray, or systray (also called the system notification area), is a tiny box on the right end of the taskbar. It displays the current time and day, little icons that represent programs running in Windows, and other tiny icons that help you do things, such as safely remove a piece of hardware you've added. (You'll learn more about that in Chapter 5.) More information about the icons can be revealed by either double-clicking or right-clicking them.

The systray in Windows XP routinely hides most of its small icons. To see all the icons, click the Show More arrows, the twin black arrows (or it might be one white arrow) at the left edge of the systray.

How to Use Windows Explorer

To help you work with folders and manage your files, Windows provides you with the Windows Explorer program. It's an easy-to-run program that you've no doubt already used while poking around your VAIO. You can open Windows Explorer (Figure 4-8) in several ways:

- Press WINDOWS LOGO KEY-E.
- Select Start | My Computer.

FIGURE 4-8   The right pane shows the contents of the selected folder, while the left pane shows the folder's *tree structure*.

- ■ Right-click the Start button, and then choose Explore.

- ■ Select Start | All Programs | Accessories | Windows Explorer.

All the files on your computer are organized into a *tree structure,* which can be seen on the left side of the Windows Explorer window. You can use the tree structure to quickly navigate to a specific folder in your computer if you know where to go. Just click a folder to display its contents on the right side of the window.

 *You can right-click an empty area in Explorer's right pane to use the View menu.*

Explorer lets you view the contents of a folder in many ways. You can change the size of icons, change the details displayed, or view miniature previews of graphics and files.

In Windows Explorer, select a folder, and then tap the View menu. Filmstrip (new in Windows XP) creates a slide show of images, with the selected image bigger than the others. Thumbnails display large icons for easy identification. Tiles display large icons with three lines of text that describe each file. If you take lots of digital pictures with the cool little camera mounted on top of the Sony VAIO TR Series notebook, or with a standard digital camera, then you'll love Explorer's Filmstrip view. Filmstrip only appears as an option when you have image files in the folder. Otherwise, it's absent from the list.

Now that you've learned how to configure many aspects of your VAIO, it's time to move on to Chapter 5 to learn how to install and remove hardware, adjust the volume or choose a different sound scheme, set up your printer, use Device Manager, and many more things.

Chapter 5

Manage Your VAIO Hardware

How to...

- Install and remove hardware
- Manage your hardware
- Use VAIO's Device Manager feature
- Set up different profiles for at-home and remote use

Whether you own a Sony VAIO desktop PC or notebook, managing your hardware will pretty much be the same. Working with standard hardware—like your keyboard, monitor, and mouse—is usually a simple task, because Windows XP is smart about adding and removing that hardware. But if you connect to a peripheral (nonessential) device like a digital camera, DVD burner, music player, or the like, you may need to manage that kind of hardware. I don't have room here to cover all the myriad ways you can tinker with your primary hardware or external devices, but this chapter gives you the basics you'll most likely need.

Install and Remove Hardware

The process of installing hardware includes connecting the device to the PC or notebook (most often via a cable to one of the USB 2.0 ports). If you're using hardware created after 1995, connecting the device usually means your operating system then finds and loads a *driver* that lets your machine talk to the hardware. Keep reading for more information on that.

Most of the external devices you'll install or remove from your VAIO PC or notebook are plug-and-play compatible, which simplifies matters. Plug-and-play is a technology that allows Windows to automatically recognize and configure plug-and-play–compatible hardware.

> **NOTE** *A* driver *is a software program that allows your computer to interact with a piece of hardware.*

Install Plug-and-Play Hardware

Installing plug-and-play hardware is one of the easiest things you'll ever do with your VAIO. Simply connect the device to your VAIO PC or notebook, turn your system on (if it's not already on) and wait. Soon, Windows XP will detect the new hardware and configure itself to work with that new device, including installing the proper

Did you know?

Three Ways to Minimize All Windows

If you've opened a ton of windows on your desktop, there are three shortcuts for minimizing them all in one shot.

- Select the Show Desktop shortcut icon in the taskbar. The icon shows up on the left side of the taskbar and looks like a square with a tiny pencil pointing to the center. If the icon isn't appearing in the taskbar, you can get it to appear by right-clicking an empty spot on the taskbar, then left-clicking Toolbars | Quick Launch. The Show Desktop shortcut icon resides in the Quick Launch toolbar. When all your windows have been minimized, click the icon again to maximize them all.

- Press WINDOWS-M. If you've never used the WINDOWS key, never fear: you're not alone. On most keyboards, this seldom-used key with a little Microsoft logo on it is found to the left of the spacebar on the bottom row of keys.

- Right-click an empty space on the taskbar and select Show The Desktop from the menu. (That option used to be called Minimize All Windows in previous versions of the Windows OS.) That should reduce all your windows to the taskbar, unless you have an unresolved issue in a program such as Outlook.

driver. Sony VAIO desktops and notebooks supply anywhere from two USB 2.0 ports on some notebooks to as many as six on some VAIO desktops. After you connect the device, a little message appears on your screen, telling you that Windows has found new hardware and is preparing to use it.

 To ensure that a device is plug-and-play–compatible, see the manufacturer's documentation that came with the device.

Install Non-Plug-and-Play Hardware

Although most hardware and accessories nowadays are plug-and-play, you may also want to use non-plug-and-play hardware, such as a favorite old mouse. In those cases, fire up the Add Hardware Wizard, shown in Figure 5-1, to guide you through

FIGURE 5-1
The Add Hardware Wizard guides you through the installation process.

the installation process. First, turn off your VAIO, unplug it from the wall, and connect the hardware to your notebook or PC. Restart your system and initiate the Add Hardware Wizard by selecting Start | Control Panel | Performance And Maintenance | System Hardware | Add Hardware Wizard. Follow the instructions that appear on the screen. You may need to insert the manufacturer's installation CD if you have one, or you may need to dig through a vendor's web site to find the latest driver. If your Control Panel is set to *classic view*, your path to the Add Hardware Wizard may be Start | Control Panel | Add Hardware | Add Hardware Wizard.

Remove Devices

Removing plug-and-play hardware is also a cinch. Unless you've added an internal device under the hood of your VAIO PC that must be extracted, you can normally remove the external hardware without shutting off the machine. First, check the *system tray* (or *systray*) at the right end of the taskbar to see if the Safely Remove Hardware icon is present. The icon looks like a PC Card with a green arrow above it. The fastest

Checking for Updated Drivers

Hardware companies commonly revise their software drivers to fix bugs, boost performance, and add features. Vendors typically post the updated drivers on their web sites, so you should periodically check their sites to see if new drivers are available. These updates often include support for newer versions of Windows. Some hardware manufacturers also allow you to sign up for driver update notifications, where the manufacturer will e-mail you when a new driver for your device has become available. You typically sign up for these via the manufacturer's web site.

way is to click the icon once. A list of devices will then appear. Click the name of the device that you want to remove. Another method is to double-click the icon with your left mouse button, select the name of the device you want to remove, and then click once on the Stop button. Another box will appear with the name of your device highlighted. Click OK. (These steps are supposed to stop the device and let you yank it out without the risk of data corruption. In my experience, however, the Safely Remove Hardware function often won't work on the first try, and you'll get this pop-up message: "The device cannot be stopped right now. Try stopping the device again later." If you get that message, try, try again. If you again get the warning, shut off your system before removing the device.)

 *A small rectangular box sits at the right end of the taskbar, displaying the time, the speaker icon, and icons for programs that Windows is running in the background. This area is known as the* system tray, *or* systray *for short.*

Manage Hardware

Windows XP gives you a couple of areas where you can manage your Sony VAIO hardware. Some hardware, such as audio devices and printers, have their own categories in the Control Panel (see Figure 5-2). Every bit of hardware on your VAIO can also be controlled from the Device Manager, although that method takes some getting used to and you have to be careful what you click.

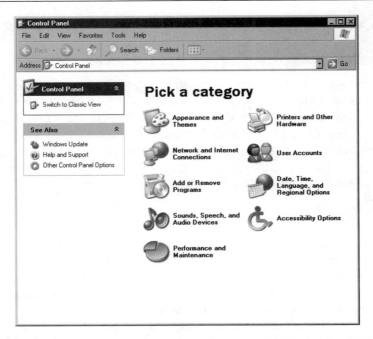

FIGURE 5-2 The Control Panel is a central area for tools to help you change preferences and settings. This is the *category view*.

Manage Sound and Audio Devices

If you travel on a crowded commuter train like I do, the first thing you'll want to know about your new VAIO notebook is how to mute a machine that's booting up. It's no fun blasting the Microsoft jingle throughout the train—the few stressed-out folks not shouting into their cell phones aren't amused to have their peace and quiet interrupted by loud reminders of the office.

On Sony VAIO notebooks, you drop the volume by hitting two keys on the keyboard (FN-F3 to mute, FN-F4 for up/down control). Some VAIO notebooks also have two dedicated volume buttons. On the VAIO TR Series, for example, the two volume buttons are on the side of the display. Once powered on, you can also adjust the volume by clicking the speaker icon in the systray, at the right end of the taskbar. That brings up the Volume window. To adjust volume from here, use your mouse to place your pointer over the horizontal bar on the volume scale; press and hold your left mouse button down while your pointer is on the bar, and then move your mouse up or down to drag the bar up or down. For more volume options, double-click

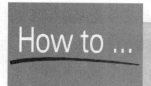 **Change Control Panel Views**

If you've owned other computers, you may recall the way the Control Panel used to look, now called *classic view*.

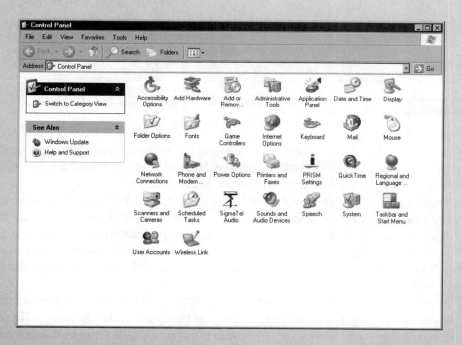

Windows XP's Control Panel defaults to a different, beginner-friendly look, called the *category view* (see Figure 5-2), but if you have a soft spot for classic view, (and who doesn't) you can switch views. To do that, first make sure the Control Panel's *task pane* is showing. The task pane (new in Windows XP) occupies the left side of the Explorer window and provides useful commands and links to related locations. To call up the Control Panel's task pane, select Tools | Folder Options | General tab | Show Common Tasks In Folders. Once the task pane is called up, you're ready to change the look of the Control Panel. In the task pane, simply click Switch To Classic View.

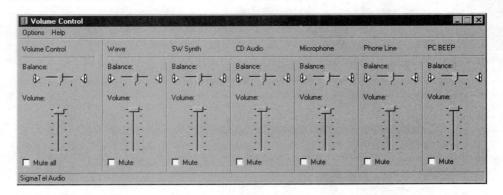

FIGURE 5-3   The Volume Control window lets you set the sound levels and balance.

the speaker icon, and you'll bring up the expanded Volume Control window (see Figure 5-3). You can then adjust the volume, balance, and other sound settings by dragging bars as you did on the pared-down Volume window.

These two volume control methods—the two-finger keyboard poke and the systray icon—work fine, if you're quick and know which keys to hit. But dedicated volume buttons are easier, and I'd like to see Sony include those buttons on all models, or start using a volume control wheel found on some Toshiba notebooks. Sony VAIO desktops have another volume option: the little knob on the speakers. Don't forget those.

Your VAIO might also make various beeps and grunts when you open a menu, close a window, or get an e-mail (depending on how your e-mail is set up). If you listen too closely, or have these sounds cranked up too high, they might start to drive you nuts. Luckily, Windows lets you assign specific sounds to individual Windows events, or you can mute the whole system.

To assign audio clips to events, drill down to the Sounds And Audio Devices Properties (see Figure 5-4), like so: select Start | Control Panel | Sounds, Speech, And Audio Devices | Change The Sound Scheme. (Your path may vary if your Control Panel is set to classic view.) In the Sounds tab, scroll down and click the name of the event whose sound you want to change, and then scroll down through the Sounds menu until you find what you want. My favorite? Assigning the musical "tada" sound to the Empty Recycle Bin "event." That's always a joyous occasion in my house.

Set Up Your Printer

Most likely, you set up Windows to work with your printer when you first cracked open your VAIO PC or notebook. If not, or if you just bought a new printer, you may need to tell Windows about it. If your printer supports plug-and-play, Windows XP

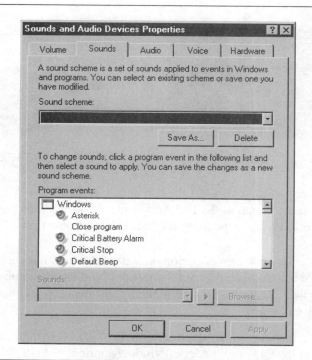

FIGURE 5-4   The Sounds And Audio Devices Properties window lets you assign audio clips to various "events," such as opening a window or emptying the Recycle bin.

will lead you through the installation automatically, because the OS comes with printer drivers for most common plug-and-play printers. Also check for a CD, because your printer might have come with an updated printer driver as well. Most modern printers connect via a USB 2.0 port, but if you want to go old school, you'll still find plenty of printers that accept those big, 25-pin parallel cables (see Figure 5-5).

NOTE   *Avoid being a frustrated printer buyer who must trudge back to the computer store: Don't forget to buy a cable when you buy a new printer.*

If you need to add a printer driver via the disk you got, insert the disc, select Start | Control Panel | Printers And Other Hardware | Add A Printer. In Control Panel's classic view, it's Start | Control Panel | Printers And Faxes | Add A Printer (which appears as a link in the upper-left corner of the window).

FIGURE 5-5   Three vertical USB 2.0 ports on a VAIO notebook and a 25-pin parallel cable

Click Next on the Welcome To The Add Printer Wizard screen (see Figure 5-6). The steps that follow vary, depending on your printer. Some tips:

- Select the network printer option only if you're on a network, which means your network manager may set things up. If you have a home network, keep in mind that Windows XP automatically installs network printers as part of the network setup.

- Windows may ask for its distribution CD to load the printer driver. If you can't find the CD, look under c:\windows\options\CABS. Windows may find the files there.

- If your printer came with its own CD, you may need to install programs from the disc to begin the printer installation. Check the documentation that came with the CD.

Finally, print a test page. If you've made it this far without a trip back to the computer store for a cable or more ink-jet cartridges, give yourself a musical "tada" salute and call it a night.

Use Device Manager

Only more experienced users should dare venture into the Device Manager (see Figure 5-7), a powerful tool that lets you inspect, manage, and troubleshoot drivers for the hardware already installed on your VAIO. It lists every device in, or attached to, your computer in an Explorer-like tree. Be cautious, because you can damage your VAIO if you click the wrong thing when manually changing settings in the Device Manager. Get help from the tech savvy if you're unsure.

FIGURE 5-6   The Add Printer Wizard guides you through the sometimes tricky steps of adding a printer.

If you're having trouble installing a device, the Device Manager can give you a clue as to what's going on. To open the Device Manager, select Start | Control Panel | System Hardware | Device Manager. (Your path may vary if your Control Panel is set to classic view.) Or try this way, which is faster: Right-click My Computer, and then choose Properties | Hardware tab | Device Manager. The Device Manager Window will open and look similar to Figure 5-7.

> **TIP**   *To expand or contract all branches of the Device Manager tree, select the top entry, and then press the little + symbol to the left to expand it, or the little – symbol to contract the tree.*

You can use the Device Manager to install a driver that's newer than the one you're currently using. However, keep in mind that newer doesn't always mean better, or more stable. If a driver isn't broken, don't update it unless the improvement will be significant.

FIGURE 5-7 The Device Manager shows all your computer's devices in an Explorer-like tree.

Set Up Hardware Profiles

A hardware profile tells Windows which devices to start when you fire up your VAIO. Profiles are particularly useful if you're traveling with your Sony laptop. For instance, when you're in the office or at home, you'll want your VAIO to recognize your network card, external mouse, keyboard, and monitor, but when you're on an airplane or in a hotel room, you won't want your laptop wasting time and battery life searching for these devices. So, to make life easier, you should create a profile for each scenario. To set up a hardware profile, follow these steps:

1. Select Start | Control Panel | Performance And Maintenance | System | Hardware | Hardware Profiles. In Control Panel's classic view, it's Start | Control Panel | System | Hardware | Hardware Profiles.

2. Choose an existing profile in the list, and then click Copy.

3. Type in a name for a new profile, and then click OK (see Figure 5-8).

How to ... Update Drivers

The best way to update a device driver is to open that device's Properties dialog box. To do so, in the Device Manager right-click the icon for the device, select Properties in the menu that pops up, and then click the Driver tab. All the Driver tabs have the same form, with basic driver information at the top, and four buttons below. The descriptions next to each button tell you what they do. Because hardware makers periodically update drivers, there may be a new driver on the manufacturer's web site. Compare the driver version number shown in the Properties dialog box to that of the latest driver for your device on the manufacturer's web site. If a newer driver exists, download it to your VAIO and follow any instructions provided by the manufacturer. Use the Hardware Update Wizard to install the new driver. This wizard uses the same screens as the Found New Hardware and Add New Hardware wizards (see Figure 5-1, shown previously).

If a new driver causes more problems than it solves—common for prerelease beta drivers—Windows XP's driver rollback feature allows you to uninstall the current driver and replace it with the previous one. To roll back a device driver: In the Device Manager, right-click the device in question, and then choose Properties | Driver tab | Roll Back Driver.

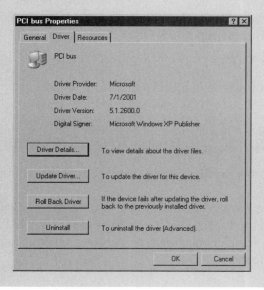

FIGURE 5-8 Windows names the default hardware profile Profile 1. You'll want to give your new profiles memorable names, such as Working Slob or Travels With Charlie.

4. In the Hardware Profile Selection section, select how Windows should load a profile during startup. Click OK.

5. Restart your VAIO.

6. On the startup screen (a black, text screen), choose the profile you want to modify.

7. Open the Device Manager (see the preceding section) and adjust the settings for each device you want to enable or disable. Close the Device Manager.

8. To modify other profiles, repeat these steps for each profile.

Now that you've learned how to manage your VAIO hardware, it's time to learn how to connect to the Internet, including examining the different types of ISP, choosing an ISP and connection type, creating a new account, and installing broadband connections.

Chapter 6

Connect to the Internet

How to...

- Choose an ISP
- Learn the different kinds of ISPs
- Choose a connection type
- Create a new Internet account
- Set up an existing Internet account
- Install broadband connections

For most people, a computer isn't much fun less unless it's connected to the vast supply of news, maps and directions, downloadable music, online games, product reviews, comparison shopping, and communication media on the Internet. To do the fun stuff, you have to get connected to the Internet. Your Sony VAIO's New Connection Wizard (see Figure 6-1) simplifies this task, but, to tell the truth, hooking up to the Internet causes stress in even the most experienced computer users. To get on the Net, you need to pay a go-between company called an *Internet service provider (ISP)*; Sony VAIOs come with software that will allow you to connect to two, or sometimes three, of the biggest national ISPs, Microsoft's MSN, America Online (AOL), or EarthLink. You can also choose your own ISP.

The goal of this chapter is to help you get your Sony VAIO notebook or desktop PC connected to the Internet. I'll describe the different types of services, the options for connecting, show you how to set up a connection automatically or manually, and tell you how to adjust the connection settings for when you take your swanky new VAIO notebook home to meet the relatives.

Choose an ISP

There are two factors that affect your Internet browsing speed: your connection from your computer to your ISP and the connection across the Internet from your ISP to the web site you're trying to access. Depending on the time of day, Internet routing issues, and the responsiveness of the web site you're trying to get on, even the fastest connections can feel slow at times. Regardless, it makes sense to get the fastest and most cost-effective connection to the Internet you can.

 *If you want to connect your VAIO to the Internet via a network (either a big corporate network or a small home network), the situation is somewhat different. For that, you'll need to read Chapter 8.*

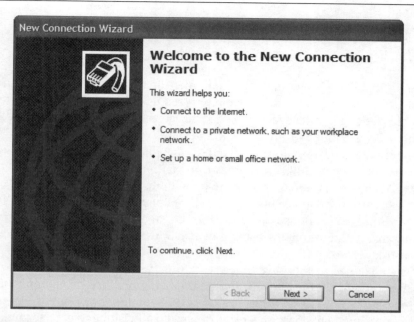

6

FIGURE 6-1   The New Connection Wizard can help you connect your Sony VAIO to the Internet.

Unless you're accessing the Internet from work, you'll probably be relying on an ISP to provide your Internet connection. In the 1990s, ISPs were often local operations, but as the market has grown, many local ISPs have been swallowed up by bigger regional or national operations. Now you have the choice of using a local ISP, a national ISP, a national online service (like AOL), or your phone or cable TV provider. Each has pluses and minuses. As I mentioned, Sony VAIOs come with Microsoft's MSN, America Online (AOL), and sometimes even EarthLink.

Luckily, Internet access pricing differences are pretty minimal these days. The widespread availability of ISPs has squeezed pricing, so for a dial-up connection, you shouldn't need to pay more than $20–$25 per month for unlimited use.

National ISPs

National ISPs are great if you travel a lot. You should be able to find a local access number in most cities, allowing you to dial in and check e-mail without incurring toll charges. For a business traveler, this is a big plus.

The Architect

I bought my Sony VAIO laptop to help me run a consulting business in construction management and residential design. Initially, I was drawn to its streamlined design, and the fact that it had the largest screen size of any comparable laptop. Because much of my computing time is spent with demanding CAD (computer-aided design) drafting and design applications, I needed a notebook computer that behaved like a graphics workstation.

My VAIO had no problem keeping up with the demands of my work, and it quickly became my portable office, managing all my e-mail, drawing files, billing, and correspondence. It also proved rugged enough to withstand the occasional beating that it received in the back of my truck when I'd drive up rutted roads to construction sites.

I soon learned how to save time by drafting "as-built" floor plans directly into my computer at the job site. The traditional, more time-consuming method of preparing "as-built" drawings involves taking building measurements in the field, scribbling them down on a piece of paper, and waiting to get back into the office to prepare the actual drawings, only to find the most critical dimension was forgotten in a sea of handwritten notes. Having a portable computer fast enough to draft with, obviated this problem and made my business more productive.

—Christopher Barlow is a project designer and aspiring architect working in the North Beach neighborhood of San Francisco. His firm specializes in developing high quality designs for residential and commercial projects. The firm's web site is www.arcanumarchitecture.com.

What's the downside? Well, if you run into a problem, it may not be easy to get personal service from a huge outfit. It's not like a local ISP where you can just charge into the office and ask for help. Check for toll-free support numbers first, and try calling one before you sign up. If you're on hold for a while, consider it a warning, no matter how good the on-hold music is.

TIP *If you need a new account, ask your friends and neighbors who already have Internet access who they prefer. Are they happy? Did they try and reject another ISP first?*

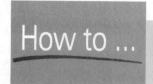

Find a Local Access Number

If you're accessing the Internet with a program bundled with your Sony VAIO, such as Microsoft's MSN or EarthLink, you'll first be connected with an 800, 866, or other toll-free number. After you set up your account, you'll get a list of local access numbers. If you want to choose your own ISP, but aren't sure where to start, you can usually find them in the Yellow Pages under Internet. Some ISPs even advertise on TV. After choosing, call the ISP's main number. From there, you'll often be dumped into a dreaded voicemail options menu. If you click the right numbers, you should eventually hear a choice for "start a new account" or "a list of local access numbers." Make sure you double-check the number you select to see if it's really local. (See the Did You Know? box titled "Watch Out for Extra Phone Charges.") Finally, you can also find local access numbers on an ISP's web site, such as support.earthlink.net/support/ACCESS/.

Local ISPs

Local ISPs aren't as prevalent as they used to be, but they can still be wonderful. You can get personal service, special deals, and local dial-in numbers. If you have configuration problems or need special service, the help of a local provider can be

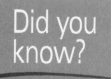

Watch Out for Extra Phone Charges

Whichever ISP you choose, pay close attention to the phone number you use to access the Internet. Without any warning, charges may appear on your next phone bill if you pick a number in a location that's too far from your house. It's a tricky process that has fooled many. Here's how it works: If you live in Cupertino, California, for instance, and see a dial-up number in the same 408 area code but in a different city (San Jose, for instance), you might think it's fine. It's in the same area code, right? Wrong (possibly). You need to make sure you're not incurring extra charges. One way to do this is to dial the operator and ask if the number you've chosen is a local number for you.

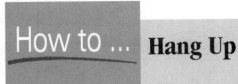

How to ... Hang Up

When you close your browser or other Internet program, your dial-up connection doesn't hang up automatically. It ties up your phone line until you disconnect it manually. To hang up, here's what you do: First, look for the little two-computer icon in your *system tray,* which is at the right edge of your taskbar at the bottom of the screen. Click the icon to see your connection status. You can also just rest your pointer on top of the icon, without doing any clicking, to see your connection status. To hang up, simply click the Disconnect button, or right-click the little icon and choose Disconnect from the pop-up menu.

invaluable. In some areas, a local ISP may be your only option for connecting to the Internet.

On the downside, some local ISPs do not provide excellent service. The little company might not have enough servers, and you might have all kinds of problems like dropped connections and lousy performance.

Internet junkies prefer traditional ISPs, which offer direct, unsanitized access to the Internet. Beginners like online services, such as AOL or MSN, because they're (allegedly) easier to use and set up, and they have their own little online communities. Online services give you an all-in-one application to browse the Web, send e-mail, create web sites, and so forth. With traditional ISPs, you choose your programs, such as Internet Explorer for browsing, and Outlook Express or Eudora for e-mail.

Online Services

Online services are another way to get on the Internet. America Online (AOL) and Microsoft's MSN both offer value-added content and services in addition to being your ISP. What kind of value-added content and services? Some people couldn't face life without their IMs (instant messages) on AOL, for instance. Or you might find all kinds of interesting content on MSN's home page, such as a notebook review from yours truly. (CNET Networks, where I'm a Senior Editor, provides some content to MSN.)

Despite some problems in coming up with enough phone lines to satisfy demand, AOL has done a good job of providing connections. And both AOL and MSN have

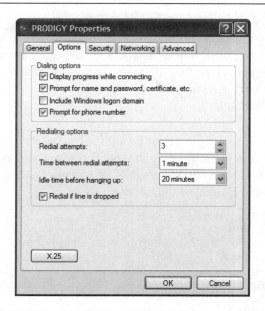

FIGURE 6-2   This Options tab will let you force a connection hang-up after a period of inactivity.

tons of local access numbers. Just make sure you're using a local number. (See the Did You Know? box titled "Watch Out for Extra Phone Charges.")

To force a connection hang-up after a period of inactivity, first get to the connection icon by choosing Start | Connect To | Show All Connections. Then, find your icon and right-click it, choose Properties, and select the Options tab (see Figure 6-2). Afterward, select a time limit from the Idle Time Before Hanging Up list.

Choose Connection Types

A *dial-up connection* uses the standard phone lines that run into your home or office to connect your VAIO to an Internet service provider. To establish a dial-up connection, you need a dial-up modem installed and configured to communicate with an ISP (which you have on your Sony VAIO). A dial-up modem (short for modulator/ demodulator) is a device inside your computer that converts the digital signals it uses into analog signals the phone system uses, and vice versa. Installing and configuring a high-speed *broadband connection* such as DSL (digital subscriber line) or cable is conceptually similar to installing a dial-up connection. To get the Internet ball rolling, plug the telephone cable from the wall jack into your modem's jack. (Make sure you don't plug it into the bigger, but similar looking, Ethernet jack, a common newbie mistake.) To establish a dial-up connection, follow these steps.

Create a New Internet Account

Read this section if you lack an Internet account and want to use Microsoft's referral service to sign up with an ISP online. The service lists only ISPs that cut a special deal with Microsoft, but with a little extra work, you can find a local ISP. If that's the case, skip to the next section.

To create a new account:

1. On the taskbar, select Start | All Programs | Accessories | Communications | New Connection Wizard (see Figure 6-1). You can also get to the wizard by clicking Start | Connect To | Show All Connections | Create A New Connection (located on the left side of the window).

2. Click Next to skip the first screen.

3. Select Connect To The Internet (it should already be selected by default), and then click Next.

4. Select Choose From A List Of Internet Service Providers (ISPs), as shown in Figure 6-3, and then click Next.

5. To use Microsoft as your ISP, choose Get Online With MSN, and then click Finish. To choose a different ISP, choose Select From A List Of Other ISPs (Figure 6-4), and then click Finish.

6. If you choose MSN, the MSN wizard will start. Or double-click Refer Me To More Internet Service Providers in the Online Services Folder window that appears. The Internet Connection Wizard starts.

7. Follow the onscreen instructions. When you're done, a new connection icon appears in the Network Connections window. Choose Start | All Programs | Accessories | Communications | Network Connections. Double-click the icon to go online, or right-click it to see its properties.

Set Up an Existing Internet Account

If you have an existing Internet account, this section is for you. First, follow steps 1–3 in the preceding section. Once you're past the Connect To The Internet screen, follow these steps:

1. Select Set Up My Connection Manually, and then click Next. Detour: If you have an AOL or other installation CD, select Use The CD I Got From An ISP, click Next, click Finish, insert the CD, and then follow the onscreen instructions and skip the rest of these steps.

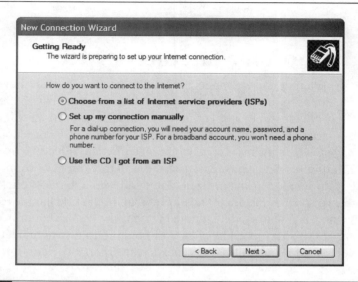

FIGURE 6-3   The New Connection Type window can help you set up a variety of accounts.

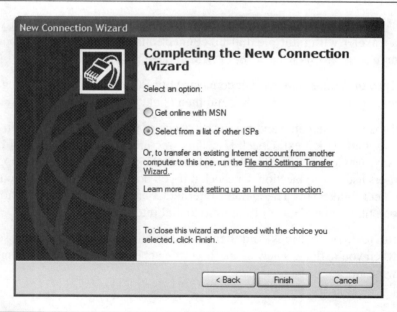

FIGURE 6-4   This window gets you started on selecting your ISP.

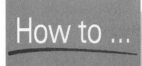

Create a Shortcut to Your Internet Service

You'll use the Internet connection icon a lot. So create a shortcut to it on your desktop. You do that by first finding the icon, which you may have called MSN, AOL, Prodigy, or something similar, in the Network Connections window (see step 7 in the preceding section). Next, make sure the Network Connections window isn't *maximized,* which means a window the size of your whole screen. You want a smaller window, so you can see part of the desktop and have room for your shortcut. If your window is maximized, don't call Maximus. Just click the little button with two squares inside it that's located up in the title bar, next to the X. (When a window is maximized, that little button is the *restore* button.) When you can see part of the desktop, right-click and hold the Internet connection icon, drag it to your desktop, and release it. Click Create Shortcuts Here from the menu that appears.

2. Select Connect Using A Dial-Up Modem, and then click Next.

3. Type a connection name, and then click Next (see Figure 6-5). If you're a traveler with multiple dial-up connections on your VAIO notebook, use names like MSN (San Jose) or MSN (New York).

4. Type the phone number that connects your PC to your ISP (including a prefix and area code, if necessary), and then click Next.

5. Type your username and password, check or uncheck the connection options, and then click Next. Check Use This Account Name And Password When Anyone Connects To The Internet From This Computer to let all logged-on users use this connection. Uncheck it if you don't want to share the connection. Check Make This The Default Internet Connection if this connection is the one that you use most of the time to dial into the Internet.

6. Review your settings, and then click Finish. As in the preceding section, when you're done, a new connection icon appears in the Network Connections window.

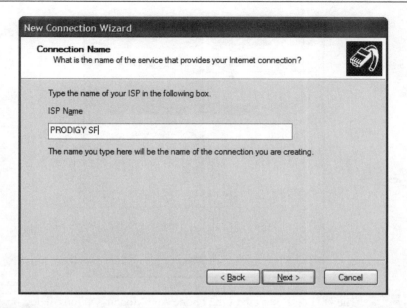

FIGURE 6-5   In this window, type the name of the Internet connection. This process will create an icon that you'll use frequently.

Create and Use Dialing Rules

If you own a sleek Sony VAIO notebook, chances are you'll want to show it off on the airplane or dazzle distant relatives. But when you're away from home and want to get online, you'll likely need to configure your modem differently, to account for the local area code and other location-specific conditions. *Dialing rules* allow you to set up configurations that your VAIO will use in each location.

Anything you do with dialing rules, you do from the Phone And Modem Options dialog box (Figure 6-6). To open this dialog box, choose Start | Control Panel | Printers And Other Hardware | Phone And Modem Options, and then select the Dialing Rules tab. You should see something similar to Figure 6-6. You can view the list of dialing locations here, as well as create and edit them.

If you want to create a new dialing location, click New to open the New Location dialog box. Start on the General tab (Figure 6-7). Enter the name you will use to identify this location, as well as the location you'll be dialing from.

The rest of the information on this tab is specific to the telephone system your computer will be connecting to at this location. Use information from the local phone service to fill in the Dialing Rules fields, along with the To Disable Call Waiting, Dial field, and the Dial Using field. If the phone you'll be using has call waiting, disable that when the modem is in use.

FIGURE 6-6   The Dialing Rules tab of the Phone And Modem Options dialog box allows you to quickly switch between the computer and modem configuration options for different locations.

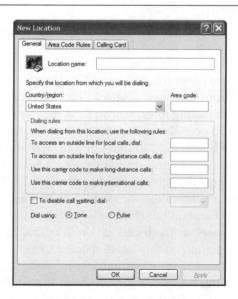

FIGURE 6-7   Start creating a new dialing location on the General tab of the New Location dialog box.

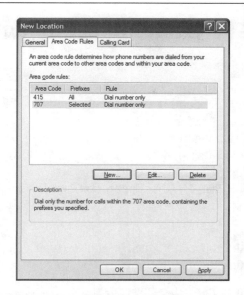

FIGURE 6-8   The Area Code Rules tab lists the rules you have defined for handling today's more complex phone-dialing requirements.

Understand Area Code Rules

Next, you'll want to look at the Area Code Rules tab (Figure 6-8). With the increasing number of phone lines in the United States, the rules for dialing within and between area codes have become more complex. You may, for instance, have to dial 1 and the area code for numbers even within your own area code. Or you may need to dial 9 to dial out from some hotel rooms. The Area Code Rules tab allows you to tell Windows how to handle these situations.

This tab lists the rules that you've defined so far. From here, you can delete existing rules, edit the ones you have, and create new ones. To delete or edit a rule, select it in the Area Code Rules list and click the appropriate button.

You edit existing area code rules and create new ones using the same dialog box. (Just the name changes, appearing as Edit Area Code Rule when editing and New Area Code Rule when adding a new rule.) To create the new rule, enter the area code for which the rule applies. If you're dialing from 408 where you are, enter "408." Then fill in the Prefixes and Rules sections of the dialog box as necessary and click OK to save this new rule, which then appears in the list.

NOTE   *Don't forget to restore the dialing location to normal when you return home.*

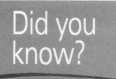

The Truth About Modem Speed

Modems are advertised to operate at 56 Kbps (kilobits per second), but you'll never see that speed. Connections are currently limited to 53 Kbps because of an arcane FCC regulation, but that kind of speed is over a perfect connection under ideal circumstances. Depending on the distance between you and your ISP, and the quality of the phone lines between you, you will see lower speeds. In reality, anything approaching 50 Kbps is good.

In order to make a near–56 Kbps connection, several conditions must be met:

- One end of the connection needs to be digital (the end at your ISP).

- One end of the connection must be analog (typically, the line connecting your modem to the phone company's equipment).

- Both ends must have 56-Kbps capability.

If you use a calling card, choose the Calling Card tab. Here you can usually select your card from the extensive calling card list maintained by Windows. Then enter your account number, PIN, and access phone numbers. If your card doesn't appear in the list on this tab, click New and fill out the information fields in the screen that appears. Once you finish with these tabs, your new dialing location is complete.

Hotels May Charge Extra

Be aware that while traveling, hotels typically charge Internet access fees, even if you're using an 800 number to get online from your room. These sometimes hefty fees will appear as phone charges on your bill. To avoid an unpleasant surprise upon checkout, ask hotels up front what fees they charge and what options they provide for business travelers connecting to the Internet. For example, many hotels now offer broadband Internet access in your room.

If you're working at one of your dialing locations, you don't need to manually configure all the dialing rules your VAIO needs. Simply go to the Phone And Modem Options dialog box and select it.

Install and Configure Broadband Connections

There are several ways to establish a broadband connection with the Internet. In many cases, you should let someone else set up these connections for you, but you may have to set one up or repair it yourself some day. The process is conceptually similar to installing dial-up connections. You need to connect some sort of device to your computer (using the Ethernet port on your VAIO) that translates information between the computer and the ISP. The two most common types of broadband connections in the United States are cable modems and DSL. To connect to the Internet wirelessly, see Chapter 9.

DSL and cable connections are growing in popularity because:

- *They're fast.* Broadband modems are 10 to 50 times faster than dial-up modems.

- *They're always on.* When your VAIO is connected to the broadband modem, it has a live connection to the Internet. There's no need to wait while the computer dials into your ISP.

- *They don't tie up your phone line.* Unless you have a very early broadband modem, all communications between your VAIO notebook or PC and the Internet goes through the cable, leaving your phone free for other uses.

Understand the Different Broadband Options

A cable connection uses a cable modem to operate over a cable TV line (coaxial cable). If you're wired for cable TV, you can get a connection through your cable company. Be aware that cable speed can drop quite a bit when too many people in your area use the system.

DSL uses a DSL modem to operate over a standard phone line without interfering with normal voice calls. It works better if you're closer to a phone-company central office. DSL offers the same three advantages over regular dial-up access that cable does, except it is usually somewhat slower than a cable modem.

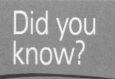

Other Broadband Technologies

Cable and DSL are the most popular broadband choices, but there are two other interesting options. One is satellite service.

Satellite systems are offered by companies like DIRECTV. These systems use a fleet of satellites that orbit the earth, and offer speeds faster than dial-up but slower than DSL and cable. You should consider a satellite connection if you live in an area with no other broadband options.

ISDN is another broadband technology that is occasionally available. This technology requires special equipment be attached to your computer, and it must be supported by both your phone company and your ISP. You should consider ISDN (integrated services digital network) only if you have no other options.

Install Broadband Connections

With the variety of available broadband connections, it's impossible to give you explicit instructions on how to install yours. The easiest approach is to have the cable company (for cable modems) or the phone company (for DSL) install it for you. You'll probably have to pay the installer, but the technician should have you up and running with minimal problems. If you're comfortable mucking around with hardware, you can install the connection yourself. But I wouldn't recommend doing this unless you're confident of your technical abilities, and you're not running a business where a connection problem would hurt your mojo.

Configure Your Broadband Connection

As with installing your broadband connection, there are too many variables to go into detail here regarding configuring the connection. If you had someone from the cable or phone companies install your hardware for you, that technician should have completed all the necessary configuration work as well. If you decide to do it yourself, the equipment you received should have detailed instructions on how to configure the setup.

Now that you've learned the ins and outs of connecting to the Internet, it's time to move on to Chapter 7 to explore Outlook Express and how to use it for e-mail or as a *newsreader* for those vast, uncensored *newsgroups*. There, too, you'll learn about web-based e-mail and how to use it, as well as how to fight the growing onslaught of junk e-mail (spam).

Chapter 7

Communicate with E-mail

How to...

- Understand the features of Outlook Express
- Use Outlook Express for e-mail
- Use Outlook Express as a newsreader
- Get something for nothing with web-based e-mail
- Fight spam and other nuisances

E-mail started out as the Internet's killer application and continues to be the most widely used Internet tool for computers and mobile devices. Blue-haired grandmas who never had any interest in electronic gizmos will buy complete desktop systems just so they can stay in the loop by sending and receiving e-mail and family photos.

Over the past several years, e-mail has in many cases replaced what is now derisively referred to as "snail mail," communications delivered by the United States Postal Service. It has also become a viable alternative to faxing, although, in some cases, where legal-type documents need hard copy signatures, old methods must prevail. But in almost all other respects, e-mail has become one of the fastest-growing phenomena in the history of international communications. In this chapter, you'll learn about using Microsoft's Outlook Express for e-mail or newsgroups, how to use free web-based e-mail, and how to fight the onslaught of spam.

Explore Outlook Express

Sony VAIO notebooks and PCs come with Windows XP, which includes Outlook Express (a.k.a., OE), a free e-mail client that Microsoft has included with Windows for several years now. Outlook Express can also be used as a *newsreader* for reading, or to post items in a *newsgroup* (the Internet equivalent of an incredibly wide-ranging bulletin board; we'll discuss newsgroups later in this chapter). OE can manage multiple e-mail and newsgroup accounts for you under a single user identity, or under different identities. That way, you can handle both your business and personal messages from the same program without mixing them up. If you'll be using your Sony VAIO as a communication tool, it's a good idea to learn about OE. Let's start by looking at the e-mail side of OE.

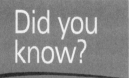

Brevity Is the Soul of E-mail Wit

When you get your first e-mail account, or if you've had one for a while, remember Shakespeare's immortal line: *Brevity is the soul of wit.* Unfortunately, people new to e-mail often feel obligated to entertain everyone they know who has an e-mail address. But the vast majority of us on e-mail have seen those jokes you're about to forward. We've seen the funny pictures. We know the outrageous stories. And we're short on time. Many of us use e-mail as a vital business tool. We're already bogged down with work messages, important personal missives, and spam. So before you send out that blanket e-mail, think. Be part of the solution, not the problem.

Use Outlook Express for E-mail

Turn on your VAIO, and Outlook Express should be easily accessible from your Windows desktop. To open the program, double-click its desktop icon (a white envelope being hugged by two blue arrows, so to speak), or choose Start | All Programs | Outlook Express.

NOTE   *Don't confuse Outlook Express with Outlook, its bigger sibling in Microsoft's Office suite. Outlook is a complex application that manages your e-mail, calendar, meetings, and more. Like many of us, you may be using Outlook in your office.*

Configure Outlook Express

The first thing you'll need to do is maximize the OE window. The opening view of OE, shown in Figure 7-1, gives you an overview of what the program can do, but you won't find it useful on a daily basis. Instead, click the Inbox in the left pane, which puts OE into its e-mail handling configuration, as shown in Figure 7-2. What's inside the selected folder appears in the bigger View pane on the right.

TIP   *You don't have to use Outlook Express for e-mail. You can try other e-mail programs like Eudora, which is free at www.eudora.com, or you can use free, web-based e-mail from Yahoo or Hotmail. See "Web-Based E-mail: Get Something for Nothing," later in this chapter, for more information.*

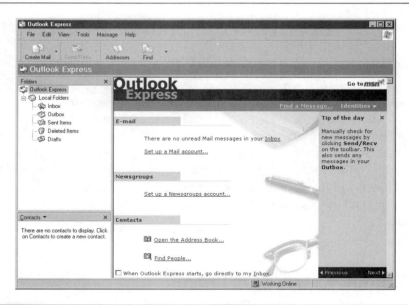

FIGURE 7-1   Outlook Express can handle all of your e-mail, contact, and newsgroup needs in one program.

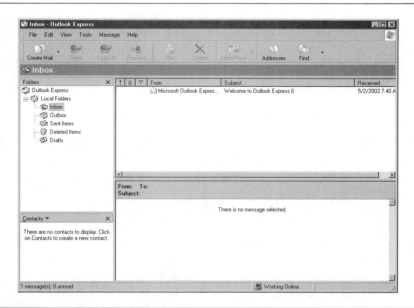

FIGURE 7-2   The Outlook Express Inbox view, which shows e-mail messages in the main window

Did you know?

E-mail Etiquette

Remember that communicating via e-mail can be problematic. Aspects of interpersonal communication that work face to face, like sarcasm, often don't work in e-mail. It only takes a few additional minutes to review your message to make sure that it is courteously worded before sending it, so please do so. The following tips will make your recipient feel that your message is worthy of attention and a response:

- Include a greeting and a closing in your message.

- Writing in all uppercase letters makes it seem like YOU ARE YELLING!

- Include text from the original message if you are responding to another person's e-mail.

- Use both uppercase and lowercase letters and proper punctuation.

- Before sending, use built-in tools like the spell checker to make sure you haven't made any major spelling blunders.

- Before forwarding that crude joke, make absolutely certain the receiver wants to see it.

7

If you plan to use Outlook Express as an e-mail client, the first step is to configure one or more e-mail accounts. Assuming you have an existing e-mail account that you want to access with OE, select Tools | Accounts, and then select the Mail tab in the Internet Accounts dialog box. You can use this dialog box to export existing accounts from other e-mail and newsgroup accounts, as well as to import and export existing accounts from other e-mail clients and newsreaders. To add your account information, tap Add | Mail, and then follow the directions in the Internet Connection Wizard, which guides you through the process.

NOTE   *We're not going to cover importing and exporting existing e-mail accounts in this quick tour. The Outlook Express help system or your company's information technology whiz can assist you in those steps.*

Create and Send Messages

The steps for creating and sending e-mail messages vary, depending on which e-mail program or online service you're using. In most cases, you first click the big button at the top of the window for composing a new message, but there are other methods as well. For example, in Outlook Express, there are three ways to create a new message: click the Create Mail button, click File | New | Mail Message, or press CTRL-N. A window then appears, prompting you to compose your message (see Figure 7-3).

Click in the To box and type the person's e-mail address. Then click the Subject box and type a brief description of the message. Click in the large box near the bottom of the window and type your message. When you're ready to "mail" your message, click the Send button above the To field.

If you receive an e-mail message sent to many people, and you wish to reply to the sender only, be careful. Don't click Reply All. Many have been embarrassed by accidentally hitting Reply All and sending a blanket message intended for one set of eyes only.

Some e-mail programs send the message immediately. Other programs place the messages you send in a temporary outbox. Then, when you're ready to send, you can do it all in one shot. In OE, you do this by selecting Tools | Send And Receive,

FIGURE 7-3   This window appears when you click Outlook Express' Create Mail button.

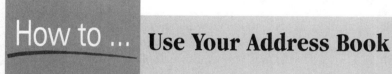

How to ... Use Your Address Book

Most e-mail programs, including Outlook Express, include e-mail address books. Instead of typing the person's e-mail address, you simply select it from a list. To quickly display the address book, press CTRL-SHIFT-B in Outlook Express. To add someone to your address book, click the button for creating a new contact, and then enter the person's name, e-mail address, and other contact information.

and then choosing Send And Receive All, Receive All, or Send All. You can also use the Send/Receive button on the toolbar at the top of the window.

By default, OE checks for new messages every 30 minutes, to which we say, are you kidding? Who can wait that long for new messages? To adjust that time, click Tools | Options | General tab, then look for the Check For New Messages Every field. In the little box showing 30, click the tiny arrows to adjust the time up or down depending on your personality type or medication level, click Apply and then OK. (See Figure 7-4.)

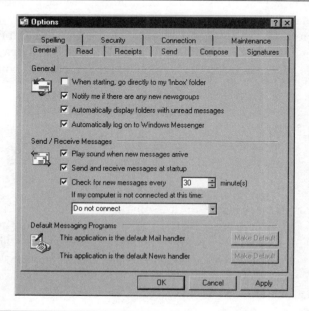

FIGURE 7-4   Use this window to make adjustments to your Outlook Express e-mail settings.

7

If you have new messages, they appear in the View pane. You can read a new message in a separate window by double-clicking it. To respond to the message, choose Reply, Reply All, or Forward in the message window's toolbar or the Outlook Express toolbar.

E-mail programs have subtle but important differences. For instance, if you're sending an e-mail in Outlook Express to more than one person, separate the names in the To box with a semicolon. But if you're sending a message to many people using your web-based e-mail account, such as Yahoo, separate the names with a comma only, not a semicolon.

Use Outlook Express as a Newsreader

The Internet's uncensored masses dwell in a crowded corner of the online house called *newsgroups* or *Usenet*. These groups cover thousands of topics of almost every conceivable interest, and new groups are born all the time. A newsgroup consists of messages and follow-up posts, which are (in theory) related to the original message. A message and its follow-ups are called a *thread*. It takes a little effort to find and read postings by these groups: to view and post messages to newsgroups, you need a *newsreader,* which looks a lot like a regular e-mail program but is more specialized.

Outlook Express lets you work with one or more news servers and allows you to view and post newsgroup messages. Your Internet service provider will provide you with the name of its news server, or if your ISP doesn't offer newsgroup access, try www.newsguy.com or www.easynews.com. Setting up OE as a newsreader is similar to setting it up as an e-mail client. If you have access to a news server, choose Tools | Accounts, and then select the News tab in the Internet Accounts dialog box.

Did you know?   Understanding Newsgroup Names

A newsgroup name is a series of dot-separated words that indicates the newsgroup's topic, such as rec.pets.cats. The first part indicates the group's overall subject area—for example, *rec* is for recreation and *alt* stands for alternative. The rest of the address indicates what the newsgroup is about, in increasingly narrow categories. Rec.food.baking is about … you guessed it. Or, peruse the far more interesting rec.food.drink.beer.

To add the newsreader account information, choose Add I News. Then follow the directions in the Internet Connection Wizard, which guides you through the process. (See Figure 7-5.)

NOTE

You don't have to use Outlook Express as your newsgroup reader. There are many free newsgroup readers, and also quite a few beefed up programs that cost a bit. Our favorite free program is Forte's Free Agent, which can be downloaded for free at www.forteinc.com/agent/index.php.

Once you have the news server account set up, OE gives you the option to download a list of the newsgroups available on that news server. This process can take a while because there will probably be tens of thousands to download. Once you have the list of available newsgroups, you can start looking for some to join (see Figure 7-6). To do this, click the Newsgroups button in the View pane. This opens the Newsgroup Subscriptions dialog box.

Once you've subscribed to some newsgroups, you're ready to start reading messages. In the View pane, click the Synchronize Account button. OE downloads the headers of all available messages in all the newsgroups to which you're subscribed. Click a message in the View pane to make it appear in the Preview pane. Double-click it to make the message appear in a separate window.

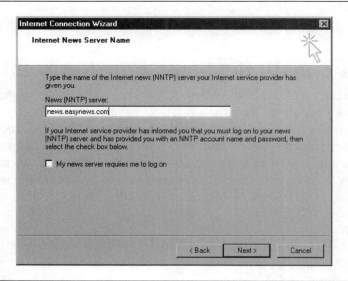

FIGURE 7-5   Before setting up newsgroup access, get your username, password, and news server address from your Internet service provider.

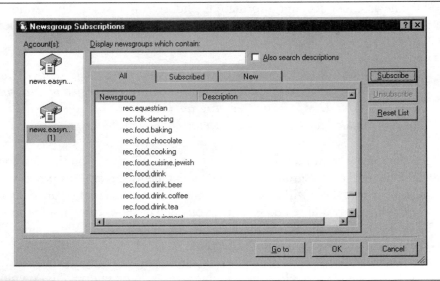

A newsgroup name is a series of dot-separated names that indicate the newsgroup's topic in increasingly narrow categories, like rec.food.drink.beer.

CAUTION *Randomly exploring newsgroups with suspicious names can expose you to material you may not want to see. Because most newsgroups are uncensored, people can, and do, post anything they want. Plus, spammers often deluge newsgroups with unwanted messages. So let's be careful out there.*

Web-Based E-mail: Get Something for Nothing

If you don't take your Sony VAIO notebook with you when you're on the road, how can you check your e-mail from the airport, for example? Luckily, if you sign up for a free, web-based e-mail account, you don't need your VAIO or a special e-mail program to send and receive e-mail. You can set up a free account at many sites, including www.hotmail.com and www.yahoo.com. From there, all you need to check your e-mail is a computer with a web browser and an Internet connection. You don't need a computer that has your e-mail account settings on it.

NOTE *Typically, free e-mail services do not provide a very big inbox, so users receiving large quantities of data, such as JPEG files, will find their storage space disappearing quickly. You'll probably want to increase your storage limit, for a fee (of course).*

Did you know?

Newsgroup Etiquette

Usenet, which is the home of newsgroups, is one of the oldest parts of the Internet. Well-established newsgroups have many guiding principles and rules of engagement that participants are expected to follow. If you break these rules in a newsgroup of meticulous and ruthless members, you might get some nasty messages in return. Before you post extensively in a newsgroup, hang out for a few days and test the waters. You should also heed this advice:

■ If you join a newsgroup, find and read its FAQ (frequently asked questions), which may answer many of your questions before you take up the group's time asking them again.

■ Learn some tricks of the trade by subscribing to and reading the newsgroups that are called news.answers and news.announce.newusers. Find out what *crossposting* to more than one group is and why it's frowned upon.

7

Web sites like Hotmail and Yahoo make signing up for free e-mail a snap. Just go to the web site, look for an e-mail button, and click it. Figure 7-7 shows the Yahoo Mail page.

Besides being able to check your e-mail from the airport or cyber-café, free e-mail has many advantages:

■ It lets everyone in your home or business have his or her own e-mail account. When your teenager starts corresponding with her chat room friends, she'll want her privacy, and she can have it (if you want her to) with her own e-mail program. If she's a typically wired teen, she'll have more than one e-mail account.

■ Free e-mail provides you with a stable e-mail address. If you change ISPs, you don't need to notify all of your friends, relatives, and colleagues that you changed e-mail addresses.

■ Free e-mail gives you another e-mail address for registering anonymously for free stuff. Whenever you register for online contests, shareware, and other freebies, you must enter your e-mail address. Use your free account, so that companies will send junk e-mail there, keeping your real e-mail address private for as long as possible—which is a perfect segue to our next topic.

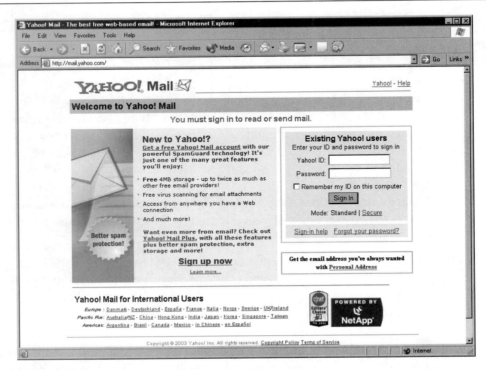

FIGURE 7-7   The Welcome To Yahoo Mail page takes you through the easy steps of creating your own free e-mail account.

How to Fight Spam

The battle between the senders of unsolicited e-mail ads and those who try to block them has reached epic proportions in the past year. In one corner are legions of spammers who find ways, through technology, dirty tricks, and perseverance to penetrate consumers' inboxes. The dirty tricks include misspelling telltale words in the subject line like "V/agra," spacing out letters like "D E B T," or confusing you with a subject line like "re: your invoice."

In the other corner are Internet service providers with vigorous spam-blocking software, organizations that blacklist spammers, and consumers armed with retail spam-blocking programs. Unfortunately, the blocking side has pretty much been given a black eye this year, with the ever-increasing spam volume about to overtake that of legitimate e-mail.

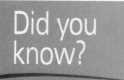

Four Mistakes to Avoid

Most spam is deceptive; the better to trick you into opening it. So you must be eternally vigilant. When you're managing your e-mail or shopping online, never:

■ Click an e-mail's devious "unsubscribe" link or follow the e-mails instructions on how to "unsubscribe," as shown here, which would appear to be a smart thing to do, wouldn't it? Heck, I used to do that several years ago, before I knew how the game was played. Unfortunately, clicking the unsubscribe link actually informs the spammer you're there.

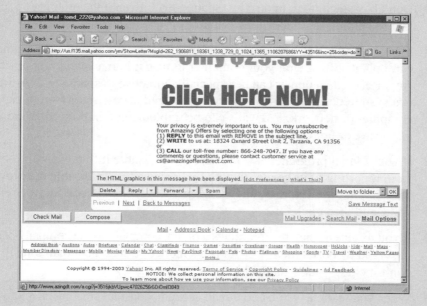

■ Forward chain letters, petitions, or virus warnings. All could be a spammer's ploy to collect addresses.

■ Post your e-mail address on a public web page, like eBay. If you must post it, you can thwart spammers' harvesting software by using "jonqpublic at yahoo.com," not jonqpublic@yahoo.com.

■ Disclose your address to a site without checking its privacy policy. And don't give the site permission to send you anything nonessential.

The spam scam imposes heavy costs on most users, who are forced to spend time deleting all that junk and can feel violated when pornographic spam makes it through the filters.

What can you do to fight spam? First, be realistic. Fighting spam promises to be a hot topic in 2004, but as the battle stands now, you can catch or filter a lot of unsolicited junk e-mail, but you can't get all of it over the long haul. Taking the following steps may keep your inbox clean for a while, but spammers scour the Web for e-mail addresses, ISPs can sell your address, and eventually you'll end up on a spammer's list. Here's what to do to slow the process:

- Use a provider that filters e-mail, such as AOL, Earthlink, or MSN. If you get lots of spam, your ISP may not be filtering effectively.

- Don't buy anything promoted in a spam e-mail. Even if the offer isn't a scam, you're helping to finance junk e-mail.

- Install a *firewall* if you have a broadband Internet account so a spammer can't plant software on your computer to turn it into a spamming machine. An unsecured computer can be especially attractive to spammers. (A firewall is a system designed to prevent unauthorized access to or from a private computer or network. Firewalls can be implemented in both software and hardware, or both.)

- If your e-mail program has a preview pane, disable it to prevent the spam from reporting to its sender that you've received it. To disable the preview pane in Outlook Express, choose View | Layout. Uncheck Show Preview Pane, and then click OK.

- If you receive a spam that promotes a brand, complain to the company behind the brand by postal mail, which makes more of a statement than e-mail. But don't include your e-mail address in the letter.

- When you set up a web-based e-mail account, consider creating an anonymous e-mail identity. That type of account can reduce the amount of spam you get. When you fill in forms or order stuff over the Internet, give them your anonymous address. The spam resulting from this transaction will be kept separate.

Now that you've learned how to use Outlook Express as an e-mail client or newsgroup reader, absorbed some tips on free e-mail programs, and know how to fight spam, check out the next chapter on how to set up a wired home network.

Chapter 8

Set Up a Wired Home Network

How to...

- Learn wired networking basics
- Plan a home network
- Buy the right hardware
- Install your network
- Use Internet Connection Sharing
- Run the Network Setup Wizard
- Navigate the network
- Share a printer

These days, every home or office that has a notebook or desktop PC usually has more than one. Maybe you use your Sony laptop on the road, and a desktop at work. Maybe your old PC resides in your den, while your new laptop hangs out in the bedroom and family room. Maybe your family's always fighting for the one phone line that connects to the Internet. Or maybe your seven-year-old son won't get off Kiddonet.com so daddy can finally get some work done. If so, then this chapter is for you.

Thankfully, setting up a home network is easier than it used to be, with Windows XP guiding you through the steps. This chapter can't cover everything relating to home networks (entire books have been devoted to the subject), but I can cover enough to make the process less painful.

Wired Networking Basics

Before you embark on establishing a home network, you need to know a few basics. In simple terms, a network is nothing more than several computers linked together in order to share an Internet connection, to share peripherals like printers, scanners, and storage devices, or to exchange information.

A local area network, or LAN, is a network designed to serve a small area, like your home office. If you have more than one computer and want to exchange files between them, or if you own multiple computers and you want to share a broadband Internet connection or a single printer, you'll want to build a home network.

Did you know?

The Differences Between Wired and Wireless

When it comes to home networking, a hard-wired network is the most cost-effective, tried-and-true solution. A wired LAN will provide more speed—and more security—than a wireless LAN. And you don't have to worry about the problems that can hinder wireless networks, like interrupted frequencies or nosy neighbors who try to glom onto your network. So, why consider a wireless home network at all?

For starters, a wireless network can be easier to install. You don't have to drag cables all over the house or drill holes in the walls or floors to accommodate them. And a wireless network is more convenient if you want to lie in your bed, untethered, with your new VAIO laptop warming your lap. Wireless also has its advantages if you need to connect your handheld Personal Digital Assistant (PDA) to the network. On the other hand, there are several drawbacks to wireless networks, including security issues and the joys of frequency problems. To learn all about wireless networking, check out Chapter 9.

8

Fortunately, Windows XP has made home-network building relatively easy. Plus, the hardware and cables required are fairly inexpensive. So where do you start? First, each computer you install on your network will need a network interface card, or NIC. (If you have a recent Sony VAIO, you're good to go. Some older computers don't have NICs.) If you subscribe to broadband Internet service, the PC receiving that service already has an NIC. To find it, just follow the cable that runs from the back of your modem to the back of the computer. The computer device the cable is plugged into is your NIC. The connector at each end of the cable is known as an RJ-45 (short for Radio Jack-45) connector, which looks like a large telephone cable. The cables from all the computers on the network connect through a device called a *hub* or *router,* which is just a small piece of hardware that acts like a traffic cop on your network.

TIP *Most computers, including new Sony VAIOs, come equipped with a standard NIC when you buy them. Check your computer documentation to find out.*

You can, however, skip the router in some cases. With the growth of home networking, a number of solutions are available where cabling and a router is not needed. For example, you can buy network adapter cards that plug into your phone jacks. The computers use the existing phone wiring in your house to communicate with each other at no expense and interruption to you. Some home networking setups use power outlets so PCs and peripherals can communicate with each other (see the sidebar "How to…Use Your Wall Outlets for a Network"). The key is to shop around and find a solution (and dollar amount) that works best for you. Plus, you can still use standard networking cabling and routers, which are not terribly expensive.

NOTE *If your network has only two computers that are close together, you can connect them with a crossover cable (about $10), which runs directly between the two PCs' Ethernet jacks. This no-hassle network is easy to set up, saves you the cost of a hub, and works exactly like a "real" Ethernet network. If you expand to three computers, you must buy a hub.*

Besides the hardware, the Windows XP software must be configured for networking. This includes turning on Microsoft File and Printer Sharing, and configuring the TCP/IP protocol so that computers can understand each other. Fortunately, in Windows XP you get help in setting all this up from the Network Setup Wizard, which we'll get into later in this chapter. If you ever wanted to know what TCP/IP stands for but were afraid to ask, here it is: Transmission Control Protocol/Internet Protocol. It's a protocol used on the Internet and is also used by many companies for running large networks.

Plan Your Home Network

Before you try to configure your Windows XP-running Sony VAIO for networking, you need to complete a few tasks to make sure your home networking adventure will be a positive one. Before moving on, keep these points in mind:

- If you only have one Windows XP computer, it needs to be the primary computer. For instance, if you're using a Sony VAIO with Windows XP and another computer with Windows 98, the Windows XP machine will be the head honcho, and all the shared peripherals and the Internet connection should be attached to the Windows XP machine.

- Make a list of all the hardware you'll need, and inspect your computers to make sure they have a network interface card. (New VAIOs do.)

- You'll need to figure out what kind of network you want, whether to use regular Ethernet cables, phone lines, power outlets, or wireless. (Check Chapter 9 to find out how to build a wireless network.) You can learn more about these different kinds of networks later in this book, on the Web, or from your local computer store. Keep in mind that some solutions offer faster transfer speeds.

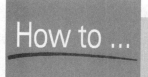 **Use Your Wall Outlets for a Network**

One of the more intriguing home network alternatives to emerge recently uses the regular old power lines that are already built into your home. Given the fact that every room in your home already has several power outlets, the advantages to this solution are obvious. Simply plug a receptacle into any power outlet in your home, plug in another one to any other power outlet in the same building, and you have an Ethernet-class network. The little adapters are very easy to set up, and they fake out your PC or router into thinking it's plugged into a standard Ethernet port.

Naturally, there are few downsides to this setup. A power-line network is slower than a conventional wired network—about the same speed as an 802.11b wireless network (approximately 7 Megabits-per-second, or Mbps). Turn on a "noisy" appliance such as a hair dryer or air conditioner and the network slows down even more, even though some of these adapters are supposed to handle interference from said appliances. Another downside is the cost: For example, one of the popular products in this field, the Netgear XE602 Powerline Ethernet adapter, costs between $80 and $100 each, and you'll need at least two to set up a network.

Still, the idea of building a home network without laying any new wires is an intriguing concept. Many companies in the network industry have formed the HomePlug Powerline Alliance to develop a common set of standards for this technology.

NOTE *If you want to share a single high-speed DSL or cable Internet connection for all your computers, Ethernet is your best choice. You can buy a hardware device for about $125 to connect your DSL or cable modem directly to your network, and these devices usually include a built-in hub.*

What You'll Need

You'll need some basic hardware to build your wired home network. Following is a list.

CAUTION *Avoid 1-Mbps networking equipment and any adapter that connects through your computer's parallel printer port. These are obsolete devices, and there's simply no need to use such slow equipment these days. If the box doesn't mention 10 Mbps or 100 Mbps on the outside, don't buy it.*

■ **Network interface card (NIC)**   As I said, your Sony VAIO most likely has one of these pre-installed, but if it doesn't, you'll need one NIC for each computer you're going to plug into your network. A NIC has an RJ-45 jack that you connect an Ethernet cable to (see Figure 8-1). If your PC didn't come with an Ethernet jack, you can buy a NIC, or an external network adapter that plugs into a USB port. For laptops, plug in a PC Card that provides an Ethernet jack. All newer NICs are plug-and-play. For installation tips, see Chapter 5.

■ **Power strip**   This device is also called a surge protector, and you're probably familiar with them. A typical power strip has six or more electrical outlets, and it attaches to the wall outlet with a short extension cord. If you're plugging in multiple computers, a printer, a scanner, or more, power strips are a must.

■ **Ethernet cable**   This is the wiring that will connect each piece of hardware and transport the data on your network. You'll use what's known as CAT5e UTP cables, which stands for Category 5 Enhanced Unshielded Twisted Pair. CAT5e cables come in pre-cut lengths ranging from 6 inches to 100 feet. For custom lengths, you (or a store clerk) can cut the cable off a spool and attach the connectors. Each cable's length shouldn't exceed 328 feet. If you're drilling through walls to lay cable, consider hiring a professional cable installer, or consider a different type of home network.

FIGURE 8-1   RJ-11 cable (left) is used for phone equipment; RJ-45 cable (right) is used for networking PCs.

- **Hub** On an Ethernet network, you connect each cable from a PC to a central connection point called a hub—a small box with a row of five or more jacks that accept RJ-45 connectors. Small green lights on the hub glow or flicker to signal an active connection between any two PCs. One port, labeled Uplink, connects to a router, broadband modem, or another hub to expand the network. The other ports usually are numbered, and it doesn't matter which port you plug which cable into. You can also connect shared peripherals, such as printers, to the hub. If you have an Internet connection, consider using a *router/ hub* instead of an ordinary hub to share the connection.

- **Gateway** If you have broadband Internet service, your service provider has already given you this piece of equipment, most likely in the form of a cable or DSL modem.

Install Your Network

Installing and configuring a network used to be incredibly complex. And while it's still no stroll in the park, the process has gotten easier. In fact, you can have a three-computer network up and running in an hour once you've bought your equipment. You'll of course need to follow the manufacturer's guidelines during the installation process, but here are some basics.

NOTE *Check Microsoft's Hardware Compatibility List before you buy network equipment. Manufacturers include D-Link, Linksys, 3Com, Belkin, Netgear, Microsoft, and SMC. No-name hardware is cheaper, but the few dollars extra that you pay for a name brand generally buys you better phone and web support, as well as regularly updated drivers.*

First, decide which rooms you want your computers, printers, and other peripherals to be in. Be sure to put them relatively close to power outlets, or you'll be stringing lots of extension cords. Turn off each of your computers and printers, as well as your gateway.

You're probably happy with where your primary PC and gateway live, so place the router in close proximity to the gateway (you may even want to stack them.) Plug the router into your power strip, but don't turn it on. Now, look at the back of your gateway. You'll see one cable (either a telephone line or an Ethernet cable) leading away from the gateway to the wall (or wherever else your broadband connection comes into your home). You'll see another cable (this one will definitely be the Ethernet cable) leading away from the gateway and into the back of your computer.

Disconnect the Ethernet cable that links your gateway to your PC by squeezing the tab on the top of the connector and gently pulling it out of the gateway's socket.

Take a short length of Ethernet cable and plug one end into the Ethernet port on the back of the cable/DSL modem; plug the other end into the port on the router that's marked "WAN." (WAN stands for wide area network, which is similar to a LAN.) Now, take the Ethernet cable that's plugged into your PC and plug the free end into your router. If you bought a cable/DSL router equipped with a built-in switch, plug the Ethernet cable into port 1.

After verifying your wiring connections, turn all your hardware back on. Check if the power indicator lights glow on everything (computer, cable/DSL modem, and router).

Share an Internet Connection

Internet Connection Sharing (ICS) is a built-in Windows feature that enables you to have one computer connected to the Internet and all other computers on the network share the Internet connection. It's free but difficult to configure. You must designate one computer as the ICS *host;* all other computers on the network, called *clients,* access the host to get on the Internet. ICS is designed for use with broadband Internet access, although you can use ICS with a 56K modem. But your 56K modem will operate very slowly if several people are trying to use the Internet connection at the same time. For broadband Internet connections, the host PC must have two Ethernet adapters: one that connects to the DSL or cable modem and the other that connects to the hub. If the host PC is switched off, the other client PCs can't get online.

NOTE   *ICS does not work with some versions of AOL. Check with AOL to see whether your version is supported. It's also possible, although unlikely, that your Internet service provider will charge you for multiple computer connections to the Internet. Check with your ISP to make sure you won't get any extra charges.*

Here are some setup and troubleshooting tips for using Internet Connection Sharing:

- The host PC needs to have Windows XP installed; the client PCs can be running earlier Windows versions, except Windows 95/3.x.

- Switch on the host PC before turning on the client PCs.

- If your DSL service has multiple static *IP addresses,* you can share a connection without designating a single PC as host. (An IP address is a string of numbers that identifies the computer. No two computers on your network can have the same IP address. The same is true on the Internet where every web site you visit is on a computer with a unique IP address.)

■ For dial-up connections, if the host computer tries to maintain a continuous connection to the Internet by dialing repeatedly, you want to turn that off. So, on the host PC, choose Start | Control Panel | Network And Internet Connections | Network Connections, right-click your ISP's icon, choose Properties | Options tab, then uncheck Redial If Line Is Dropped.

■ For dial-up connections, a client computer's browser or e-mail program may report a "server/page unavailable" error before the host computer gets online. Wait a moment, and then try the browser or e-mail program again on the client PC.

Run the Network Setup Wizard

Once you have all of your hardware and your computers are connected to each other, you can run the Network Setup Wizard, which will set up home networking on your computers. The Network Setup Wizard is supported only on computers using Windows 98, Me, or XP. The following steps walk you through the Network Setup Wizard:

1. On your Windows XP computer, choose Start | All Programs | Accessories | Communications | Network Setup Wizard (see Figure 8-2).

2. Read the information on the Welcome screen and click Next.

3. The next window gives you more information about home networking. Make sure you have completed the preparation tasks listed, and then click Next.

4. The Select A Connection Method window appears, as shown in Figure 8-3. The button options here ask you to describe how the XP computer connects to the Internet. Select the desired button, and then click Next.

5. The Internet Connection wizard appears. In the box listing all the entries in your Network Connection folder, select your connection to the Internet, and then click Next.

6. If you're using a dial-up connection, the wizard will prompt you to dial a connection to the Internet.

7. In the provided window, enter a description for your computer as well as a desired computer name. Take my advice and give the computer a very descriptive name. If you go with something like "tom 1" or "tom 2", instead of "Sony GRT in Den"—(assuming you'll be able to remember which computer is "tom 1"), you'll likely be sorry.

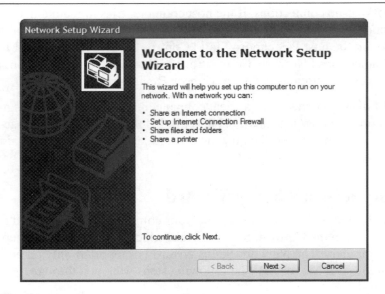

FIGURE 8-2   Use the Network Setup Wizard to start configuring your home network.

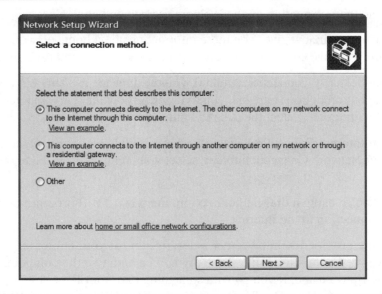

FIGURE 8-3   Selecting a connection method

8. Review the changes that will be made to your computer and click Next. Windows XP automatically configures all of your computer's software and hardware components for networking, according to the selections you made when running the wizard.

9. Click Finish. You will need to restart the computer for the new changes to take effect.

Once you've run the Home Networking Wizard on the XP computer, you need to run the wizard on each computer that you want to include in the network. Once that's done, it's time to test the network. Choose Start | My Network Places to see the shared folders and disks that your PC can detect on other computers on the network. If you're running an earlier version of Windows, the icon may be called Network Neighborhood.

Navigate the Network

After your home network is up and running, you can explore the contents of the shared disks, folders, and files on the other computers on the network. To explore the network, follow these steps:

1. Choose Start | My Network Places, also called Network Neighborhood on older versions of Windows. (See Figure 8-4.)

2. To see icons for each computer on the network, click View Workgroup Computers in the task pane on the left side of the window.

3. Double-click shared items to open them, just as though you were working in your My Documents folder.

4. You can easily move and copy items between networked computers by using the Windows Explorer window you have called up. For tips on how to do that, see Chapter 3.

5. To use Search Companion to find shared network items, choose Start | Search (or press CTRL-E in Explorer). Choose Browse from the Look In drop-down list, click My Network Places, and then click OK.

Share a Printer

A *local printer* connects directly to your computer through a USB, parallel, serial, or infrared port. Your printer's manual describes the simple steps of attaching it to your computer. Newer printers attach through a USB port; older printers attach through

FIGURE 8-4   My Network Places shows shared disks and folders on the network, including the ones on the host PC.

a parallel or serial port. You can also use a cableless connection if both your printer and your computer have infrared lenses.

When you connect a printer, Windows XP often recognizes the device and searches its collection of built-in drivers to run the printer. If your printer doesn't show up on XP's built-in list, you can use the driver on the CD or floppy that came with the printer. Your printer will most likely support plug-and-play, which lets Windows detect and configure a connected device automatically. For more on plug-and-play, see Chapter 5.

When you share a printer connected to your computer, everyone's print jobs go through your copy of Windows, slowing down your system. Big networks like the kind you may have at work use a computer dedicated to printing (print server) to expedite complex print requests.

FIGURE 8-5   On the Sharing tab, type a short name in the Share Name pane.

After your printer is installed, you can begin using it, but others on the home network will undoubtedly want to print, too. To share the printer with them, follow these steps:

1. On the host computer, choose Start | Control Panel | Printers And Other Hardware | Printers And Faxes.

2. Right-click a printer icon; choose Sharing.

3. Select Share This Printer, and then type a share name for your printer, as shown in Figure 8-5. Use a name with no spaces or punctuation.

4. To share the printer with users with different Windows versions, click Additional Drivers, choose the environment and operating system for the other computers, and then click OK. Click OK on the next screen as well.

5. After you've set up a shared printer, others on the home network can add it to their own Printers And Faxes window and print with it.

So now you know the basics of building a wired home network. If you prefer to work without wires, check out Chapter 9 and learn all the gory secrets of constructing a wireless home network.

Chapter 9 Go Wireless

How to...

- Understand wireless networking basics
- Tap into an existing wireless connection
- Set up a wireless home network
- Secure your Wi-Fi connection

In Chapter 6, you cut your teeth on connecting to the Internet via two traditional methods: old-school dial-up and faster broadband. Both ways require wires and cables. Now, we'll take it up a notch and talk about getting on the Net through a wireless connection.

The advantages to using wireless technology (Wi-Fi, for short) are many. First and foremost is the freedom to go online without being literally tied to your desk. It also omits the clutter of a dozen cables running from each computer throughout your house back to one centralized modem. Sure, you could hide the cables inside your walls. But the headache and expense of this route seem ridiculous when compared to the relatively little time and money it takes to get a wireless network going.

While I'm an overall fan of wireless, the technology still has some imperfections. Tenuous security, limited range, and other factors can prove frustrating. This chapter provides a breakdown of the potential security and range pitfalls involved in wireless pursuits and how to skirt them. Before that, I'll walk you through the different wireless technologies and help you decide which one is right for you. I'll also show you step-by-step how to tap into an existing wireless connection and establish your own Wi-Fi network.

Understand Wireless Networking Basics

You don't have to be a genius to understand how wireless works. You've used a cordless phone, right? In the same way that a cordless phone talks to its base by sending signals through the air, a wireless computer sends signals through the air to talk to a wireless base station, which is usually called an access point or router. We'll talk more about access points and routers later in this chapter.

With the glut of wireless computers, phones, and many more devices on the market, a virtual traffic jam of wireless signals travels through the air at any given moment. To help minimize the mayhem, wireless device manufacturers design their products to emit signals at different frequencies. Think of the different frequencies as the lanes on a freeway. When each type of device runs within a specific frequency, it helps all of the signals they send out to travel as quickly and smoothly as possible. For example, your cordless phone, wireless computer, and cell phone may run at respective frequencies of 900 MHz, 2.4 GHz, and 850 MHz. If all these devices ran at 2.4 GHz, and you used each one inside your house at the same time, none of them would function as efficiently.

The Wi-Fi Trifecta

While the basic idea behind wireless is fairly easy to grasp, plenty of intimidating words and acronyms exist in the Wi-Fi world. You don't need to know them all to set up a simple wireless connection. That said, you should still become familiar with three key terms.

> TIP   *Whenever I'm scratching my head over a technological term, I turn to www.pcwebopedia.com. It's an awesome resource for every tech expression under the sun.*

9

802.11b

802.11b (pronounced eight-oh-two-dot-eleven-b) is the most common type of wireless technology available for PCs. It runs at the same 2.4 GHz frequency used by a lot of other wireless devices. That translates into one of 802.11b's biggest weaknesses: Its signals are more likely to butt heads with other common signals. 802.11b signals also transfer data at a measly maximum of only 11 Mbps (megabits per second) compared to the 54 Mbps and faster speeds of the newer wireless technologies, 802.11a and 802.11g, that I describe next. Still, 11 Mbps is plenty fast considering a dial-up connection transfers data at around 50 kbps (kilobits per second), or less than one percent of 802.11b's speed. The last major factoid about 802.11b is that a computer equipped with the technology can communicate with a base station from up to 150 feet away. This isn't an amazing range, but it's also not as bad as it gets. Be aware that walls and doors generally cut the range in half. But if you place your base station in the middle of your home (provided the house is of average size), your VAIO should still be able to connect to it from anywhere throughout your home. Even with an 80-foot effective range, the typical Wi-Fi base station covers 20,000 square feet of horizontal and vertical floor space, meaning it can reach floors above and below the one it's on.

If you count yourself among the average Joes and Janes who want to get away from their desks every once in awhile to send a few e-mails, 802.11b is for you.

Did you know?

Wi-Fi Has Morphed from Its Original Meaning

The term *Wi-Fi*—short for Wireless Fidelity—was originally cooked up by the Wi-Fi Alliance, an international nonprofit group formed in 1999 to certify the interoperability of 802.11-based wireless computing devices. The Alliance initially intended the term to refer to 802.11b only. But once people started calling later-generation wireless standards (see the following sections) Wi-Fi as well, the Alliance decided to eliminate confusion around the term and open it up to all three standards. Check out www.weca.net for more background on this scintillating topic.

NOTE *Your wireless VAIO won't always achieve the maximum speeds I just mentioned. In fact, it usually won't. Life, in the form of competing signals and many other factors, often gets in the way. The best you can expect is about 60 percent of top speed, so the typical Wi-Fi connection usually yields about 7 Mbps of throughput in the real world. For accessing the Net throughout your home or small office, this speed is more than fast enough. In comparison, the typical DSL or cable connection can only provide about half the speed.*

802.11a

802.11a is the follow-up to 802.11b. It runs at a 5 GHz frequency that few other devices share, making its signals less susceptible to obstruction. But because 802.11a runs at a different frequency than 802.11b, the two can't communicate with each other—putting the multitude of 802.11b base stations at coffee shops, airports, and elsewhere off-limits to 802.11a users. Another 802.11a perk is its 54 Mbps maximum data-transfer speed. However, its comparatively short 100-foot communication range is a bummer. And don't forget that both speed and range are generally slower and shorter in real life.

Got a lot of wireless devices around the house and like to access large files over the Web, including videos and music? 802.11a will fit your bill.

CAUTION *If you're using a VAIO notebook, think twice before settling on 802.11a. It'll drain your laptop battery faster than either 802.11b or g.*

802.11g

802.11g is the latest wireless standard that's a hybrid of both a and b. Like 802.11b, it runs at 2.4 GHz, which opens up the possibility of signal interference but also allows you to connect to all of those 802.11b base stations out there. 802.11g's 150-foot maximum range also falls in line with 802.11b's. Yet 802.11g is at least as fast as 802.11a, featuring max speeds from 54 Mbps to more than 100 Mbps. 802.11g pulls off the speed feat by doing a more efficient job of squeezing data into its signals and moving those signals through the air. Of course, the same rules of range and speed limitations that I mentioned before still apply.

All of these elements combined put 802.11g in position to become the de facto standard in wireless computing. If you plan to use your wireless VAIO everywhere you can, go with 802.11g. Its faster speed and backward-compatibility with 802.11b base stations make it a no-brainer.

Check out the following table for a short breakdown of the three main Wi-Fi types.

Wireless Technology	Frequency	Max Speed	Real-World Speed	Range	Best For
802.11b	2.4 GHz	11 Mbps	7 Mbps	150 feet	Basic web surfers and e-mailers
802.11a	5 GHz	54 Mbps	22 Mbps	100 feet	Gadget-lovers with lots of wireless gizmos
802.11g	2.4 GHz	100+ Mbps	20 Mbps	150 feet	Technophiles who go online everywhere

Dual Band

Never ones to miss an opportunity, some wireless manufacturers have now created devices based on all three types of Wi-Fi. The devices are called *dual band,* which signifies their ability to run at both the 2.4 GHz and 5 GHz frequencies of 802.11b, a, and g. Dual-band devices combine the best of all three Wi-Fi types. They can connect to any type of wireless base station, achieve the faster speed of 802.11a and g, and avoid all the signal bumping. This flexibility comes at a premium price, however: Dual-band devices can cost hundreds more than those based on one Wi-Fi technology.

Tap Into an Existing Wireless Connection

Now that you know what type of wireless you want, you can start thinking about the equipment you'll need. This will depend on whether you plan to hook up with an existing wireless connection or create your own. Let's start with linking up to an existing connection.

Bluetooth Offers a Quick Alternative to Wi-Fi

If you have the very simple wireless desire to zap brief info between devices, such as transferring a phone number from your cell phone to your VAIO, Bluetooth may be for you. This wireless standard operates in the 2.4 GHz frequency, transmitting data at a comparatively pokey 500 kbps with only a 30-foot range. On the flip side, Bluetooth-enabled devices require almost no setup in order to communicate with each other.

Required Components for Tapping into an Existing Connection

Thankfully, you don't have to worry about whether your VAIO's operating system is Wi-Fi compatible, since all VAIOs come with Windows XP, and Windows XP supports wireless.

The primary piece of hardware you'll need is a *wireless adapter* for your VAIO. Wireless adapters based on each Wi-Fi flavor come in several shapes and sizes. The main type of adapter for desktop PCs is an internal PCI card that fits into one of the system's PCI slots. For notebooks, two types of cards are available:

■ Mini-PCI cards are much smaller versions of desktop PCI cards that fit inside the mini-PCI slot inside your laptop. In general, you can't crack a notebook open to install a mini-PCI card yourself; the installation happens at the factory before you receive the machine.

■ PC Cards are external cards that you can add to one of your laptop's PC Card slots. This is a good option for people who ordered their notebooks without wireless but want to add it later. Just remember that most VAIO notebooks come with only one PC Card slot, so once you fill it with a wireless card, you can say sayonara to other cards.

TIP   *If you're about to buy a new VAIO, and you're toying with the idea of using wireless at some point, do yourself a favor and order the machine with an internal wireless card. They eliminate the hassle of having to install a card on your own.*

The latest craze in wireless adapters is the USB adapter. It looks a lot like the pack-of-gum-sized thumb drives I described in Chapter 4. You can use them in the

USB 2.0 ports of a VAIO desktop or notebook, providing a level of freedom you don't get with a card that's made exclusively for desktops or laptops. A drawback to USB adapters is that they disrupt the feng shui of your machine by jutting out a few inches from the side, as you can see in Figure 9-1.

CAUTION *No matter how much we pray, we all know that computer equipment can be problematic. Get a good warranty with whatever adapter you choose. Settle for nothing less than one year; three years is ideal. Telephone support is equally important for those times when you're ready to toss your adapter out the nearest window. Go for a toll-free phone number that you can call 24 hours a day, seven days a week, and make sure the manufacturer doesn't apply a service charge for each call.*

How to Tap In

Any wireless adapter worth its salt will come with a setup guide, which you should follow to install the hardware. Though they may vary slightly, most guides will take you through the following steps.

TIP *Many manufacturers are foregoing hard copies of setup guides and user manuals in favor of electronic versions that ship on CD. If you don't see hard copies, check the box for a CD.*

FIGURE 9-1   USB adapters don't make for an overall pretty picture, but they're super easy to install and remove.

Install the Adapter

Because some wireless adapters are based on the same plug-and-play technology we discussed in Chapter 5, you can pop those adapters into your VAIO and let Windows XP do all of the configuration work. When you insert adapters that aren't plug-and-play, the Found New Hardware wizard will appear on the screen. Follow the wizard's instructions, which will prompt you to insert the installation CD that accompanied your adapter. Keep going until you've completed all of the onscreen instructions.

 *Some adapters require you to insert the CD first so that the appropriate drivers and other software are installed before you insert the hardware. Be sure to check the setup guide to confirm the proper order of events.*

Check the Connection

After the installation, you'll see a tiny new icon in the lower-left corner of the screen that looks like two monitors, as shown here.

For the first minute or so, the icon will have a red X through it, which means the card hasn't yet detected the presence of a wireless base station. The red X will then disappear, and the two monitors in the icon will blink on and off like the icon shown here.

When this happens, give yourself a pat on the back—you're connected. If you rest your pointer over the icon, a small yellow box will appear that gives you the name of the network you're connected to, the speed of your connection, and your signal strength. Signal strength will range from Very Low to Excellent.

You may see a second or even third icon that looks like two monitors in the bottom-left corner of your screen. That's because Windows XP uses the same icon to represent any kind of Internet connection you have—whether it's dial-up, Ethernet, wireless, or another type. So if you have a 56k modem or Ethernet card installed along with your Wi-Fi card, they'll show up as dual-monitor icons as well. To tell which is which, simply rest your pointer on each one until the descriptive yellow box appears.

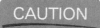

Certain adapters include software that overrides the double-monitor icon and replaces it with a unique icon, such as a single monitor with an antenna on top. Read your adapter's directions thoroughly so you know what type of icon to look for.

If the red X remains, you can try to connect to the network yourself. Right-click once on the wireless dual-monitor icon, and then select View Available Wireless Networks. A dialog box will appear, shown in Figure 9-2, with a text box that lists Available Wireless Networks. The name of the network you're trying to connect to should appear inside the text box. To connect, click the name once to highlight it, and then click Connect at the bottom of the dialog box.

TIP   *Some VAIO notebooks, like the V505 series, include hardware switches on their edges for turning wireless on and off. Make sure the switch is turned on when trying to connect to a wireless network.*

Don't see any network names inside the text box? All is not lost. Click the Advanced button to the left of Connect. Another dialog box like the one in Figure 9-3 will appear with three tabs up top. Click the Wireless Networks tab. Make sure to check the box in front of the words Use Windows To Configure My Wireless Network Settings. Then look to see if the name of the network appears in the text box under

9

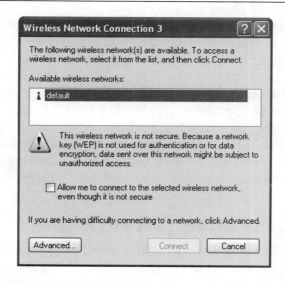

FIGURE 9-2   The names of available wireless networks should appear in the text box.

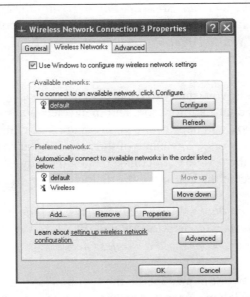

FIGURE 9-3   Click the Refresh button if the name of the network you want doesn't show up inside the text box.

Available Networks. If the name doesn't appear, click the Refresh button to the right of the text box.

When you see the network name in the box, click it once to highlight it, and then click Configure. Another dialog box will appear; click the Association tab shown in Figure 9-4. The network name should appear at the top of the window. Underneath the name, you'll see two tiny checkboxes for Data Encryption and Network Authentication, and a third checkbox that says The Key Is Provided For Me Automatically. If either of the first two boxes are checked, and the third box is unchecked, that means you need to type in a key code before you can access the network. At this point, you'll need to consult the person who manages the wireless base station that you're trying to connect to, since he or she is probably the only one who knows the code. However, if the third box is checked, you don't need to type in the key. Click OK and check the dual-monitor icon to see if the red X has disappeared.

Set Up a Wireless Home Network

If you're like me, the thought of setting up a network—a cluster of two or more computers that are linked together—invokes images of long hours, lots of cursing, and even some manual labor laying cable. Thankfully, the reality of installing your own wireless network is nowhere near this nightmare.

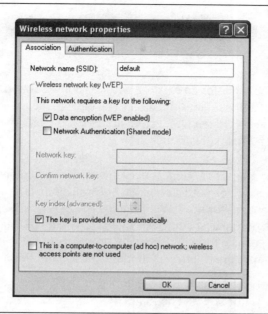

FIGURE 9-4. If you need a key code to connect, get the code from the person who manages the wireless base station.

Required Components for Setting Up a Network

In addition to the wireless adapter we talked about under the "Tap Into an Existing Wireless Connection" section earlier, you'll need a few more pieces of equipment to establish a Wi-Fi network:

- A broadband connection (a DSL or cable modem)
- Either a wireless access point or a wireless router
- A *Cat-5* cable for each wired computer that you want to connect to a router

We covered broadband connections in Chapter 6, so let's jump into wireless routers and access points.

Wireless Access Points

A wireless access point is like a subway station for wireless PCs. You use a cable to plug the access point into your broadband modem. When PCs send out their Wi-Fi signals, all of the signals converge on the access point (provided the computers are within range of it). The access point then routes the signals out to the broadband modem.

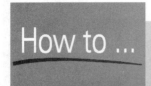

Find a Wireless Hot Spot

Hot spot is another name for an existing wireless connection in a café, airport, or other public place. Some establishments let you tap into their wireless connections for free, but most still charge a fee. Here are five hints on how to find hot spots of both the free and for-pay varieties.

- Search for a hot spot online. Several web sites, including www.jiwire.com and www.wi-fihotspotlist.com, have search engines that comb the whole country looking for hot spots. Simply type in your ZIP code or city/state to find the one nearest you. The engines generally pick up everything, from hot spots sponsored by independent providers to those backed by the big three hot-spot providers: T-Mobile, Boingo, and Wayport.

- Go to Starbucks. The huge conglomerate seems to have at least one store on every major street. The majority of these stores are now equipped with 802.11b wireless connections, courtesy of T-Mobile. However, if you don't already pay for a regular Wi-Fi service plan with T-Mobile, you'll have to buy a one-day, $10 pass to get on the Net.

- Keep your eyes peeled for free access at mom-and-pop coffee shops. A few months back, I noticed that the independently owned café down the street from me offers free Wi-Fi. So I started watching out for similar deals at other joints and learned they're out there.

- Look for wireless warchalk—a specific set of graffiti-esque symbols scribbled on a wall, table, or other surface that indicate the presence of a hot spot. To learn more about warchalking, head to www.warchalking.org.

- Go to the public library. The library systems in big cities like New York and Boston have just begun to offer no-cost wireless access. It might not be as cush without a cappuccino in your hand, but hey, it's free.

Wireless Routers

Wireless routers are simply Wi-Fi access points with a twist: They accommodate wired PCs as well. Routers, such as the one in Figure 9-5, include access points inside, plus up to four ports where you can plug in your cable-bound computers. This is a cool way to go when you don't want to outfit all of your systems with wireless adapters.

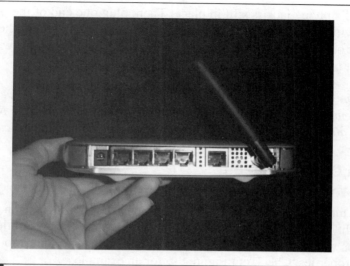

FIGURE 9-5   Most routers combine wireless access points with about four ports for wired PCs.

How to Set Up the Network

For starters, follow the steps from the preceding section to install a wireless adapter in your VAIO, if it doesn't have one already. Then, move on to installing the access point or router.

Chances are, the setup guide for the access point or router you choose is going to be chock-full of daunting language. Buried (hopefully not too deep) within that language should be reasonably simple directions for installing the device. The directions will likely guide you through the following procedure.

Pick an Unobstructed Spot

Competing signals aren't the only things that can impede your Wi-Fi flow. Walls, windows, mirrors, and a host of other building elements may block wireless signals. Try to anchor your router in the highest, most wide-open spot you can. Ideal places include the top shelves of bookcases and on top of the refrigerator. If nothing else, keep it away from walls consisting of concrete or steel.

Plug In Your Access Point or Router

To be safe, turn off all equipment, like your VAIO and broadband modem, that's currently running. Unplug the modem cable from any computers it's attached to. Using the same cable, plug the modem into the designated port in the access point or router. Make sure the telephone cable running from the back of your modem to your wall's phone jack is still in place. Then, plug one end of the power cord that came with your access point or router into the device, and put the other end into a power outlet. The device probably includes status lights that glow when you've connected it properly.

Some access points and routers require you to configure the device using a computer that has a wired (that is, Ethernet) connection to the Net. Consult the directions for the specific procedure required by your particular device.

Establish Communication Between Your VAIO and Wi-Fi Base Station

From there, turn on your VAIO. Look for the My Network Places icon on your desktop screen. Right-click the icon, and left-click Properties. A window entitled Network Connections will appear. Right-click the Wireless Network Connection icon, and left-click Properties. Check out Figure 9-6 for an example.

Another Wireless Network Connection window will then materialize, as shown in Figure 9-7. Click the General tab at the top. Within that tab, click Internet Protocol (TCP/IP) to highlight it, and then click the Properties button.

FIGURE 9-6   In the Network Connections window, right-click Wireless Network Connection, and then left-click Properties.

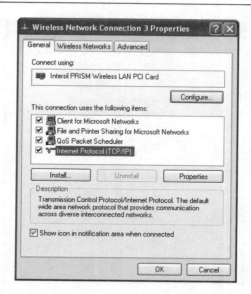

FIGURE 9-7 Click Internet Protocol (TCP/IP), and then click Properties.

9

You've come to your last window called Internet Protocol (TCP/IP) Properties (Figure 9-8). The directions for your access point or router should tell you whether your computer can obtain IP and DNS server addresses automatically. If the directions say your computer can, click the corresponding ovals in the window, and then click the OK button at the bottom. If they say it can't, click the ovals in front of Use The Following IP Address and Use The Following DNS Server Addresses, then enter the IP and DNS addresses provided for you in the directions. If they say no but provide no addresses—it's time to call tech support.

NOTE *Every modern access point and router gives you the choice of static IP addressing (pick your own) or dynamic addressing (with a built-in DHCP server). Make things easy on yourself by sticking with dynamic addressing to get the thing up and running.*

Get Your Modem and Wireless Base Station Talking

The final step is to get your cable or DSL modem talking to your access point or router. First, reset them both by unplugging each device from its respective wall outlet. Plug them both back in and wait for the appropriate status lights to glow, indicating that the devices are once again at full-steam. Restart your VAIO as well.

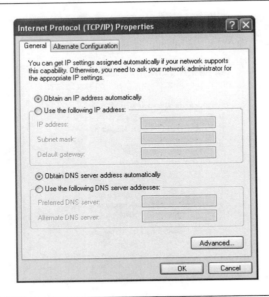

FIGURE 9-8   Check the directions for your access point or router to see if they supply IP and DNS addresses.

Open a new Internet browsing window in your VAIO using whichever browser software you choose, such as Internet Explorer, Netscape Navigator, or Opera.

The browser window will show you an error page since you're not yet on the Net. In the long Address box at the top of the window, type the Internet address listed in the setup guide for your router or access point. The address will probably start with http://192.168.0., followed by several numbers.

A password window will appear, prompting you to enter the default username and password listed in the setup guide. From there, follow the onscreen instructions. Be sure to program a new password, change the SSID, and establish a WEP key. If it sounds like I'm speaking Greek, skip to the "Secure Your Wi-Fi Connection" section later in the chapter for further explanation.

NOTE   *Some access points and routers require you to enter specific information from your ISP, such as Host Name and Domain Name. Keep your ISP's customer service phone number handy in case you need to call for the info.*

Once you've completed these last tasks, it should be easy to tell whether all of your hard work paid off in a wireless connection: Just open a new browser window, type in a web link, and see if your site comes up.

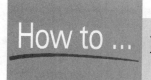 **Extend Your Wireless Range**

On paper, a 150-foot wireless range might not seem short. But if you're lucky enough to live in a 2,000-square-foot house, 150 feet takes on all new meaning. A few products on the market help you extend the reach of your wireless equipment. Just remember: Extended reach means more room for hackers to bust into your wireless connection (see the following "Secure Your Wi-Fi Connection" section to find out more about wireless hacking and how you can prevent it).

- Enhanced *antennae* let you send your signals in a specific direction or over a longer distance.

- *Repeaters* sit at a midpoint between your wireless VAIO and access point or router. They intercept signals that are too weak to make it all the way between the VAIO and access point or router, refresh the signals, and send them out anew.

- *Signal boosters* make wireless signals stronger and louder, increasing the likelihood that they'll reach their target.

Before you run out and buy one of the three, do some more research on their particular ups and downs. And by all means, make sure the one you choose supports your existing wireless equipment.

9

If you get an error message, don't be discouraged. With all of the equipment and steps involved in setting up a network, there's a good chance you inadvertently skipped something. Go back through each step to ensure they're all complete. If all else fails, take advantage of the good warranty you were sure to get with your equipment and call tech support.

Secure Your Wi-Fi Connection

Wi-Fi critics often cite weak security as the technology's most serious shortcoming. Breaking into wireless connections has been notoriously easy for computer hackers. It's not hard to understand why, with Wi-Fi signals exposed for up to 150 feet before reaching their destination at a router or access point. Most of us don't have much

Did you know?

WPA Improves Wireless Security

There's a new security standard in town that should strengthen your ability to ward off unwanted wireless intrusions. WPA, or Wi-Fi protected access, is the next-generation of WEP. WPA protects your WEP key and makes sure that only the users you have approved can access your connection. Some access point and router manufacturers have started offering WPA as an upgrade for devices that already offer WEP. Check the specs or call the manufacturer to find out if a WPA upgrade is part of the package.

to worry about, since we aren't sending secret files over our wireless networks. But that doesn't mean your nosy neighbor won't try to mooch your wireless connection.

Two basic security measures can help deter casual Wi-Fi thieves who try to glom on to your connection. The way to implement these measures should also be covered in the user manual of whatever access point or router you buy.

SSID (Service Set Identifier)

An SSID is a fancy term for a unique wireless connection name. The manufacturer of the access point or router you just installed probably assigned a generic SSID to the device, such as Default or Wireless. These are the first words a hacker will try when attempting to break into your wireless connection. A good setup guide should show you how to change the SSID immediately upon installing your access point or router.

WEP (Wired Equivalent Privacy)

WEP is the technical name for a secure password. Again, the setup guide for your access point or router should take you through the process of establishing a WEP key. I want to warn you that your device could require you to establish a key that's 26 (or more) characters long. That's a whole lot of characters to type in. Even then, WEP keys aren't foolproof. Our advice is to change your WEP, and change it often.

I've given you a lot to chew on in this chapter, but trust me—once you go wireless, you won't go back. Now, go forward to Chapter 10, where we'll talk about snapping digital shots with the tiny VAIO TR notebook.

Part III

Cool Things to Do with Your VAIO

Chapter 10

Take Digital Photos and Video with Your VAIO TR Series Notebook

How to...

- Use the integrated camera
- Use PictureGear Studio to crop, organize, and print your photos
- Share your pictures with friends and family

Nine info-packed chapters ago, we went over all of the different designs among VAIO desktops and notebooks. Now we'll spend some time talking about one of those designs in detail—the TR Series laptop. If you plan to skip ahead to the next chapter because you don't have a VAIO TR, don't split just yet. In addition to discussing TR Series particulars, we'll also talk about a cool Sony software program shared by all VAIO desktops and notebooks: PictureGear Studio. This program lets you do just about anything with your digital photos, from tweaking their look to arranging them in albums. Finally, I'll give you a few quick tips on how to share your shots with family and friends.

Use the Integrated Camera

You already know from reading Chapter 1 that the 3.1-pound TR is one of the tiniest VAIO notebooks. Despite its small size, the TR includes its own digital camera, which Sony coined the Motion Eye. I'm going to tell you how to operate the camera in a minute, but first, let's talk about its nuts and bolts.

Camera Specifications

The 3.2-inch-long Motion Eye camera certainly doesn't look like your regular point-and-shoot. You might not even notice it at first, since it's built right into the lid above the screen. Within that tiny camera are components similar to those found in the average digital camera.

The Semiconductor Within

Digital cameras, including the Motion Eye, are powered by internal, dual-circuit semiconductors. The typical camera's semiconductor is called a *CCD,* or *charge-coupled device,* meaning both of the semiconductor's circuits are on at the same time. However, the semiconductor inside the TR's camera is based on *CMOS* (c-moss) technology—short for *complementary metal oxide semiconductor*—in which only one circuit is on at a time. This allows the TR to conserve power by running just one circuit instead of two.

 **Sony TR World Guru**

I have been an avid fan of Sony's subnotebooks for many years. During the spring of 2003, when Sony announced the TR Series notebook in Japan, I was thrilled, as it seemed to be the notebook I was looking for. As a mobile professional, the TR's integrated 802.11a, 802.11b, and Bluetooth wireless technologies were extremely compelling.

To my dismay, the U.S. domestic model only shipped with an 802.11b solution. Despite these noticeable omissions, I purchased a Sony VAIO TR1AP notebook because it was still better than any other subnotebook in its class. Before purchasing the notebook, however, I was dismayed to find little information about it, and the reviews that I did find completely missed the point on this unique product. Luckily, I am multilingual and can speak, read, and write Japanese, so I was able to find information on the TR series in Japanese. Still, there wasn't enough information about this tiny but mighty laptop, and I decided to create a web site based on my experiences and research.

I now run Sony TR World, a forum dedicated to the Sony TR subnotebook (www.siliconpopculture.com/sonytr). In conjunction with the forum, I run a technology review site (www.siliconpopculture.com), where I have reviewed the Sony TR and many of its accessories (even imported ones). Additionally, I've written several how-tos about unofficially upgrading the Sony TR to 802.11a/b/g, adding integrated Bluetooth, and adding a DVD-RW drive. The forum has exploded in popularity, because it not only offers the most information about the notebook on the Web, but also its members are helpful and technically adept and use their TRs for things that Sony probably never envisioned; they provide the additional support needed.

I'm thankful that Sony decided to release the TR Series in the U.S. since many of its better Japanese products tend to not make it overseas; however, Sony doesn't need to reconfigure and sell less-functional models in the U.S. From my experience, Sony's customers are advanced users who are willing to pay for all of the bells and whistles.

There are still lots of people who don't have clue about this great product, and I'm constantly demonstrating and "selling" the TR Series to curious patrons at my local coffee house. Perhaps Sony can make some new commercials showing off this laptop, as I believe it's one of the best.

—Victor Chen, founder of Sony TR World
and siliconpopculture.com, is a technology consultant
and application developer in the Los Angeles area.

10

Image Resolution

Another important fact to know about the Motion Eye is its *resolution,* a term that determines just how sharp your pictures will appear. When you see a picture on your computer display, what you are actually seeing is a specific pattern of light that is distributed across tiny dots, called *pixels* (short for picture elements), on hundreds or even thousands of horizontal and vertical lines. The more lines and pixels you have, the sharper your picture will turn out—and the larger its file size will be. Resolution refers to the total number of pixels on each line, and the total number of lines in the picture. The Motion Eye's resolution is 640×480, meaning each picture it produces can have a maximum of 480 lines with 640 pixels on each line. That gives you a maximum of 307,200 pixels in each photo.

If you don't need the highest-quality shots and want to save some storage space on your hard drive, you can knock the Motion Eye's resolution down below 640×480. I tell you how in the "Capture Pictures and Video with the Motion Eye" section that follows.

TIP   *640×480 is a sufficient resolution for obtaining decent-looking, albeit small, photos. But if you want super-sharp shots, you'll have to go for a megapixel camera, which emits images with one million or more pixels each. The hottest cameras nowadays offer 6 megapixels, or 6,000,000 pixels, per image.*

Image Format

When you take pictures or videos with a digital camera, the camera records those images in a format that dictates the way the captured info is organized. Some formats, like *TIFF* (*tagged image file format*), organize the info so that the resulting photo is as clear and sharp as possible without as much regard for the size of the image file. Other formats, such as *JPEG* (pronounced *j-peg* and short for *joint photographic experts group*), care less about absolute perfection in the image's appearance and more about file size. Like most digital cameras, the Motion Eye captures images in JPEG format. Some high-end cameras support JPEG, TIFF, and even more formats.

I don't mean to imply that the Motion Eye's images will look like one big blur. In fact, the naked eye often can't distinguish between TIFF and JPEG images. But when images need to be published in a book or preserved for posterity, TIFF is a better bet.

NOTE   *Not all image-editing and viewing programs can read all image formats. If you want to ensure your images are readable by the widest variety of programs, save them in JPEG format.*

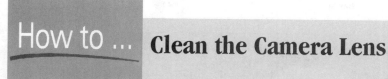

Clean the Camera Lens

Just like any camera lens, you've got to keep the TR's lens clean—but not by rubbing it with a Kleenex or shirttail. Go down to the local camera store and buy the same soft cloth and lens cleaner you'd get for any other camera you care about. Then follow the lens cleaner directions to apply it properly. Or, try using optical tissue and a little rubbing alcohol.

Vertical Rotation

One of the niftiest things about the Motion Eye is that it rotates 180 vertical degrees, letting you snap shots in front of, above, or behind your laptop. Unfortunately, it doesn't rotate horizontally, so you can't take pictures to the left or right of the notebook, unless you turn the whole notebook in those directions.

Focus Wheel

The last stop on our TR camera tour is the focus wheel. The wheel conveniently runs all the way through the top and bottom of the camera, letting you adjust the focus no matter how the camera is positioned: facing front, on its back, or flipped upside down to face backwards.

Capture Pictures and Video with the Motion Eye

Firing up the Motion Eye to take photos and video is literally as easy as pressing a button. The button in question is the Capture button to the right of the TR's display.

You can use the Motion Eye camera in three modes: Still, Movie, and Web Camera. Each mode specializes in a different kind of image. Still mode lets you snap one-off shots. Movie mode allows you to capture up to 120 minutes of continuous video footage. And Web Camera mode permits you to upload near real-time images to a web site. In this next section, I'll explain how to use each mode to its full advantage.

Still Mode

Once you hit the Capture button, the TR's Network Smart Capture software program window (Figure 10-1) surfaces on the screen. This program polices all of the Motion Eye's capabilities. In the top-left corner of the Network Smart Capture window,

10

FIGURE 10-1 The Network Smart Capture window is the central command post for all of the Motion Eye's operations.

you'll see a list of the three Motion Eye modes. Click the Still option. You'll know you're in Still mode when the bar underneath the word Still turns yellow.

You should have already noticed that the large preview screen in the middle of the Network Smart Capture window is showing whatever is currently in front of the camera lens. If the preview screen isn't reflecting your desired subject, then rotate the Motion Eye and/or the TR so that the preview window shows the subject. Remember, you can use the wheel on the top or bottom of the camera to bring your subject into sharper focus.

Your subject should now be showing inside the preview window. While it's the right person, place, or thing, the image might appear too dark, grainy, or otherwise unsatisfactory. This is where the camera's settings come in. You can adjust the settings before you take the shot, helping the final picture look better even though you're taking it under less-than-ideal conditions.

TIP *If you think your image preview looked better before you started messing with it, you can go back to the beginning by clicking the Default buttons in the various tabs we just talked about.*

We're almost done with our discussion on Still settings, but before we move on to actually taking a photo, let me draw your attention to a few other setting options. You can access all of these options by clicking the Select Capture Menu icon.

- *Self Timer* instructs the Motion Eye to capture the subject in the preview pane 10 seconds after you press the Capture button.

- *Auto Shutter* tells the camera to take a picture every time the subject in the preview pane moves to a new position.

- *Digital Zoom* commands the Motion Eye to zoom in on (or out of) the subject. But unlike the optical zoom lens on a regular camera, which gets you physically closer to your subject by extending out of the camera's face, Network Smart Capture's Digital Zoom feature merely magnifies the image inside the Motion Eye's line of sight and reduces its resolution.

NOTE   *At this point, you've probably noticed the button on the right side of the screen that looks like a magnifying glass with an X in the middle, and you likely assumed it allows you to zoom. Well, you're both right and wrong on that score. This is the Magnify button that lets the visually challenged zoom in on anything—except the subject in the Network Smart Capture window. For enlarging images in the Network Smart Capture preview pane, you have to use the Digital Zoom feature I just described.*

10

Now that you have all of your settings arranged, you're ready for the *pièce de résistance*—taking a picture. Just click the Capture button underneath the preview pane in the Network Smart Capture window, or easier still, press the Capture button on the screen's right side one more time. In one fell swoop, you've both completed the shot and saved it in the area you already designated when you adjusted your settings.

A miniature version of the shot you just took will appear to the right of the preview window. To see a bigger version of it, double-click the shot with your left mouse button, or click the light blue icon (that looks like a filmstrip) to the right of the Network Smart Capture window. The program then whisks it over to the preview pane. If it's a keeper, navigate to the place where you elected to store your shots and give it a proper name other than the number assigned to it by the Motion Eye. To rename the shot, right-click the shot, and then click the Rename option in the menu. From there, just type in the new name.

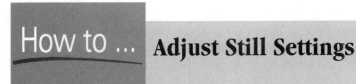

How to ... Adjust Still Settings

Gone are the days of twisting your 35 mm camera lens this way and that. With digital cameras like the TRs, you can do all the adjusting electronically, ensuring the end result comes out clearly.

1. To get to your Still settings, click the little briefcase icon in the bottom-left corner of the Network Smart Capture window. Another window will appear like the one shown here, called Still Image Setting. Click the Camera Adjustment tab at the top of this window.

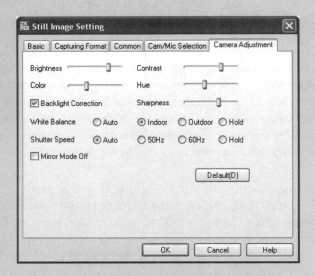

2. You'll then see a slew of image-adjustment options for Brightness, Contrast, Sharpness, and more. Play around with these settings by positioning your pointer on the sliders, pressing and holding your left mouse button, and then dragging the sliders left and right until you get your desired effect. You'll instantly see the results of your tweaking in the preview portion of the Network Smart Capture window. Notice that the Still Image Setting window also lets you optimize images according to indoor and outdoor conditions. You can even adjust the backlighting, which helps when you're shooting into a sunset or other bright light, by clicking inside the Backlight Correction box.

3. Next, click the Capturing Format tab at the top of the Still Image Setting window. This is the tab that lets you set your image resolution from a maximum of 640×480 to a minimum of 80×60. You can also adjust the Quality by dragging the slider just like you did for Brightness, Contrast, and other options in the Camera Adjustment tab. Keep in mind that the higher the resolution and image quality, the bigger the photo file you have to store on your TR. At max resolution and highest quality, a photo will be about 2MB. That may not sound like a lot, but you'll be surprised how fast your hard drive can fill up.

4. Last but not least, be sure to specify where you want your files saved. Click the Basic tab, and then click the Browse button. A small Browse For Folder window will appear. Scroll up and down through this window until you see the location where you want to save your shots. Click the location name to highlight it, and then click the OK button at the bottom of the window.

CAUTION   *When you're done typing the name, be sure to click anywhere* outside *the name box you're typing in. Otherwise, the new name won't stick but will revert back to what it was originally.*

10

Movie Mode

Movie mode works a lot like Still mode, with a few notable exceptions. First, make sure you're in Movie mode by clicking the word Movie on the left side of the Network Smart Capture window. Again, a yellow light will appear under this option to let you know where you are. Point the camera at the subject of your video just as you did when taking still shots. A preview of the subject will appear in the preview window.

Now, adjust the settings for your movie in much the same way you did for your still shots. Click the briefcase Settings icon in the lower-right corner of the Network Smart Capture window. Click the Camera Adjustment tab to fool around with brightness, color, contrast, and more.

Next, click the Capturing Format tab (see Figure 10-2). The options in this tab are slightly different than the corresponding tab for Still mode. Since the Motion Eye records all video in 160×112 resolution to keep video files from becoming too huge, you can't adjust this setting. But you can opt for lower or higher quality, as well as Noise Reduction to minimize the effects of anything that could cause the video to distort.

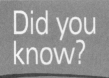

Motion Eye Software
Offers Special Effects

If you're feeling artsy or just want to goof around, check out the Effects feature of the Network Smart Capture software, as shown here. It puts one of 27 filters on the image to make it appear as if it's been sketched, painted, warped, embossed, and more. But I should warn you: You have to set your desired effect before you take your shot—you can't apply it to a picture you've already taken. To add special effects after you've snapped a shot, you'll need to use another photo-editing program like Adobe PhotoShop or Jasc Paint Shop Pro.

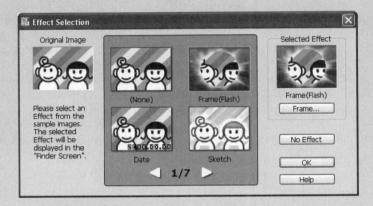

To apply one of these effects, click the Select Capture Menu icon in the bottom-right corner of the Network Smart Capture window, next to the briefcase Settings icon. Click Effect, and then use the forward and back arrows in the Effect Selection window to look at all of the effects. Choose one by clicking it once to highlight it, and then click the OK button. A preview of your image with the new effect you just applied should show up in the preview pane of the Network Smart Capture window.

Don't expect to see a full-screen rendition of the video you shoot with the Motion Eye. At 160×112, your video will be only slightly larger than a postage stamp.

The Capturing Format tab is also the place where you can adjust the Maximum time to record. The time starts at one minute and maxes out at 120 minutes; to adjust it, click and hold the up or down arrows until you reach your desired time. Whatever

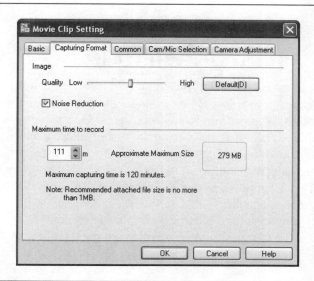

FIGURE 10-2   The Capturing Format tab in Movie mode varies slightly from the corresponding tab in Still mode.

time you choose will appear underneath the preview pane in the Network Smart Capture window, along with a timer to keep you apprised of your video's progress. Just to give you an idea of the difference in video file size between the two extremes: A one-minute video file recorded at decent quality measures about 2MB, while a 120-minute video with mid-range quality measures nearly 300MB.

Finally, click the Basic tab to select the place where you'd like to store your video files. After you've made your selection, the remaining storage space you have in that location will surface underneath the preview pane, to the right of the timer I just described.

At this stage, you're all set up to begin recording. To roll your virtual tape, click the record button beneath the preview pane in the Network Smart Capture window, or click the Capture button to the right of the display. If you want to stop recording before your preset time is up, just click the Record button again—which should now say Stop—or press the Capture button again. The first frame of the clip you just shot will appear to the right of the preview pane. Delete it by clicking the trash can icon, or rename the file in its saved location.

Adjust the Sound for Your Video Recordings   When recording video to your TR, you can't use the laptop's volume up and down buttons to set the video's volume level. You have to adjust the volume level for the TR's integrated microphone,

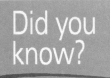

Sony Splits the TR's Hard Drive in Two

If you choose to save your video file to your hard drive, you'll notice that the amount of remaining storage space listed under the preview pane seems awfully small compared to the space you thought remained. Don't panic—the rest of your space is still there. The TR is registering the rest of the space as its own entity. In other words, the system thinks it has two hard drives instead of one.

Desktop and laptop manufacturers, including Sony, often *partition,* or split up, the hard drive to improve system performance. Dividing the hard drive into two smaller sections lets the system call up files more quickly. Think about it: When you tell your system to retrieve a certain file from a 40GB hard drive, it takes more time for the system to search through 40GB of material for the file than it would to search through 20GB.

You can tell if your hard drive has been split in two by going to Start | My Computer, and then looking under the Hard Disk Drives portion of the My Computer window that appears. If you see two Local Disk icons that say C: and D:, you know the manufacturer has partitioned the hard drive. To find out exactly how big each portion is, click the portion to highlight it, and then look at the small white Details window in the lower-left corner of the My Computer window.

which is the device that will actually be capturing the sound to accompany your video. To adjust the microphone's sound output, follow these steps:

1. Go to Start | Control Panel | Sounds, Speech, And Audio Devices | Sounds And Audio Devices. A window called Sounds And Audio Device Properties will then pop up.

2. Choose the Audio tab at the top of the Sounds And Audio Device Properties window. Under the Sound Recording section in the middle of the window, click the Volume button.

3. Another window will appear called Recording Source. Locate the Microphone volume scale in that window and click inside the tiny checkbox that says Select at the bottom of the scale.

4. From there, just place your pointer on the Microphone volume bar, click and hold your left mouse button, drag the bar to the level you desire, and release your left mouse button.

If sound really means a lot to you, you should consider using an external microphone, which you can plug into the TR's microphone port.

10

TIP *Those whoops, zips, and other sound effects of the Network Smart Capture software getting on your nerves yet? You can turn them off by clicking the Briefcase Settings icon in the lower-right corner of the main Network Smart Capture window. Another window will appear onscreen called either Still Image Setting, Movie Clip Setting, or Web Camera Setting, depending on what mode you're in. In all three windows, you'll see a Common tab at the top. Click the tab, and then click to uncheck the box next to Enable Sound Effects.*

Web Camera Mode

If you've ever been far away from someone you care about, you've probably wished you could peek in on what the person is doing at any given moment—and vice versa. Web cameras, or webcams for short, can help in that department. These devices snap consecutive images at intervals as close as seconds apart, and then upload them one-at-a-time to web sites where you can view them. While the effect is noticeably choppy compared to regular video, it's still a nice way to make you feel like you're seeing the person in real time when face-to-face visits aren't an option.

The Motion Eye's third and final function is as a web camera. After altering the camera settings for Still and Movie modes, you should now be an old pro at making these adjustments. To change the settings once again for Web Camera mode, click the words Web Camera to the left of the Network Smart Capture window, and then click the briefcase Settings icon. Go to the Camera Adjustment tab first to tweak the appearance of the webcam's image. Then head over to the Capturing Format tab to set your image resolution and quality.

Next, click the Capturing Interval tab (Figure 10-3). This is where you tell the Motion Eye how long it should wait between snapping shots. Click inside the tiny oval in front of the words Capture At Intervals, and then click and hold the up or down arrows next to minutes (m) and seconds (s) until the counter reaches your desired time. Or, choose Auto Shutter that, as you remember from our talk about this function in the "Still Mode" section, takes a photo any time the subject moves.

Now go to the Send tab. Things start to get a little tricky from here as you tell the TR where to upload the webcam's images. Beneath the words Upload Method, you'll see a rectangular white box with a blue arrow next to it. Click the arrow. Three options will then appear under the white box.

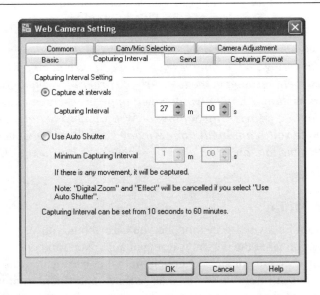

FIGURE 10-3   Tell the Motion Eye how long to wait between webcam shots by adjusting the capturing interval.

- **Upload To Web Page By FTP**   This option tells the Motion Eye to send its images to a web page using FTP, or file transfer protocol, technology. The technology is a typical method for sending or receiving files between your computer and a *server,* or another computer that manages image files like the ones you're sending. To use the FTP method, you must know several details about the server that's accepting the transfer, including the username/ID, password, and host name/address. The only way to get this info is to ask the person who set up the server.

- **Upload To VAIO Media Photo Server**   If you travel down this road, you have to set up your VAIO Media Photo Server first. Skip ahead to Chapter 13, where I take you through setting up VAIO Media servers step-by-step.

- **Do Not Upload**   This option means just what it says.

TIP   *Executing your first FTP transfer can be a daunting task. To learn more about the process, check out www.ftpplanet.com/. The site offers a new user's guide to FTP, as well as discussion forums where you can chat with other people on the topic.*

The last settings step is to click the Basic tab and navigate to the spot on the TR where you'd like to store your webcam images.

Unlike Still and Movie modes, you can't press the Capture button on the display's right side to set the webcam in motion. Instead, you have to click the Start button below the preview pane. The window for the Web Camera Reservation Wizard will appear, like the one in Figure 10-4. The wizard allows you to specify a certain date and time that you'd like the webcam to start, plus it reviews some of the settings, such as upload method, that you already determined earlier. Perform the various, self-explanatory actions in each of the wizard's four consecutive steps, and then click the Finish button at the bottom of the wizard's final screen. A window called Confirm Web Camera Setting will appear, sporting the highlights of the details you just arranged. Click the OK button, and a small window will appear in the middle of the screen, indicating through a diamond-shaped line that the webcam is transferring files to the server you've chosen.

If you want to go back and review the webcam images you sent to your friends and family, you can access them in the same storage place you specified on the Basic tab—unless you checked the Upload Without Saving The Captured Images box on the Send tab.

NOTE   *Although the Motion Eye's webcam mode lets you shoot video of a sort, you can't add sound in this mode. Rather, what you see is literally what you get in Web Camera mode.*

10

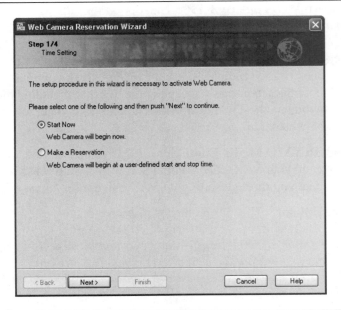

FIGURE 10-4   The Web Camera Reservation Wizard helps you specify certain webcam settings, such as start time and image upload location.

Use PictureGear Studio to Crop, Organize, and Print Your Photos

We've all been there: After shoving several years' worth of photos into shoeboxes, you wake up one day to thousands of pictures that are begging to be put in albums. Using your TR to take tons of digital shots may have freed you from the physical clutter of hard-copy photos, but that doesn't mean your hard drive has been spared the digital muck of too many electronic shots. To help you wade through it all, Sony includes its PictureGear Studio program with the TR, as well as its other VAIO desktops and notebooks.

I don't have sufficient space to describe every last function of PictureGear Studio. But I do have space to tell you about the program's coolest, most useful features. If you ever want to know more, you can always fall back on the program's user guide.

To launch the PictureGear Studio application, follow this path: Start | All Programs | PictureGear Studio | PictureGear Studio (again). A menu window will appear, like the one shown here, listing the program's five main functions: Import Photos, Binder, PhotoCollection, PhotoAlbum, and PrintStudio.

Populate Your Photo Collection

The first thing you'll want to do is populate your PhotoCollection, so you can draw from the images in your collection to create pages in your Binder and PhotoAlbum. Open PhotoCollection by clicking the PhotoCollection icon in the center of the menu window. When the PhotoCollection window appears (Figure 10-5), look to the window's left, where you'll see the default Category list assigned by Sony. You can delete those sections by right-clicking the section name, and then left-clicking Delete Category. You can also create your own new sections by clicking the Create Category button beneath the Category list. The button looks like a square file bin with a red flower on top.

10

FIGURE 10-5   Create your own Categories within your PhotoCollection, or stick with the ones Sony gave you.

To bring photos into your collection, click the Explorer icon (which looks like a yellow file folder) next to the Category heading. Then, click the system components in the left-hand window until you reach the location where you've stored your pictures. Once you've reached that location, your photos will appear as thumbnail-sized images in the center pane. From there, click the green-square icon to the left of the yellow folder icon, which will return you to the Category list. Your photos should still be showing in the center pane. Start moving the photos you just found into their appropriate categories by clicking and holding on the file you want to move, and then dragging it over to the appropriate category. Repeat the preceding process for photos you have stored on your TR in other places.

TIP   *The Import Photos option is a means to the same end as the Still Mode function of the Network Smart Capture software—it allows you to capture images directly from the Motion Eye into the PictureGear Studio program. Otherwise, you have to manually drag-and-drop the photos you took using Network Smart Capture from their stored location on the TR into the PictureGear Studio program.*

Correct and Crop Images

Once your images are organized in your PhotoCollection categories, you can start tinkering with their look and shape. Double-click the thumbnail image you want to work with. A larger version of the image will appear in the center pane, with a range of icons at the top for Correction, Trim, and even Décor. Click Correction to alter the image's brightness, hue, sharpness, red eye, and other qualities.

Next, move on to Trim, where you can resize your image. When you click the Trim icon, you'll notice that your photo appears in a new, smaller window framed by eight tiny red squares with the resolution in the middle. You can crop the image by dragging these squares to expand or contract the image's borders, as shown in this photo of my dog, Lucky, in Figure 10-6 (and yes, he does cross his paws all on his own).

The last choice I'll highlight here is Décor, which allows you to draw, type, and stamp on the image like I've done to the shot in Figure 10-7.

Create a Binder or Photo Album

Now that you've put plenty of photos in your collection, you can start arranging them in your Binder or PhotoAlbum. To open either of these features, click their respective icons in the PictureGear Studio main menu.

FIGURE 10-6   Drag and drop the red squares to trim your image down to size.

FIGURE 10-7   The Décor feature lets you add everything from cartoon-like animal stamps to geometric shapes.

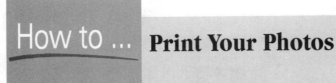

Print Your Photos

Printing your photos is as painless as pressing a couple of buttons. Did you install your printer yet? If not, backtrack to Chapter 5, where we talked about installing hardware.

To print a shot, follow these simple steps:

1. Locate the picture in your PhotoCollection. Click the photo to highlight it.

2. Click the Print icon at the top of the PhotoCollection window.

3. Click and hold your pointer on the up arrow next to your photo to specify how many prints you need.

4. Click the Select Paper icon at the top of the window. Under the Select Paper menu on the window's left side, click the manufacturer name of your printer. If you don't see your printer, click Standard Paper.

5. Choose the format you want in the center pane by clicking to highlight it. Then click the Print button at the top of the window.

6. A preview of the print will appear in the center pane. If it fits your bill, click the Print All button on the window's right. Or, you can retrace your steps and alter the print by hitting the Back arrow at the top of the window.

Make a Binder

Sony designed the Binder portion of the PictureGear Studio program to resemble a regular three-ring binder, down to the rainbow-colored tabs that separate each section. The default Binder is arranged according to the sections, called Titles, in Figure 10-8. Delete the preset Titles by right-clicking the Title, and then choosing Delete. Create your own Titles and even assign colors to them by clicking the Create Title button under the Title list.

Once you have your Titles set, click the Title name you want to start adding Binder pages to, then click the New Page icon at the top of the Binder window. Your Photo Collection will appear inside your Binder window. Click the photo you want to add to the Binder page. An Input Information window will appear where you can enter

FIGURE 10-8   The Binder's preset Title sections include Recipes and Diary, but you can always delete the presets and add your own Titles.

pertinent info that you'd like to list on the page. Click the OK button in the upper-right corner, and a preview of your page will appear in the next window.

Make a Photo Album

Creating a PhotoAlbum isn't all that different than making a Binder page. Within the PhotoAlbum window, click the New Album icon at the top of the window. The program will then present you with two options to create an album either manually or with a wizard. The former is a longer process than the latter, allowing you to design the minute details of each page.

On the flip side, creating your album with the wizard is a simple process involving just a few steps. First, click the Create An Album With Wizard option. A list of all the photos in your Photo Collection will appear on the subsequent screen. Highlight each picture you want to include in the album by clicking it once, and then click

10

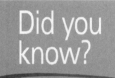

PictureGear PrintStudio Designs Greeting Cards

How many times have you been late sending a birthday card because you're too lazy to go out and buy one? Digital greeting cards, like the ones offered by the PrintStudio portion of PictureGear Studio, can save your behind. This feature lets you design your cards, like the one shown here, from the comfort of your own computer. You can then shoot them over to friends and family by e-mail, saving you the trouble of scrounging around for a stamp. In addition to its card-creation duties, PrintStudio also lets you make labels, table placeholder cards, and even your own sketchbook.

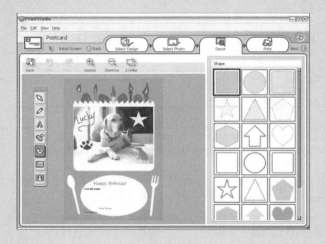

Create The Album With The Selected Photo(s) button. The following window lets you choose from among dozens of backdrops for each page in the album; click the one you like. Finally, select the picture layout for each page. The next thing you'll see is your completed album.

Share Your Pictures with Friends and Family

Before I wrap up this chapter, I want to tell you about a few easy ways to share your photos beyond the obvious print-and-mail process.

■ **E-mail 'em**   Since you already have your e-mail squared away after setting it up in Chapter 7, e-mailing your pictures to the people you love should be a snap. But for the love of Pete, don't start wantonly sending dozens of photos to folks. Even the smallest image files can be too big for some e-mail systems, causing them to crash or, at the very least, work very slowly. Make sure to save the images you want to e-mail as JPEG files at low resolutions, as well as at the lowest quality setting you can get away with.

■ **Upload the images to an FTP site**   Your more tech-savvy friends and family probably have access to an FTP site where they can receive info. Review the "Web Camera Mode" section earlier in this chapter to learn more about establishing FTP communication.

■ **Burn your pics to disc**   If you don't want to sacrifice photo quality in favor of smaller file size, try burning your photos to a CD or DVD. How in the heck do you do that? I tell you all about it in Chapter 12.

You've now nailed the basics of capturing pictures and video with the TR's integrated Motion Eye camera. These concepts will help you in the next chapter, where we discuss making movies in more detail.

10

Chapter 11

Make Movies with Your VAIO

How to...

- Connect your digital camcorder
- Use Sony's DVgate Plus video software
- Use Sony's Click to DVD program

Now that you've taken baby steps toward capturing video in Chapter 10, we'll move on to more advanced video capturing and editing techniques. First things first: Is your digital camcorder at the ready? You'll need it for the kick-off portion of this chapter, where I tell you how to connect the camcorder to your VAIO. Then I'll describe how to import and edit video using Sony's DVgate Plus program. Finally, I'll help you navigate through Click to DVD, the video software that Sony bundles with VAIO desktops and notebooks that include DVD+RW drives.

Connect Your Digital Camcorder

Before you blow the dust off the ol' camcorder and try to plug it into your VAIO, you need to determine whether the camcorder is compatible with your computer. If it's an *analog* recording device, the answer is almost always no (see the Did You Know? sidebar "You Can Convert Analog Video to DV" later in this chapter to learn about the rare exceptions). Used to be that most camcorders were analog devices, just like VCRs. Camcorders translate images into electronic signals, which then stick to magnetic videotape. Have you ever copied the contents of one VHS tape to another? If so, you probably noticed the contents of the second tape don't look as clear as the first. That's because analog recording devices can't reproduce analog signals in exactly the same way each time, causing copied tapes to look different than the original.

These days, almost all camcorders are *digital* devices that translate images into an infinite number of combinations of just two numbers—0 and 1—and then record those numeric patterns onto digital videotape. There's no ambiguity involved in repeating a set of numbers, so digital patterns reproduce perfectly no matter how many copies you make. Since computers are also digital devices, it's easy for them to recognize DV (digital video). You've probably already guessed that getting your VAIO to read video from an analog camcorder is like trying to mate cats and dogs. To do so, you'll need a digital camcorder or video capture device to make this whole shebang work with most VAIOs.

Modern digital camcorders include either a USB 2.0 or IEEE-1394 (a.k.a., iLink or FireWire) port for connecting the thing to your computer. As you know from reading about these ports in previous chapters, they support *plug-and-play*—meaning, you just plug them into your VAIO's USB 2.0 or iLink port, and in a perfect world, the computer recognizes the camcorder.

> **NOTE** *Most camcorders don't come with the proper cord for connecting to a computer, so you'll probably have to buy one at your local computer store.*

Once you plug the camcorder into your VAIO, the Windows XP Digital Video Device window appears (see Figure 11-1). The window indicates that the computer has detected the camcorder and prompts you to choose from among the video capture programs that are installed on your VAIO. Unless you've installed your own third-party video editing software, such as Adobe's Premiere, your choices likely consist of the Sony programs that came with your VAIO—DVgate Plus and/or Click to DVD. Your VAIO will subsequently send the video from your camcorder to the program you've chosen.

FIGURE 11-1   You can choose which software program will receive your imported video in the Digital Video Device window.

You Can Convert Analog Video to DV

Using your VAIO to view and edit all of the old home videos you made with your analog camcorder isn't impossible. But with most VAIOs, you'll need either a digital camcorder or video capture device before you can transform those videos into DV. Follow the steps listed in your digital camcorder's user guide to learn how to make the conversion, which will likely involve connecting your VCR or analog camcorder to the digital camcorder using an S-video or composite video cable. For video capture devices, such as Pinnacle Systems' Dazzle device, you must connect your analog camcorder to the device, and then plug the device into your VAIO. Again, follow the specific instructions included with the equipment in order to achieve a proper connection.

A couple of VAIOs, such as the RZ Series desktop, don't require a DV camera or video capture device to read analog video. These VAIOs ship with one of two (or both) things—Sony's Giga Pocket hardware and software solution, and/or Windows XP Media Center Edition (MCE)—that make it possible to plug an analog recording device directly into the computer. Check out Chapter 13 for more on both Giga Pocket and Windows XP MCE.

Use Sony's DVgate Plus Video Software

All Sony VAIO desktops and notebooks ship with DVgate Plus, the company's basic video importing and editing software. You can use this program to save video to your VAIO's hard drive, manipulate that video, and then send it back out for recording on external media, like digital video tape, or to your VAIO's hard drive.

> **TIP**
>
> *Talking about Sony's software is going to take up all the room I have for this chapter. But I wanted to at least let you know about another movie-making program that comes with your VAIO—Windows Movie Maker. Microsoft built this software into Windows XP to help you manipulate your video footage. Consult the Help file for the program to learn more about its capabilities.*

Import Video via DVgate Plus

Before we go any further, I recommend you do the following two things:

- Plug your digital camcorder into a power outlet. You're going to need a full charge to get through all of the awesome tasks that await you in this chapter.

- Set aside plenty of time to make your movies. Even if you hurry, it can take upwards of an hour for every minute of final video you edit.

Now, let's tackle the task of importing video to your VAIO using DVgate Plus. The program recognizes two types of digital camcorders:

- Straight-up DV camcorders that record video to digital videotapes.

- A newer type of digital camcorder, called *MicroMV*, which records video to tapes based on MPEG-2 technology. MPEG (m-peg) stands for *Motion Picture Experts Group*, the body that created the technology. Like the JPEG image technology we talked about in Chapter 9, MPEG technology arranges video information in a space-saving way, helping huge video files remain somewhat reasonable in size. MPEG-2 is the name for the second-generation of MPEG technology and stands for video that features a resolution between 720×480 and 1280×720 at 60 fps (frames per second).

TIP *Gabbing about all the different types of digital camcorders and their functions is beyond the scope of this book. But if you want to nose around inside the world of the camcorder, you can pick up another tome in the How to Do Everything Series, called—you guessed it—How to Do Everything with Your Digital Video Camcorder.*

11

Remember the Digital Device Selection window in Figure 11-1 that appears when you plug a digital camcorder into your VAIO? To import video right to DVgate Plus, you'll want to left-click the DVgate Plus option under the words What Do You Want Windows To Do, and then click the OK button.

A couple of new windows will crop up: The DVgate Plus window will appear in the background, while another window called Mode Select Guide (Figure 11-2) will surface in the foreground. The Mode Select Guide conveniently holds your hand through the first few choices you'll make about how you want DVgate Plus to handle your video. As the window instructs, turn your digital camcorder on, and then click the Next button. The program presents you with a second window that includes

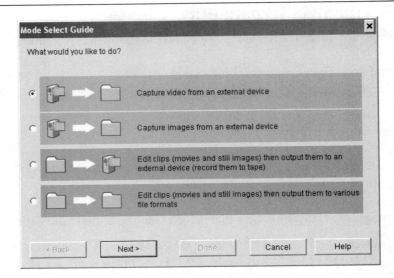

FIGURE 11-2   The Mode Select Guide provides four choices for manipulating your video.

four choices, two for importing video to your VAIO, and two for editing and exporting video that you've already imported. Ignore the last two for now while we discuss capturing video through the first two choices—Capture Video From An External Device, and Capture Images From An External Device.

Capture Video from an External Device

Now that you're a movie producer, you'll need raw footage from which to mold your epic masterpiece. The Capture video from an external device option allows you to import that raw footage you've shot with your digital camcorder into your VAIO. Within the Mode Select Guide window, choose this option by clicking once inside the tiny circle that precedes it, and then click Next. The program will detect your digital camcorder and present you with three more options to capture video through: Auto, Manual, or Batch Capture mode.

Auto Capture   Choosing the Auto Capture mode tells DVgate Plus to pull all available video off of your digital camcorder's tape. To get the ball rolling, click once inside the tiny oval in front of the Auto Capture option. The Mode Select Guide window will finally fade from view, leaving the DVgate Plus window alone. You'll notice the Auto Capture tab appears in the foreground of this window (Figure 11-3).

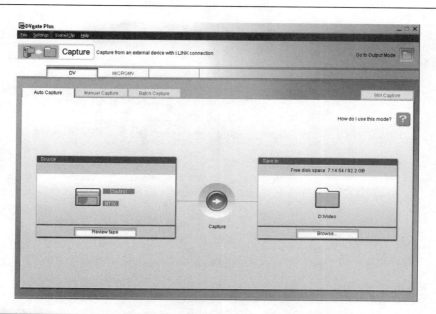

FIGURE 11-3   Auto Capture mode imports all available video from your digital camcorder to your VAIO.

You're almost ready to begin importing video, but before you do, make sure to alter a few important settings. In the upper-left corner of the window, click Settings, and then click Capture. The Capture Settings window will appear with two tabs up top—DV and MicroMV (Figure 11-4). The appropriate tab for your camcorder type should already appear in the foreground. From here, you can choose whether you want to set time or size limits for each segment of video you import. If you're using a MicroMV camera, you can save your videos in just one file format, MicroMV or .mmv. But if you're sporting a DV camera, you can specify the file type you want to use for your saved clips. Your choices include AVI 1.0, AVI 2.0, or Audio Only.

NOTE   *Short for Audio Video Interleave, AVI is the video standard developed by Microsoft and used most in the computing world. This digital technology consecutively intertwines pieces of video and audio data, resulting in the seamless video files you see and hear on your computer.*

Finally, tell the program where to save the video you import by clicking the Browse button beneath the Save In box, and then navigating to the place you'll put the video.

11

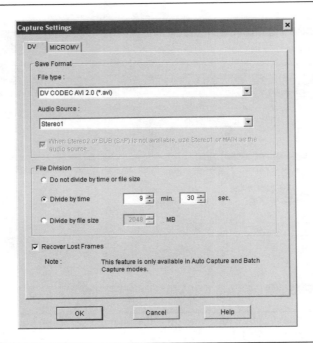

FIGURE 11-4   Determine important time and file-type settings for your movies in the Capture Settings window.

Now that your settings are all in order, click the round, red Capture button in the middle of the screen to begin importing.

NOTE   *DVgate Plus gives imported video clips some pretty funky default names that include more than a dozen numbers. For example, one of my video clips was named lucky-20040101212953-01. Believe it or not, there's rhyme and reason to the numbers. The first eight numbers indicate the four-digit year, two-digit month, and two-digit day that you imported the video to your VAIO. The next six numbers specify the military time when you took the shot, which in my case was 21:29:53, or about 9:29 P.M. The final numbers after the dash are the serial number your VAIO assigns to the image. Of course, you can always change the default names to whatever you want by right-clicking the name, left-clicking Rename, and then typing in the new name. Like we talked about in Chapter 10, don't forget to click outside the name box in order to set the new name in stone.*

How to ... Copy DVDs

How to ...

- Understand the brief history of DVD ripping
- Know what you can copy and why
- Pick a copying program
- Copy a DVD
- Burn your copy back to a blank DVD

To copy or not to copy: That is the question many DVD watchers are asking these days. Judging by the number of folks I see watching DVD movies on their Sony VAIO laptops (and other devices) while riding the commuter train, the number of people creating their own DVD movies, and the amount of e-mail I get on the subject, this is a huge question. This special section covers what you can and can't legally copy (and why), some history of the DVD-ripping controversy, and how to rip.

A Brief History of DVD Ripping

Although I'm not a lawyer, I'd be remiss if I didn't warn you up front that under current U.S. law, it is illegal to copy a commercial, protected DVD movie—even if you own the DVD and the copy is for personal backup only. For this how-to section, I stayed away from protected, commercial DVDs and copied a DVD I burned myself of my family's home movies. I don't advocate the illegal copying of protected DVDs. The problem with copying a commercial DVD is not so much the copying itself, but the breaking of the Content Scrambling System (CSS) copy protection used by commercial DVD movies. The Digital Millennium Copyright Act (DMCA), passed by Congress in 2000, defines the law in this controversy, but at least one company—321 Studios—has challenged the law in court on the basis of *fair use*, the long-standing consumer right to make a single copy of digital media for noncommercial use.

Easy to Crack the Code

The problem for the movie industry is that the Content Scrambling System, which uses only a 40-bit key encryption for copyright protection, is remarkably easy to crack. When the quest to "rip" (digitally copy the files from a DVD) began, it didn't take long for DeCSS—a program that removes the CSS protection—to show up. The origin of the DeCSS program is a bit murky, but you may recall the incident a few years back where a young European student was arrested and his computer seized for publishing the program on his web site. He was quickly released and his equipment returned. Or

you might recall the young rock-and-roll hacker who put the DeCSS instructions in a song. Whatever the method, governments and the entertainment industry remain adamant about controlling the copying of commercial DVDs.

What You Can Copy and Why

Why are they so vehement? Visit many Asian or South American countries and you'll see copied DVDs selling on the street for less than $5— and that's a conservative figure. The entertainment industry loses billions of dollars annually to this black market piracy, but there's little that they can do about it when it's happening on foreign soil. The industry is more concerned with preventing DVD piracy in the U.S. and Europe.

Some Limited Options

You do, however, have some limited DVD-copying options. One of the most intriguing solutions comes from a startup called Molino Networks (www .molinonetworks.com). This year Molino launched a digital media receiver, called the Media Mogul. It's about the size of a DVD player and can make full, uncompressed copies of up to 200 DVDs and store them on its own internal hard drive. The movies are available for instant playback through a connected TV, A/V receiver, or home-theater system. As for copyright issues, the Media Mogul system uses CSS security/ encryption. It also adds a new auditing function that asks you to validate that you still own a DVD through a two-minute, one-time-only process that pops up about two-weeks after a DVD is imported. The system makes it impractical to import a rented or borrowed DVD, the company says. Check the end of this chapter for more on Molino.

That's the legal situation, but the fact is DVD copying is becoming commonplace in certain circles, and with compression technologies, movies are even being traded and downloaded over the Internet. (At the risk of sounding like a broken DVD, er, record, I don't advocate the illegal copying of protected DVDs or the downloading of an illegally copied DVD from the Internet.). So now that you know the history, just how do you copy a DVD legally?

Pick a Copying Program

C opying a noncommercial DVD, i.e., one made by yourself or someone else that doesn't contain copy-protected material or claim restricted use, can be pretty easy, although it's time consuming. Remember, I'm only copying my home movies. Any of the more popular commercial mastering software suites, like Nero Burning ROM or Easy Media Creator, will do it, as long as you have about 10GB of free hard-drive space for the program to use for its temporary files. (Skip ahead to the "How to Copy a DVD" section for detailed copying instructions). Dedicated DVD copy programs such as Pinnacle's InstantCopy and Intervideo's DVD Copy take the process further, shrinking larger movies so they fit on one blank DVD and making raw copies—that is, the bit-by-bit contents of a disk—no matter what the content is.

The Best Things in Life Are Free

Unfortunately for you, but fortunately for companies such as 321 Studios that want to sell you DVD-copying software, the press has been remiss in explaining this software, because most of it is actually free. You don't need to pay 321 Studio's high prices. Most notably, there's been little discussion of free programs like SmartRipper and DVD Decrypter. You can use both to copy a nonprotected DVD legally, for instance your home movies. And although it's illegal and I don't condone it, both programs will also copy commercial movies to your hard drive. SmartRipper was at the heart of 321 Studio's first product—DVD Copy Plus— a product that backed up DVD movies to CD.

As I mentioned, 321 Studios has been testing the Digital Millennium Copyright Act in court on the premise that consumers have the right to make a single backup copy of media they purchase. Whether the court action is truly consumer activism or a ploy so 321 Studios can continue selling its highly profitable software is anyone's guess. But judging from 321 Studio's first product—the aforementioned DVD Copy Plus with its public domain software (a program you don't need to buy), bundled with some not-so-helpful advice—I lean toward the profit-margin theory. But I digress (call me a cynic).

Ripper-Free Versions

Probably the best kept secret is DVD Shrink, an easy-to-use, free program that both copies and shrinks DVDs. It foregoes 321 Studios DVD X Copy's annoying habit of placing a 15-second must-view watermark at the front of every movie. DVD Shrink will also copy a copy—something DVD X Copy would never do until the new RF (Ripper Free) version hit the scene in 2004. (The RF version was forced upon the company by a court injunction). DVD Shrink also allows you to back up just a portion of your movie and remove menus.

How to Copy a DVD

To copy a nonprotected DVD movie of, say, your family vacation, you could use programs such as SmartRipper or DVD Decrypter, but they require a higher level of DVD-related knowledge, so I'll stick with DVD Shrink. Once you know DVD Shrink, you'll be able to get up to speed with the other programs. (At the risk of boring you to tears, let me reiterate that I'm not advocating you copy commercial, protected DVDs.)

1. Download and install DVD Shrink. (You can download DVD Shrink from www .filepop .com/cat/m_253.htm).

2. Make sure you have about 10GB of free hard drive space on your VAIO for the program to use for its temporary files.

NOTE

See Chapter 15 for more on freeing up hard drive space.

3. Place your DVD in the DVD-ROM drive or burner.

NOTE

Many drives throttle down to a slower speed when they sense a movie disc. Consult your drive's documentation to see if there's a way to bypass this behavior.

4. Once the DVD is in the drive, fire up the DVD Shrink program (see Figure 1), and then select the Open Disk icon.

5. A dialog box will pop up asking you to chose between DVD drives if you have more than one optical drives on your system, as shown in Figure 2. Select the appropriate drive and sit back for a minute or two while DVD Shrink analyzes the movie to see if it needs shrinking, and if it does, which files are more important and, therefore, should be shrunk less.

6. Once it's analyzed the movie, the program may default to Full Disk (as shown in Figure 3) or Backup mode. Backup mode copies all the contents of a DVD including the menu structure and extra features. DVD Shrink will show you how much it's shrinking each title (menus, movies, and extra features are all referred to as *titles*) and allow you to vary the percentage of shrinkage. When you increase the compression on one title, the compression of the main movie is reduced automatically for higher quality. You can even turn extra features into slideshows to save maximum space or disable audio tracks and subtitles to further raise the quality of the main title—the movie.

Figure 1. DVD Shrink's opening window

7. Once you're satisfied with the compression levels, simply click the Backup button. Up pops a dialog box (see Figure 4) that lets you select the destination directory. It's a good idea to copy the DVD to a new, aptly named folder. In about 30 to 40 minutes (assuming you have a relatively fast VAIO) your DVD will be backed up to your hard drive. A dialog box, shown in Figure 5, allows you to monitor the back-up process.

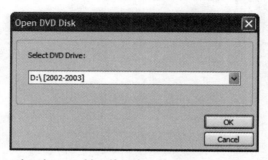

Figure 2. This window allows you to chose between drives if you have more than one optical drive on your system.

Figure 3. DVD Shrink's Full Disk mode

TIP

You can remove menus and special features in DVD Shrink's Re-Author mode (look for the icon at the top of the program). In many cases, this will eliminate the need to compress the main feature.

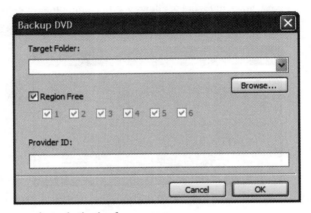

Figure 4. This dialog box lets you select a destination for your copy.

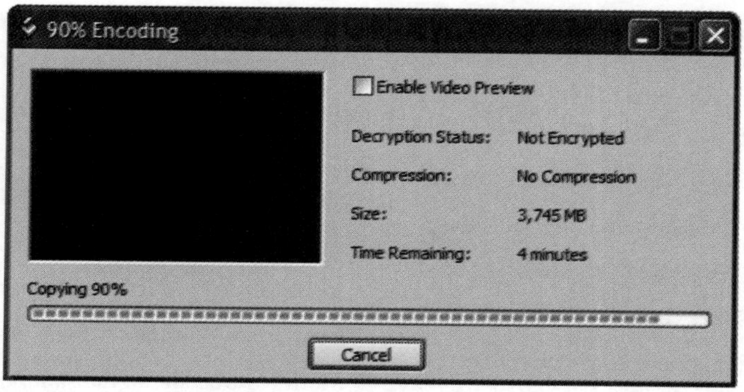

Figure 5.   Monitor DVD Shrink's backup process

Burn Your Copy Back to a Blank DVD

O nce you've backed up your DVD movie to your hard drive, you'll probably want to burn it back to a blank DVD, though some folks back up movies to their notebook hard drive to watch on the road. Unfortunately, not every mastering program will burn on a blank DVD Video disc, which differs subtly (but fatally for burning purposes) from a data DVD disc. Nero Burning ROM will burn on a blank video disc, but you may need one of the copy programs I mentioned previously or a good DVD authoring program.

A Primer on DVD Structure

B efore I get into the particulars of burning a DVD movie, it pays to know a bit about the nitty-gritty of a DVD movie structure. AUDIO_TS and VIDEO_TS folders should be on every disc. AUDIO_TS may sometimes be missing (it's really only for DVD Audio discs), and both folders may sometimes be found in lowercase. But for maximum compatibility with drives and players, both folders should be present and in uppercase. If you rip a movie and just wind up with a bunch of folderless files, you'll need to create these folders yourself.

All the DVD movie files go in the VIDEO_TS folder, which is where every DVD movie player looks for them. The files you see may seem mysterious, but are easily explained. A .ifo file is an information file that tells a DVD player what's on the disk, which files are to be played, the order in which they are played, and so on. A .vob file is a video object, a bit of a misnomer since it includes both video and audio, i.e., the movie and the soundtrack. Because of file system limitations, a .vob file is never larger than 1GB (1,073,741,824 bytes) and most movies require 4 to 6 .vob files, which are played contiguously to form the entire movie. A .bup is a backup of the .ifo file. A good movie player can handle small defects in a .vob file, but a damaged .ifo file can ruin its whole day.

> **TIP**
>
> When it comes to buying blank DVDs for copying, you get what you pay for. Cheap media gets hardly any quality control back at the plant. So expect bad discs if you go the cost-cutting route.

Find the Movie

If you're burning with a DVD copy program or authoring software, you must generally select an option such as "Burn From Disc Structure" or "Search For Movie On Disc." What you're looking for is the folder on your hard drive containing the AUDIO_TS and VIDEO_TS folders that you copied the movie to, perhaps "My Movie." Sometimes you can point to this parent folder, but often you'll have to select the VIDEO_TS folder for the program to find the movie. In other words, you might have to select "C:\ My Documents\My Videos\My Movie" or "C:\My Documents\My Videos\My Movie\VIDEO_TS".

TIP

If you're burning a lot of coasters (bad discs), check for firmware upgrades for your drive and reduce write speed if necessary.

Once you've found where you saved the movie, it should be as simple as inserting a blank disc and clicking Burn. Burning a movie will take about an hour at 1X speed, 30 minutes at 2X, 15 minutes at 4X, and less than 9 minutes at 8X.

Congratulations, you've backed up your movie. For more information on burning CDs and DVDs, or if you want to use Sony's Click to DVD program, turn to Chapter 12.

Media Mogul: Promising New Home Device?

And now, as promised, here's more information on California-based Molino Networks, which this year introduced its home media library device named the Molino Media Mogul. The device stores digital content in its native format, instead of ripping the content into a different format. This process, according to the company, lets consumers import movies and CDs in minutes, instead of the much longer chunk of time it takes to rip a DVD onto your personal computer. The basic version of the Media Mogul features a 300GB hard drive. Later in 2004, the company is expected to start selling a 1000GB (or Terabyte) version, dubbed the Media Mogul TB. Look for both products to be available direct from Molino's web site in the summer of 2004.

In addition to its massive storage capacity, the Media Mogul doubles as a CD/DVD player and can even burn photos and music to CD-Rs. It also features a built-in six-in-one flashcard reader for interfacing with the little media cards used in digital cameras and other devices and a front-panel FireWire port for easy compatibility with digital camcorders. What makes the Media Mogul different is that it preserves all recorded content in its original format, thus preserving the fidelity and interactive features. Plus, Media Mogul is the first device to integrate Gracenote's (www.gracenote.com) VideoID and CDDB music database, letting you easily organize, access, and store both music and DVD libraries and search by a broad variety of criteria, such as CD or DVD title, favorite artist or actor, and movie or music genre. Whether this device lives up the hype remains to be seen, but it sounds promising.

So there you have the basics on what sorts of DVDs you can legally copy, what types you can't copy, and how to copy them. Of course, the legal conundrum could change in the next 10 to 15 years. (Remember, I don't advocate the illegal copying of protected DVDs.) It's far too early to tell, but perhaps the fair use doctrine, combined with ever-increasing technological advancements, will break the DVD-copying stalemate.

Did you know?

You Can Get a Final Glimpse of Your Video

If you'd prefer to view the contents of your tape one last time before importing it, click the Review tape button in the Auto Capture tab. The Control External Device window will appear, which includes the same playback controls included on your actual camcorder. By clicking these onscreen control buttons, shown here, you can command your camera to execute actions like play, reverse, forward, and more in the same way you would if you were pressing the corresponding buttons on the digital camcorder itself.

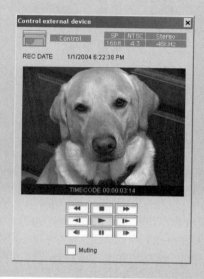

Manual Capture   Manual Capture mode provides you with a bit more control than Auto Capture, allowing you to start and stop capturing at any point within your video. To get into this mode, you can click inside the tiny circle in front of the Manual Capture option tab from within the Mode Select Guide window. Or if that window has already disappeared from view, you can simply select the Manual Capture tab next to the Auto Capture tab in the DVgate Plus window.

TIP   *Hankering to get the Mode Select Guide window back after it's vanished? From within the DVgate Plus window, follow this path: Settings | Mode Select Guide.*

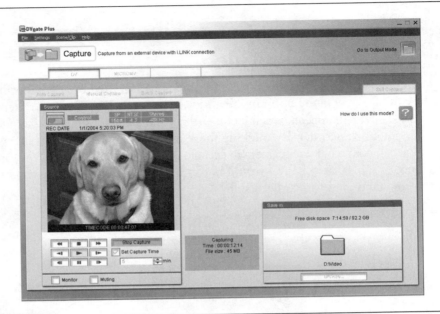

FIGURE 11-5 Manual Capture mode lets you start and stop video at whatever points you wish.

When you're in Manual Capture mode, your screen will look like Figure 11-5. The left side of the screen will contain playback controls similar to those you just saw in the Control external device window, and they serve the same purpose—to control your camcorder. On the right side of the screen lies another Save In box like the one you used in Auto Capture, to indicate where your VAIO should store imported video. Plot the course to your video-saving destination by clicking the Browse button, and then adjust your settings by going to Settings | Capture.

Once you've commanded your camcorder to begin playing your video, you'll notice a rectangular button to the right of the camcorder playback controls that turns red and says Start Capture. Just click this button at the point where you want to start importing video to your VAIO, and then click the button again (which now says Stop Capture) to cease importing. Or, you can command the camcorder to stop on its own by clicking inside the checkbox that says Set Capture Time, and then clicking on the up and down arrows underneath to determine the number of minutes you want to capture. You can start and stop importing as often as you like; your VAIO will record each beginning and end as a separate video clip.

Batch Capture   Batch Capture mode works well for capturing multiple video sessions that you've recorded to one tape, or for dividing one long video session into several individual scenes that you create on the fly. To get into Batch Capture mode, follow the same steps you used to enter Auto Capture and Manual Capture modes.

The Batch Capture tab resembles the Manual Capture tab (Figure 11-6), with one additional item in the middle: a Scene List section, where DVgate Plus lists each individual session that it captures from your digital camcorder. To make it easy for you to identify these sessions, the program includes the first and last frame of each session.

Before you begin Batch Capture, adjust your settings and browse to the location where you want to save your imported video. The method you use to capture will depend on the type of capturing you want to do. If you want DVgate Plus to import every individual session on your digital camcorder's tape, click the Scene Scan button to the right of the onscreen camcorder playback controls. The program will then begin populating the Scene List section of the screen with all of the individual sessions on your tape.

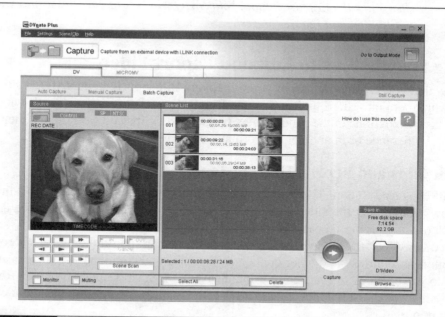

11

FIGURE 11-6   In Batch Capture mode, all of the individual clips on your videotape line up one after the other in the Scene List.

If you want to manually divvy up the tape into your own sessions, click the Play button in the onscreen playback controls (it's the center button that looks like an isosceles triangle pointing right). When the video hits your desired start point, click the IN button to the right of the playback controls. Click the OUT button when you reach the point where you want the clip to end.

After the program has imported each session into the Scene List, you can edit the list before finally recording it to your VAIO. To delete sessions, click the session to highlight it, and then click the Delete button beneath the list. You can also alter the list's order by clicking and holding on the scene you want to move, and then dragging it to its new position in the list. All of the other scenes will automatically reshuffle themselves to accommodate the new order.

When you have all of your session ducks in a row, you're ready to capture them to your VAIO. Go ahead and let your finger do what it's been itching for—click the round red Capture button, and your Scene List will start saving to your VAIO.

You don't have to delete unwanted scenes from your list so you can import the ones you do want. Just click each scene you want to save to your VAIO. Then, click the Capture button. Your VAIO will record only the scenes you've highlighted and ignore the rest.

Use DVgate Plus to Edit and Export Video

Now that you've imported all of your video and still shots to your VAIO, it's time to whip them into shape and ship them off to their final destination. That's where the last two options in the Mode Select Guide—edit clips and save them either to digital videotape or in another file format—come in.

Edit Clips and Record Them to Tape

Edit Clips And Record Them To Tape is the first of two Output modes. This mode allows you to alter the video sessions you saved to your VAIO and then send them back out to your digital camcorder for archiving on tape.

When I say alter, however, I don't mean you can manipulate your video's brightness, contrast, and other quality settings like you could the still images and video you captured in Chapter 10 using the Network Smart Capture program. Rather, I use the term loosely to indicate that DVgate Plus lets you cut time from the clips you imported.

Choose this mode from either the Mode Select Guide window, or click the Output icon to the right of the words Go To Output Mode in the upper-right corner of the DVgate Plus window (Figure 11-7).

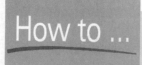

Capture Still Shots from an External Device

Whenever I'm watching home movies, I see at least one priceless expression flicker across the face of a family member or friend—and I always wish I had a picture of it. DVgate's Still Capture mode lets you preserve those fleeting moments as still shots. Here's how to do it:

1. Click the Still Capture tab to the far left of the DVgate Plus window, or click option number two, Capture Images From An External Device, from within the Mode Select Guide window.

2. The Still Capture tab will then appear in the foreground, as shown here, with camcorder playback controls on the left, a still shot preview window in the middle, and a Save In window on the right.

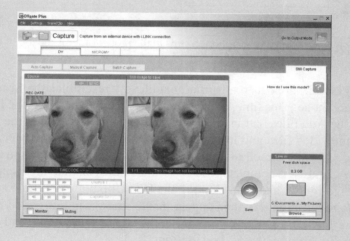

3. Click the Play button in the onscreen digital camcorder controls. The video will begin playing above the controls.

4. When you reach the point where you want to take a still shot, click the Capture 1 button to the right of the controls. A preview of the shot will appear in the middle window. You can also opt to take 30 consecutive stills by clicking the Capture 30 button.

5. Click the round red Save button to save the image(s) to your VAIO.

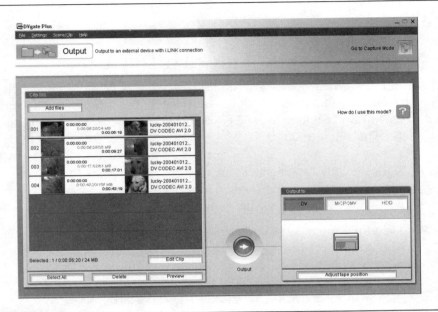

Arranging your imported clips in the proper order is the job of Output mode.

A Clip List will appear in a format that closely resembles the Scene List you Batch Capture mode. This time, you have no choice but to populate the list yourself by clicking the Add Files button above it. You must then navigate to the place where you stored the video files you imported, and choose the clips you want to include in your final recording. Each of your choices will then show up in the Clip List.

Once the Clip List is complete, you can whittle down an individual clip by clicking the clip to highlight it, and then clicking the Edit Clip button at the bottom of the list. The clip in question will then appear inside a new window called Edit Movie Clips (Figure 11-8). From there, you can set the clip to start later or end earlier than it did originally through one of three options:

- Click the IN and OUT buttons to the right of the preview screen when you see that the video has reached your desired start and end points.

- Click the up and down arrows next to the IN point and OUT point timers.

- Drag and drop the IN and OUT flagged tabs beneath the preview pane to your desired start and end points.

FIGURE 11-8   Slash time from the beginning or end of your clips within the Edit Movie
Clips window.

11

When all of your clips are at the lengths you like them, make sure they're in
the right order by clicking the ones you want to move to highlight them, and then
dragging and dropping them into position as you did with the clips in the Batch
Capture section earlier. If you want to preview the final product in its proper order,
click the Preview button below the Clip List, and the video will play in the preview
screen just as it does on your digital camcorder tape. Last but not least, get your digital
camcorder tape cued up to the right spot by hitting the Adjust Tape Position button
to the right of the DVgate Plus screen, at the bottom of the Output To box (which
should have either the DV or MicroMV tab highlighted in orange, depending on the
type of camera you're using). The onscreen camcorder playback controls will appear,
permitting you to rewind or fast forward to a free spot on your tape.

All of your video toils have finally reached their culmination: It's time to record
the movie you've produced to tape. This last step is a bit anticlimactic, as all it requires
is for you to click the circular red Output button in the center of the DVgate Plus
window.

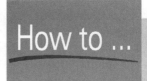 **Insert Still Shots into Your Movie**

One way to ensure your audience doesn't nod off during your movie is to mix things up by inserting still shots between video clips. You can add the shots to your Clip List just like you would a video session. Then you can tell DVgate Plus how long the shot should appear in the video by clicking the Edit Clip button beneath the list. The Edit Still Image Clips window will appear with a Playback Duration timer that lets you set the length of time for the shot to appear between 1 and 60 seconds, as well as the number of frames the shot should appear in. You can also resize the image to fit the entire screen.

Edit Clips and Output Them to Various File Formats

The last stop on our DVgate Plus journey is the Edit Clips And Output Them To Various File Formats option. In a nutshell, this option allows you to edit and organize your clips, and then save your completed movie in one of a handful of digital file formats to your VAIO's hard drive. In addition to the file formats we've already talked about in this chapter (AVI 1.0 and 2.0, MicroMV, and MPEG-2), you can also save your movies as MPEG-1 files. MPEG-1 is merely an older version of the MPEG standard in which movies max out at 352×240 resolution at 30 fps.

Get into this mode through either the Mode Select Guide window or the HDD (short for hard drive) button in the Output to box in the DVgate Plus window. After the HDD button turns orange, you'll notice that the button beneath it, which formerly said Adjust Tape Position, now says File Output Settings. By clicking this button, you can adjust several key settings for the video you're about to save to your VAIO's hard drive, including a couple you haven't seen before:

- **Sample rate**   If you have an analog-camcorder-to-digital camcorder setup, the sample rate indicates the speed (measured in Hertz, or Hz) that the program uses to convert analog signals to digital patterns. The general rule is the higher the Hz, the better your movie quality will be.

- **Movie aspect ratio**   Aspect ratio determines the length-to-height proportions of your video. In an aspect ratio of 4:3, for example, the height is three-quarters of the width.

CAUTION   *Be sure to preview the video in the aspect ratio you've chosen. Improper proportions can make the picture look like a fun-house mirror.*

You can also adjust a few settings that should be familiar to you at this point, including video length and storage location.

Now that your settings are in order, go about creating your Clip List and editing the clips in the same way you did in the preceding section. When you're finally ready to record, just hit the round red Output button in the middle of the window.

Use Sony's Click to DVD Program

Chances are you'll want to share the movies you just made with other people. If your videos remain on digital tape or inside your VAIO's hard drive, your family and friends must either have DV devices of their own to accommodate your tapes or travel to your place, where you can sit them down in front of your VAIO. A more practical sharing solution lies in Sony's Click to DVD software, a program that allows you to capture and edit video clips, and then burn them to easily portable DVDs. You can even create colorful title menu screens, just like commercially produced DVD movies. There's just one catch: Your VAIO has to ship with a DVD+RW drive, since you can't burn a DVD using any other type of optical drive. (If your VAIO doesn't have a built-in DVD-burning drive, you could always buy and hook up an external drive.)

You Can Burn Your Movies to CD, Too

If your VAIO didn't come with a DVD+RW drive, that doesn't mean you can't put your movies on an optical disc. VAIOs without DVD+RW drives usually ship with DVD/CD-RW combo drives, which, as you remember from Chapter 2, both burn files to CD-R or CD-RW discs and play pre-recorded DVDs. These VAIOs also offer CD-burning software, such as DigiOn's Drag 'n Drop CD. Together, the two can help you copy the videos you saved to your VAIO's hard drive onto CD-R or CD-RW discs. Skip ahead to Chapter 12 to get the skinny on the whole process. But beware: While the typical DVD can hold about 90 minutes of video, the average CD can handle only about 15 minutes of footage.

CAUTION *Commercial DVD players can't read video files on CD-R or CD-RW discs. So if you're going to burn your movies to either of these two media types, you'll have to view those movies on your computer.*

The Click to DVD program has three main phases: Capture Video, Import Pictures, and Create DVD.

Capture Video

Capturing video clips using Click to DVD is pretty similar to the process you used with DVgate Plus. Once your digital camcorder is plugged into your VAIO, and you've launched the Click to DVD program, the Start screen appears (Figure 11-9). This is the place where you both choose a title-screen backdrop and tell the program that you want to import video from your digital camcorder. You can preview the different backdrops by scrolling left-to-right through the various offerings on the left-hand side of the screen, and then clicking the choice you'd like to preview. It will then appear in the larger preview window above the list of choices. You can also choose animated or still versions of most backdrops, depending on your preference. Don't forget to type in the title of your DVD in the DVD Title field above the preview pane.

Next, tell the program what type of media you're importing in the Select Type column, to the right of the backdrop info column. Click once inside the box in front of Video. You must then choose whether you want the program to capture your clips using highest, standard, or long-play quality. The choice you make will determine

FIGURE 11-9   Click to DVD's Start screen allows you to pick from among various themes for your title-screen backdrop.

how big your resulting movie files will be. Remember, the higher the quality, the higher the resolution, and the bigger the file.

A new window will then appear with the words Capture Video in the upper-left corner. Sitting slightly right of center are two capture options—Automatic Capture and Manual Control. The former option sucks in all the available video on your tape; just click the Capture button underneath the option, and the program does the rest. The latter choice prompts an external device control panel to surface like the one in DVgate Plus. You can use the panel to begin your digital camcorder's playback, which will appear in the preview pane to the left of the panel. Clicking the Capture button beneath the panel begins the recording of a specific video clip. Hitting that same button, which now says Stop Capture, ends the clip. The first frame of each clip appears below the preview pane.

Edit Video Clips

If you want to slice any more time off the clips you just captured, hit the Edit Video button that shadows the Capture Video button at the top of the Click to DVD window. The same clips that lined the bottom of the Capture Video window will shift to the top of the new Edit Video window (Figure 11-10). Click the one you want to edit to highlight it, which also causes the first frame of the clip to appear in the large

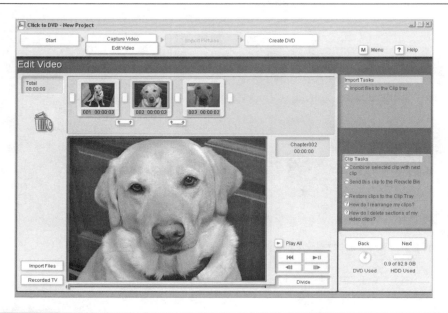

FIGURE 11-10   The Edit Video window lets you preview and cut time from your clips.

preview window underneath the clip. Unlike the IN and OUT sliding tabs offered by DVgate Plus, Click to DVD includes just one tiny pink sliding tab that moves left to right beneath the large preview pane. That means you can only cut time from the beginning of your clip, rather than from both the beginning and end.

Got your clips at the length you want 'em? Now put them in the proper order by dragging and dropping them into place like you did with the clips you imported into DVgate Plus. You can preview the whole deal by clicking the Play All button to the right of the preview window.

Import Pictures

There's not much to talk about regarding Click to DVD's Import Pictures function. Unlike DVgate Plus, which lets you capture still shots from video and then insert those shots into your movie, video and still shots in Click to DVD are like oil and water: They don't mix. Instead, Click to DVD allows you to create photo albums or slide shows from still shots you've already taken and stored on your VAIO. These albums are separate entities from your live-action movies.

To create one of these albums or shows, check the Pictures box under the Select Type section of the Click to DVD Start window. Then click the circle in front of your activity of choice—Create Album, Create Slide Show, or both. When you've made your selection, click the Import Pictures button at the top of the screen. A new window will then appear listing each shot you've imported against a blue background. You can then delete any shots you've decided you don't want in the final album.

 *In another deviation from DVgate Plus, Click to DVD doesn't allow you to include still shots in your video, so the program doesn't feature image-editing settings.*

The Create Menu

Polish up the presentation of your photo albums, slide shows, and video-clip list in the Create Menu window (Figure 11-11). Depending on the media you're working with, choose either Video Menu or Picture Menu from the options lining the left side of the window. The backdrop you chose will reappear on the next screen, with your imported

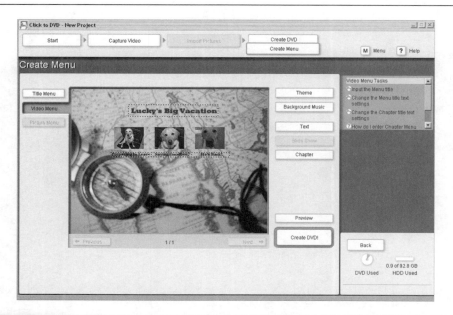

FIGURE 11-11   Finalize the small details of your photo album, slide show, or movie in the Create Menu window.

video clips or still shots spread across the top of the page. You can add titles to each individual clip or shot by clicking the Text button to the right of the preview pane. If you'd like to set your creation to music, click the Background Music button above the Text button to navigate to your chosen music file. Click the Preview button for one last look at your creation, and then burn away by hitting the big Create DVD! button.

It might take you awhile to reach Spielberg status, but you're now a bona fide movie producer. As I promised you earlier in this chapter, let's move on to burning DVDs and CDs in Chapter 12.

Chapter 12

Burn CDs and DVDs

How to...

- Understand the differences between CDs and DVDs
- Use Windows XP's CD writing wizard to copy files to CD
- Use EasySystems' Drag 'n Drop CD+DVD to copy files to disc

I hope you didn't start reading this chapter with matches in one hand and a stack of DVDs or CDs in another, because contrary to the literal interpretation of its title, Chapter 12 is not about setting your discs alight. Like we talked about in Chapter 2, the term "burn a CD (or DVD)" means copying Microsoft Word documents, spreadsheets, songs, pictures, or other data files to disc, which your VAIO's CD-RW or DVD±RW drive does by using its built-in laser to burn the data onto the disc's surface.

While the process of burning a CD or DVD is similar for both types of discs, the discs themselves differ. I'm going to begin by giving you a rundown of these differences, and then I'll tell you how to get your VAIO to burn CDs and DVDs using either the built-in wizard in Windows XP or the extra software Sony has loaded onto your machine.

Understand the Differences Between CDs and DVDs

Unless you've lived in a cave for the past couple decades, you're probably familiar with CDs and DVDs. These ubiquitous, donut-sized objects store most of today's music and movies. They have also become an important portable-storage staple in the computing world, since they can store hundreds and even thousands more megabytes of data than the few-megabyte capacities of portable storage dinosaurs like floppy, Zip, and LS-120 disks.

The words CD and DVD stand for *compact disc* and *digital video disc/digital versatile disc,* respectively. Both are types of *optical discs,* which means lasers are responsible for burning data to, and reading data from, microscopic craters on these discs. As you'll remember from Chapter 2, other types of storage disks, such as hard drives, hang onto their data magnetically.

When CDs came on the scene in the 1980s, everyone marveled at their ability to store up to 650MB of data (today's CDs can store about 700MB). The DVDs that surfaced in the next decade looked exactly like CDs yet blew them out of the water in storage capacity, holding anywhere from 4.7GB to 17GB of info. Some pretty

Did you know?

There Are More Ways than One to Refer to Burning Discs

Throwing around the phrase "burn a CD" is certainly the hippest way to refer to copying data to a disc. But if you're ever privy to a conversation between technophiles, you may hear them talking about "writing" or "recording" files to disc. Rest assured, all three terms refer to the same thing.

technical improvements account for the substantial increase in storage capability, including a greater number of those tiny craters on DVDs and superior lasers in DVD drives.

TIP

I'd need a lot more room than what I have here to wax on about all of the technical variations between CDs and DVDs. If you're yearning to learn more about the technical minutiae of DVDs versus CDs, check out www.pctechguide.com/10dvd.htm.

Familiarize Yourself with Various CD and DVD Formats

Varying storage capacity is the tip of the iceberg when it comes to the differences between CDs and DVDs. Each type of disc also comes in an assortment of flavors to suit a range of needs.

12

CD-ROM

You can learn a lot about a CD-ROM's function by defining its acronym: Compact Disc-Read Only Memory. In light of this definition, it will make sense to you when I say that the only thing your VAIO can do with the data on a CD-ROM is read it. Unlike the discs you'll learn about next, you can't copy your own files to CD-ROMs. The computer games and software programs you buy come on CD-ROM.

CD-R

A CD-R, or Compact Disc-Recordable, gives you one shot at copying data to the disc. After that, it's not possible to erase the data you've recorded and rewrite the disc with new data. If you'd like to write a section at a time, you can do so using packet-writing software, which essentially lets you create an archive that you can keep adding to until you get to the disc's 700MB limit.

CD-RW

CD-RW stands for Compact Disc-Rewriteable. Since you're getting the hang of these acronyms by now, you've likely deduced that CD-RWs allow you to record, erase, and re-record data as often as you'd like.

DVD-ROM

A DVD-ROM (Digital Video/Versatile Disc-Read Only Memory) is the DVD version of a CD-ROM. There's nothing for your VAIO to do with these discs but read their info. They're used mostly to store movies and huge software packages.

DVD-R and DVD+R

Our discussion of different optical discs has gone pretty smoothly up to this point, but things get a little stickier when talking about DVD-R and its rival technology, DVD+R. Short for Digital Video/Versatile Disc Recordable, DVD-Rs and DVD+Rs are just like CD-Rs, letting you record data to disc only once. But keep in mind that both types of DVD Recordables can hold much more data than CD-Rs can. Although DVD-Rs and DVD+Rs serve essentially the same function, there's still a fundamental difference between the two: their supporters. When the major computer manufacturers got together in the sandbox about a decade ago to hammer out the details of the emerging DVD Recordable standard, they couldn't play nicely. Therefore, some of those manufacturers splintered off into a rival group that developed their own standard. The result was two very similar technologies differentiated by the – and + symbols in their names. DVD-R technology has traditionally been supported by the DVD Forum, which includes Panasonic, Toshiba, Apple, Hitachi, NEC, Pioneer, Samsung, and Sharp. On the other hand, DVD+R has been backed by the DVD+RW Alliance, which includes the likes of Philips, Sony, Hewlett-Packard, Dell, and Yamaha.

Things in the DVD realm have been a big mess ever since, with many DVD drives having difficulty reading one or the other of these DVD technologies. Fortunately for you, Sony has begun shipping all of its VAIOs with *multiformat* drives that can read and write to both types of discs.

DVD-RW

DVD-RW is the acronym for Digital Video/Versatile Disc-Rewriteable. Again, DVD-RWs are like much bigger (storage wise) versions of CD-RWs. They're also the standard of choice for the computer behemoths that support the DVD-R technology we chatted about earlier.

To DVD-R or To DVD+R?
That Is the Question

With both DVD-recordable camps telling you their technology is best, how do you decide which type to use when, say, burning your camcorder movies to disc? The short answer is that if you've bought your DVD player relatively recently, it probably won't have trouble playing either type of disc. If you have an older player, however, you might consider using DVD+R or DVD+RW discs. These discs are (theoretically) unsusceptible to *linking loss,* which can occur during the burning process and cause discs to become incompatible with read-only devices like DVD players and DVD-ROM drives.

DVD+RW

You guessed it—DVD+RW also stands for Digital Vide/Versatile Disc-Rewriteable. It's the DVD Rewriteable standard supported by the same companies who've fallen in line behind DVD+R.

Read the breakdown that follows for a quick guide to all of the different types of discs and situations in which you'd use them.

Optical Disc Type	Average Storage Capacity	Writeable	Rewriteable	Best For
CD-ROM	650MB	No	No	Store-bought computer software
CD-R	700MB	Yes	No	Archiving moderate-sized documents
CD-RW	700MB	Yes	Yes	Replacing your old floppy, Zip, and other portable storage disks
DVD-ROM	4.7GB	No	No	Store-bought computer software and movies
DVD-R	4.7GB	Yes	No	Archiving home movies or photo albums
DVD-RW	4.7GB	Yes	Yes	Replacing old portable disks—especially for big multimedia files
DVD+RW	4.7GB	Yes	Yes	See DVD-RW

12

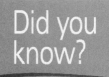

DVD-RAM Stores Giant Files, Too

As if the DVD storage scuffle wasn't complicated enough, another DVD-based standard, *DVD-RAM,* is also available. The term is short for Digital Video/Versatile Disc-Random Access Memory. Unlike the temporary storage provided by the RAM we discussed in Chapter 2, DVD-RAM is a long-term storage solution that's similar to DVD+RW, since you can write and rewrite data to DVD-RAM. But because DVD-RAM comes in cartridge form, the DVD drives that currently come with VAIOs can't accommodate it. You'll need to buy an optional DVD-RAM drive should you want to use this type of storage. The extra purchase might be worth it if the huge 9.4GB DVD-RAM cartridges appeal to you.

Get to Know the Different Types of CD and DVD Drives

Wouldn't it be nice if the various kinds of CD and DVD drives corresponded precisely with the different types of discs? If only life was that simple. Instead, the drives that are available for your VAIO desktop or laptop have their own specific sets of rules as to what discs they will and won't accept. This can actually be to your advantage, since some drives accept several of the different discs. It's just learning about them all that can be a pain. I've made it easier on you by outlining the different types in the sections that follow.

CD-ROM Drive

The role of a CD-ROM drive is cut-and-dry—it reads data from CD-ROMs, CD-Rs, and CD-RWs. Most CD-ROM drives feature a speed of about 40X for reading CD-ROMs and 16X for CD-Rs and CD-RWs.

DVD-ROM Drive

Theoretically, DVD-ROM drives should be able to read data from all types of CDs and DVDs. Due to the chaos of competing DVD technologies, however, some older DVD-ROM drives may not recognize all DVD types. The average DVD-ROM drive speed is 8X for DVDs and 24X for CDs.

How to ... **Understand Optical Disc Drive Speed**

In case you're wondering about drive speeds, read this quick primer on how to interpret the various speeds of these drives. Let's start with a CD drive that claims to read data at 40X. The X in that speed rating stands for "multiplied by 150KB per second." In other words, at peak performance, the drive reads data at 40 times 150KB per second, or 6MB per second.

The X in DVD drive speed ratings stands for a higher 11MB/second data throughput rate. So, a DVD drive with an 8X read speed can read 88MB of data per second.

Now that you know how to interpret these speed ratings, don't freak out if your drive has a lower rating than others on the market. In most cases, you'll hardly notice a difference in the performance of different drives. However, you will notice if you make a habit out of burning long movies or other huge multimedia files to disc. If that's your poison, then make sure you get a drive with the fastest burning speeds possible.

CD-RW Drive

A CD-RW drive can perform three tasks. First, it can record CD-Rs and CD-RWs. The drive can also erase and rewrite CD-RWs. Finally, it can read CD-ROMs, CD-Rs, and CD-RWs. Therefore, CD-RW drives feature three speeds. A standard speed among CD-RW drives is 24X/10X/24X, or 24X to record, 10X to erase and re-record, and 24X to read data.

12

DVD/CD-RW Drive

DVD/CD-RW drives don't quite combine the best of the CD and DVD worlds, but they come close. These drives can perform all of the functions of a CD-RW drive, and they can also read all types of DVDs. An average DVD/CD-RW speed is 24X/10X/24X for CDs, and 8X for reading DVDs.

DVD+RW Drive

DVD+RWs drives do it all—read, write, and rewrite data to both CDs and DVDs. The typical speed for a drive of this type is 4X/2X/2X for DVDs and 24X/10X/24X for CDs.

CDs and DVDs themselves feature speed ratings as well, which helps you determine the speed at which you should set your drive to record data (if the burning software that controls your drive allows you to alter its speed). Learn more about how to set this speed in the upcoming section on "Use EasySystems' Drag 'n Drop CD+DVD to Copy Files to Disc."

For the visually inclined, here's all of the preceding optical disc drive info in table format:

Optical Drive Type	Disc Types Supported	Average CD Speeds (write/ rewrite/read)	Average DVD Speeds (write/ rewrite/read)
CD-ROM	CD-ROM, CD-R, CD-RW	none/none/40X (CD-ROM) none/none/16X (CD-R, CD-RW)	none
DVD-ROM	CD-ROM, CD-R, CD-RW, DVD-ROM, DVD±R, DVD±RW	none/none/24X	none/none/8X
CD-RW	CD-ROM, CD-R, CD-RW	24X/10X/24X	none
DVD/CD-RW	CD-ROM, CD-R, CD-RW, DVD-ROM, DVD±R, DVD±RW	24X/10X/24X	none/none/8X
DVD±RW	CD-ROM, CD-R, CD-RW, DVD-ROM, DVD±R, DVD±RW	24X/10X/24X	4X/2X/2X

NOTE *A few storage manufacturers, including IBM, Iomega, and LG, are just now shipping the first multiformat DVD drives that support DVD-R, DVD+R, DVD-RW, and DVD+RW, as well as DVD-RAM cartridges. Sony has not (yet) joined the fray.*

Use Windows XP's CD Writing Wizard to Copy Files to CD

Rocket science is not required to burn files to a CD or DVD using your VAIO. How you go about this process will depend on whether you bought your system with a CD-RW, DVD/CD-RW, or DVD±RW drive. If you count yourself in the CD-RW or DVD/CD-RW group, you can use Windows XP's built-in CD Writing Wizard that I describe next to copy your files to CD-Rs or CD-RWs.

If you're a member of the DVD+RW drive camp, you can't rely on Windows XP, because the operating system doesn't yet include a DVD writing wizard. In that case, you'll need to use the EasySystems' Drag 'n Drop CD+DVD software that Sony provided with your VAIO to copy files to DVD. Skip ahead to the next section for some step-by-step tips on how to use this software.

> **CAUTION** *Be sure to shut down all other applications before burning a disc. Lots of other activity can spoil the burn.*

The easiest way to copy a file to CD with the CD Writing Wizard is to follow this course:

1. Move your pointer over the file in question, and right-click the file.

2. A cascading menu will appear. Click the Send To option, which will trigger another cascading menu. Click the CD-RW or DVD/CD-RW drive within the second menu.

3. A yellow balloon will appear in the taskbar at the bottom of the screen, alerting you that you have files waiting to be written to the CD. The balloon will ask you to click it to see the files. Do as it asks, and the drive window will appear like the one in Figure 12-1. The file you just sent to the drive will reside inside this window.

> **NOTE** *If you don't click the balloon within 10 seconds or so, it will disappear. To get to your files after this disappearing act, go to Start | My Computer | DVD/CD-RW Drive.*

> **TIP** *You can add more files to the drive window by dragging and dropping them into this window.*

4. Click the Write These Files To CD option underneath the CD Writing Tasks heading on the left side of the drive window. The first CD Writing Wizard window (Figure 12-2) will surface onscreen. Click inside the rectangular box mid-window to name your CD, and then click Next.

12

FIGURE 12-1   The files you've chosen to burn appear inside your recordable drive window.

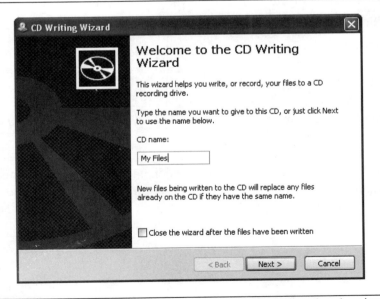

FIGURE 12-2   The CD Writing Wizard gets you started on the path to burning a CD.

TIP
If you don't want to copy all of the files that appear in the drive window, you can copy only the files you want by holding down the CTRL key, then clicking on each of your desired files to highlight them. When you select the Write These Files To CD option, the drive will copy just the highlighted files.

5. The next CD Writing Wizard window will appear (Figure 12-3), telling you that the wizard has begun copying your files to the CD. A green status bar shows you the progress of the process, while the Estimated Time Left section tells you how much time remains before the process is complete. When the wizard's almost finished with its handiwork, the words Performing Final Steps To Make The CD Ready To Use will appear in the window.

6. As the wizard wraps up the process, it instructs the drive to pop out the CD. The window then shows its final message. You have successfully written your files to the CD.

TIP
For professional-looking CD labels, check out HP's new LightScribe technology. The software burns images and text right onto the top of the disc itself using the drive's own laser.

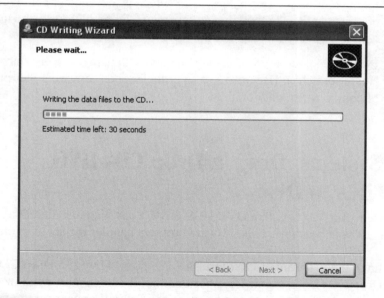

FIGURE 12-3   Once the wizard has begun to work its magic, the green status bar will tell you how much longer you have to wait.

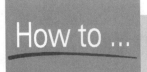

Take Care of Your Discs

I've ruined my fair share of discs by failing to care for them properly. Following a few common-sense rules can help you avoid making the same mistakes.

- You can accidentally douse your discs with water or let them get a little dusty without ruining them. But whatever you do, don't expose your discs to anything hard that will scratch their surface. Scratches ruin discs for good by causing them to skip.

- Fingerprints and other smudges can also hamper the proper playback of your discs. Make sure to handle them only on the edges. If they do get smudged, wipe them very delicately with a soft, dry cloth.

- Store your discs away from direct sunlight. Although optical discs don't warp nearly as easily as cassette tapes, prolonged sun exposure can eventually corrupt your data.

- Keep your discs inside a *jewel case,* which is just another name for a hard plastic case like the kind that commercial CDs and DVDs come in. It will help to protect against all of the dangers I just mentioned.

- Don't label your discs by writing on them with ballpoint pen, which could create scratches. Use only a soft permanent marker, like a Sharpie—and of course, write only on the top of the disc.

Use EasySystems' Drag 'n Drop CD+DVD to Copy Files to Disc

If you styled your VAIO with a DVD+RW drive, Sony also installed Drag 'n Drop CD+DVD on your machine. This software program handles the act of burning both CDs and DVDs.

To launch the program, go to Start | All Programs | Drag 'n Drop CD+DVD | Drag 'n Drop CD+DVD (again). Rather than a full-screen start window, a small, rectangular stack of what looks to be three blocks will appear on your screen. Each block represents one of the program's three functions: to burn music, data, or backup discs.

The first step in all three options is to drag and drop the files you want to burn onto the corresponding block. For example, if you have a song you want to record to CD, you should drag the song file on top of the Music block and release it. The block will swirl around, letting you know that your file is transferring to the Music window. A tiny orange arrow will then appear in the upper-right corner of the Music block. You can either hit that arrow to begin recording immediately, or you can double-click the box to open the larger Audio CD Layout Window (Figure 12-4). Let's talk more about this window in the following Burn Music CDs section.

Burn Music CDs

Launching the larger Audio CD Layout Window allows you to view more information about the burn process, including Track Info and Total Time remaining. You can also initiate burning from within this window. But before you begin the task, take a minute to adjust some important music-burning options. To reach these options, go back to the initial Music block and right-click it, then choose Options. The Music CD Options window will appear (Figure 12-5), within which you can choose your burn speed by clicking the down arrow at the top of the window. You can also choose to test out the viability of your CD before you burn it.

FIGURE 12-4   The Audio CD Layout Window displays pertinent info about your music, including track listings and remaining time left in your burn.

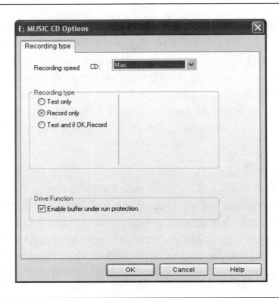

FIGURE 12-5   Set the speed at which your VAIO will burn your CD in the Music CD
Options window.

NOTE   *As you can see in the Music CD Options window, the program only supports
the copy of music files to CD. That's because most conventional CD players
use different codecs, or compression/decompression techniques, than
DVD players (many of which rely on the MPEG-2 codec we discussed in
Chapter 11). So, if you burned your music to DVD, the majority of CD players
wouldn't be able to play the music on that DVD.*

If you'd like to burn music directly from one CD to another (or to your hard drive),
just right-click the Music block, and then choose Record Music from your Audio CD
option. Another window like the one in Figure 12-6 appears, allowing you to pick
which tracks you want to record and where you'd like to save them.

NOTE   *Drag 'n Drop CD+DVD does not support copying the ever-popular MP3
(or MPEG, audio layer 3) music format to CD. Again, most commercial
CD players only recognize WAV (a definition-less acronym that stands for
a joint Microsoft-IBM audio standard) or WMA (Windows Media Audio,
another Microsoft format) files. Therefore, the program only records those
two types of audio files to CD. You can still record MP3s to CD, you just
need to convert the files first—which you can do with any one of the hundreds
of conversion programs available. Go to www.download.com to find one.*

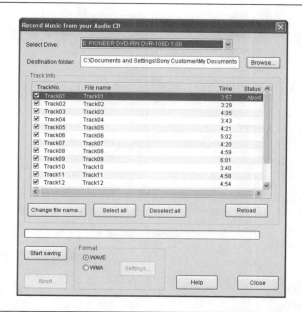

FIGURE 12-6 You can copy music right from one CD to the next with the Record Music From Your Audio CD option.

Burn Data CDs or DVDs

The Burn Data mode offers a bit more flexibility, letting you copy all sorts of data files, including Word documents, spreadsheets, PowerPoint presentations, photos, videos, and much more to CD or DVD.

Once you've dragged your desired files onto the Data block and dropped them in, you can initiate the burning process in the same way you did with Music files. Don't forget to adjust your Options first in the Data Disc Options window (Figure 12-7). You'll notice that this window provides you with more choices than the Music CD Options window. For starters, you can pick from one of two *file systems* for your CD, which tells the program how to organize your data on the disc. Without going into all the technical jargon surrounding the two choices—ISO 9660 Level 1 and Joliet—I'll simply tell you to choose Joliet if your data includes long filenames. Joliet supports names up to 64 characters long, while ISO 9660 Level 1 supports names with only eight characters or less.

Again, you can double-click the Data block to call up the larger Data Layout Window (Figure 12-8). Detailed info about both your recordable disc and the files you're about to burn appears here. You can right-click your disc's name to change it, as well as start your copying job.

12

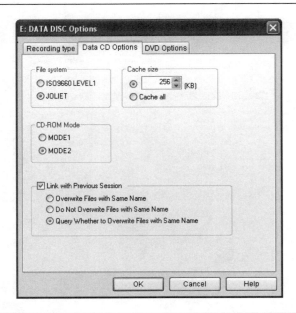

FIGURE 12-7 Specify file systems, modes, cache, and more within the Data Disc Options window.

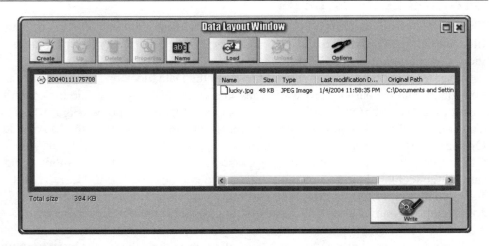

FIGURE 12-8 The Data Layout Window gives you more detail about your CD or DVD, as well as the data you're about to burn to it.

How to ... **Ensure a Successful Burn**

While your disc-burning software does the bulk of the file copying work, there are still a few things you can do to help the process along.

- Make sure you have plenty of main system RAM installed in your VAIO. Burning discs generally requires a lot of it.

- Don't use cheap discs. While you may be tempted to buy those extra-economical bulk packs of discs, beware that they're more likely to contain imperfections which can cause them to fail.

- Close all other programs before burning, and don't mess around with your computer during the process.

- Try to *defragment* your hard drive before burning. For more on defragmenting, visit Chapter 15.

- Take your time and burn your discs at slower speeds. It may take an extra couple of minutes, but your discs will have an even better chance of turning out error-free.

12

Burn Backup Copies of Your Discs

Disc Backup mode is similar to Music and Data modes, but instead of dragging and dropping single files onto the block, you drag and drop the entire contents of the disc you just burned. Navigate to the disc by going to Start | My Computer, and then finding the appropriate disc icon under the Devices with Removable Storage section. Your disc is most likely residing in your VAIO's E: or F: drive. From there, just drag and drop the disc icon onto the Disc Backup mode block.

This mode doesn't offer a larger window, but you can still set your options just as you did in Music and Data modes. When you're done, click the orange arrow on the Disc Backup block to begin burning.

It's time to move on to the multimedia big time—using your VAIO as a digital video recorder. Ready? Great. Now get going to Chapter 13.

Chapter 13

Turn Your VAIO into a Personal Video Recorder

How to...

- Get started with Giga Pocket
- Get to know four media programs
- Hook up your TV to your VAIO
- Download channel settings
- Adjust recording settings
- Record shows from the Internet
- Edit video capsules

Unless you've been in a coma for the last few years, you've undoubtedly heard the word TiVo, as both a noun and a verb, or perhaps you've used a TiVo yourself. The verb form goes something like this: "I TiVoed Letterman last night. Watched it this morning. Hilarious." TiVo is the most well-known of the many personal video recorders (PVRs, also called *digital video recorders*) on the market, a market that looks to grow by leaps and bounds as these set-top devices get cheaper, are offered by more companies (like digital cable TV services), and continue to replace dusty old VCRs.

But if you have a VAIO PC or notebook running Sony's innovative Giga Pocket software and hardware, you don't need a separate personal video recorder like TiVo. You can easily record your primetime addictions to your hard drive and quickly retrieve them for playback anytime. Or you can burn them onto a DVD. (You could even burn much smaller files onto a CD. See Chapter 12 for more on burning CDs and DVDs.) You can also easily convert your old VHS tapes to DVD.

Keep in mind, however, that not every VAIO runs Giga Pocket. All five lines of VAIO desktop PCs include Giga Pocket, which is part software and part built-in TV tuner hardware. Only two notebooks, however, the new A Series and the GRT Series, currently have the Giga Pocket package. Two of the VAIO desktops, the new RA Series and the RZ Series, also include Microsoft's Windows XP Media Center Edition 2004. (See the Did You Know? box, "Sony and Media Center Edition.") I'll concentrate on Giga Pocket and related applications in this chapter.

Get Started with Giga Pocket

Using a remote control or your keyboard and mouse, Giga Pocket brings all of your favorite shows to your desktop, which you can watch in full-screen mode, or in a smaller window, with other programs open next to it like a web browser

Did you know?

Sony and Media Center Edition

Sony did not immediately embrace Microsoft's answer to the personal video recording wave, the latest iteration of which is called the Windows XP Media Center Edition 2004 (MCE 2004) operating system. At first, Sony only included its own Giga Pocket suite of hardware and software for PVR functionality. Now, however, the company offers MCE 2004 software on two PCs, which works in conjunction with the Giga Pocket hardware.

There are many significant differences between Giga Pocket and MCE 2004—too numerous to go into detail here. For starters, MCE 2004 is a full operating system, while Giga Pocket is a combination of hardware (a TV tuner) and software (MPEG2 encoder) that allows for TV viewing, PVR function, and conversion of analog content to digital. If you have the new RA Series or RZ Series desktop, Giga Pocket "offers a subset of the functionality of MCE," as Sony puts it. For more on MPEG and MPEG-2, check Chapter 11.

Also, MCE 2004 integrates music and digital photo features, while Sony keeps those functions separate from Giga Pocket. Sony's multimedia applications include PictureGear Studio, SonicStage and SonicStage Mastering Studio, DVgate Plus, Click to DVD, and VAIO Media. Although these programs are not integrated into the OS interface, they let you do a ton with your digital content, besides just watching it, listening to it, or burning it. With Sony's applications you can manipulate, edit, create, network to other PCs or devices, or carry out other actions.

13

on one side of the screen. Sure, watching live TV on your VAIO is great, but what's really cool is to tell your VAIO what to record ahead of time (or, if you like, just as the program starts) so you can watch that episode of *Arrested Development* or the big game when you feel like it. Additionally, you're not limited to storing these shows on your VAIO hard drive. Using the video file conversion feature of Giga Pocket, small recorded video files can be saved on a Memory Stick and then played back on a Sony CLIE or CyberShot. Or you can burn them to a DVD for playback on your VAIO or your DVD player.

Before you start hooking up your TV to your VAIO, it's a good idea to get to know a little something about the programs you'll be using. The first thing to do is click the VAIO TV icon on your desktop, which brings up a window detailing four media programs (Figure 13-1). These Sony programs let you record and watch your favorite TV shows, which are recorded on your VAIO's hard drive so you can watch them later, edit them, or record the shows onto a DVD (or other media). Giga Pocket

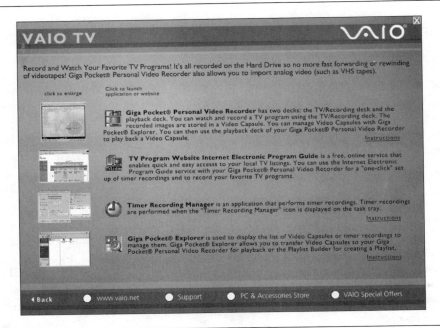

FIGURE 13-1   Use these four programs when you're recording live TV to your hard drive.

Personal Video Recorder also allows you to import analog video (such as live TV or VHS tapes), and easily convert them to digital clips on your system, using DVgate Plus. From there, you can edit your clips and then burn them onto blank DVDs.

Get to Know Four Media Programs

Here are the four programs listed on the VAIO TV window:

- **Giga Pocket Personal Video Recorder (PVR)**   This application has two main functions: the TV/Recording deck and the playback deck. You use the TV/Recording deck to watch TV or record the channel you're watching. Recorded video is stored in video capsules to your hard drive. You can then use the playback deck of your Giga Pocket Personal Video Recorder to play back a video, or use another media player instead.

- **TV Program Website Internet Electronic Program Guide**   This is a free, online service that lets you quickly access your local TV listings. You can use the Internet Electronic Program service with your Giga Pocket Personal Video Recorder for a quick set up of timer recordings and to record your favorite TV shows.

- **Timer Recording Manager**   An application that performs timer recordings. Timer recordings are performed when the Timer Recording Manager icon is displayed on the task tray.

- **Giga Pocket Explorer**   Use this to display the list of recorded shows (a.k.a. "video capsules") or timer recordings. Giga Pocket Explorer also allows you to transfer video capsules to your Giga Pocket PVR for playback and lets you create a play list.

NOTE   *On some models, playback of video capsules while TV recording is in progress does not work as smoothly as that during normal operation where no recording is being performed. Why? Because while recording is in progress, recording has a higher priority than playback.*

Hook Up the Hardware

Now that you know a bit about the software you'll be using, it's time for the hookup. First, make sure the *coaxial cable* that connects to your TV or set-top box can reach your VAIO. Your coax cable may be coming from your TV, your VCR, or your set-top box, depending on how your TV is set up. On VAIO PCs, the coax cable hooks directly into a coax port on the front or side of the PC. (Figure 13-2). On the VAIO

13

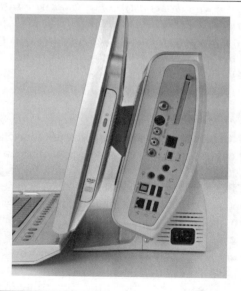

FIGURE 13-2   Coax cable hookup on one of the VAIO PCs (next to the PC card slot).

FIGURE 13-3   Coax cable hookup on VAIO laptop. You also need a small converter cable that Sony includes.

GRT Series laptop, the coax cable first connects to an included converter cable, and then into the VHF/UHF port on the side (Figure 13-3). On the new A Series laptop—Sony's flagship desktop replacement with a 17-inch screen option that will eventually replace the GRT Series—the TV tuner hardware has migrated from the notebook to the docking station, so you connect the coax cable to the back of the docking station. You also need to connect to the Internet, so make sure your cable of choice (or your wireless signal) is in place.

NOTE   *Coaxial cable is a wire that consists of a center wire surrounded by insulation and then a grounded shield of braided wire. The shield minimizes electrical and radio frequency interference. Coaxial cabling is the primary type of cabling used by the cable television industry and is also widely used for computer networks.*

Download Channel Settings

Once those cables are in place, you need to download your channel settings. Don't worry, Sony makes it easy. Connect to the Internet, then open the VAIO TV icon on your desktop, and click the icon next to TV Program Website Internet Electronic Program Guide, or iEPG (shown in Figure 13-1). A web page opens, and after you click through an acceptance page, a ZIP code page, and a page about your particular TV service, you get to the Download All Channel Settings page. Your page should look similar to the one shown in Figure 13-4.

After you download your channel settings, a TV Setup Wizard appears (see Figure 13-5). The TV Setup Wizard also appears when you run other programs for the first time, including Giga Pocket, the Timer Recording Wizard, and the Timer

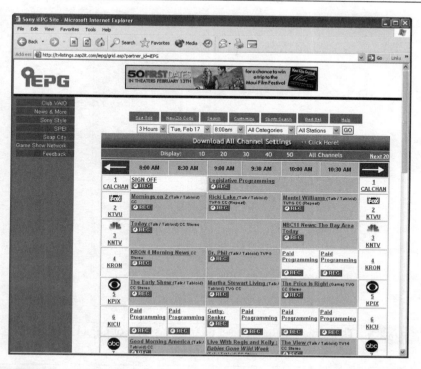

FIGURE 13-4   The iEPG web service lets you download your channel settings or record shows by hitting REC.

Recording Manager. You can also launch the TV Setup Wizard by choosing Start | Control Panel | Printers And Other Hardware, and then clicking the TV Setup icon. With this wizard you can do many things, such as adding and deleting channels, modifying your TV setup, adjusting picture quality, connecting to the online electronic program guide, and setting up a parental lock (see Figure 13-6).

> NOTE   *Giga Pocket may not be compatible with some cable TV channels. Contact your cable TV provider for more information.*

If you plan to share your TV shows or other media with family members on a small home network, be sure to click the Giga Pocket Server tab when you're configuring the TV Setup Wizard. Create a password so you can connect to another VAIO Giga Pocket server on the same network. Once connected, you can access the files in that computer's Giga Pocket Explorer with your own computer. After making adjustments in the TV Setup Wizard, press OK.

13

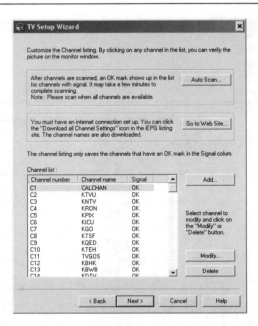

FIGURE 13-5   This wizard helps you set up many aspects of Giga Pocket.

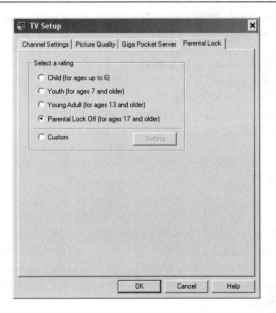

FIGURE 13-6   Setting up a parental lock on TV content

Start Recording TV Shows

Once you've downloaded your channel listings, fire up the Giga Pocket Personal Video Recorder. You'll find that application by selecting Start | All Programs | Giga Pocket. Hold your pointer over Giga Pocket and a submenu appears. Choose Giga Pocket. (If you'll be using Giga Pocket a lot, create a copy of the folder on your desktop. You do that by right-clicking and holding the pointer on the main Giga Pocket folder and dragging it to the desktop. When you release, select Copy from the submenu.)

If you've connected everything properly, when you open up the Giga Pocket program, you should start seeing a live TV show in the Giga Pocket window on your VAIO after a few seconds. If you need help or need more details on the Giga Pocket window, click the Help button on top of the program. A well-organized help section opens (see Figure 13-7). You can change channels or adjust the volume on the left

13

FIGURE 13-7   Giga Pocket's help section

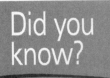

Swap Photos, Songs, and Videos with VAIO Media

Watching live TV on your VAIO or saving TV shows to your hard drive is a great attribute. But you'll also want to get away from a PC tethered to a coax cable and a TV, not stay in front of it to watch one of the last episodes of *Friends*. Sony's VAIO Media program frees you from your computing shackles by letting you view your shows, listen to your music, and access additional multimedia files using PCs or other devices on your home network.

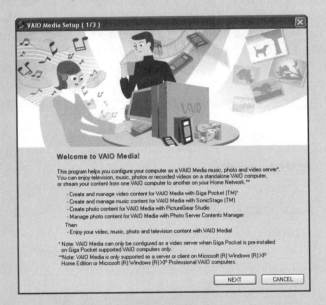

Say you have a VAIO desktop in your office and a wireless VAIO notebook like the Z1 Series in your family room. Using Giga Pocket and VAIO Media, you can record a show on your VAIO PC, and then instruct that PC to make the show play on your notebook in the family room. You do that by using the VAIO Media software to make the office PC act as a *media server*. That way, you can watch the show from the comfort of your couch, your bed, or wherever else you like to hang. The same goes for songs, slideshows, and the like. If you buy Sony's Room Link adapter, you can even watch the shows stored on your hard drive on a regular television. For more on setting up wired and wireless home networks, see Chapters 8 and 9.

FIGURE 13-8   Watch or manage your TV shows from this Giga Pocket Explorer window.

side of the Giga Pocket screen. Or hit the Record button on the right side of the screen to start saving the live TV show to your hard drive.

If you're new to recording TV shows on your hard drive, check your progress early and often before you start recording like mad, because these files eat up tons of hard drive space. Hit the stop recording button on the Giga Pocket viewer and find where your clip is stored. If you don't know the path, open Giga Pocket Explorer, which is in the Giga Pocket folder that you opened a minute ago. (Did you take my advice and copy it to your desktop?) With the Giga Pocket Explorer window open, you'll see the My Cabinet icon (Figure 13-8), which contains your video capsules. If you're still not sure (like me) what the exact path is to your recorded TV show, right-click the My Cabinet icon and click Cabinet Information. You'll see the folder's path on the next window. With Giga Pocket Explorer open, double-click a video

13

FIGURE 13-9   You can watch your shows with various media players, including Windows Media Player.

capsule you want to play, and it starts playing in the Giga Pocket player. You can also watch the clip with Windows Media Player (Figure 13-9), Real One's player, InterVideo WinDVD 4, or other media players.

You can also operate Giga Pocket with the included remote control (which Sony likes to call the "remote commander"). You operate the remote by first hooking up the included IR receiver into a USB 2.0 connector on your VAIO.

Record Shows via the Internet

Search for a TV program you want to record through the Internet on iEPG, or the Internet Electronic Program Guide—that's the web page you used to download your TV listings. Next, set the timer with a click of your mouse. By recording directly on your hard disk, you don't need to worry about the hassles of rewinding or changing videotapes, although you will have to keep an eye on how fast your hard drive is filling up. Once the record timer is set up, your VAIO remains in stand-by mode until the designated recording time.

NOTE   *Bookmarks can be attached to favorite scenes. You can then jump to those scenes by selecting the bookmarks, which are shown on the Giga Pocket window.*

Another feature of Giga Pocket is *Slip Playback,* which lets you watch a TV show even while it's being recorded. For instance, you can watch a show from the beginning even if it's in the middle of recording when you get home—no more waiting for the program to finish recording. Also, if you're interrupted while watching a program, simply start recording and Giga Pocket will allow you to go back and continue where you left off. The Film Roll feature lets you watch only the scenes that you want, and fast forward to the show that's currently on air.

TIP   *You can't start Slip Playback for approximately 10 seconds after recording starts.*

Set and Adjust Recording Times

You can also set timer recordings or make adjustments to existing record times by opening Giga Pocket Explorer. Then select New Recording from the Time Recording Menu. The New Timer Recording—Set Channel, Start Date And Time dialog box opens. This box is pretty much self-explanatory, with choices for time, channel, recording start date, and more. The Control Start Time box is a handy feature: it lets you set the recording time back three minutes to allow for a possible discrepancy between your computer's clock and the actual broadcast time. If you don't need to adjust the recording start time, uncheck Control Start Time. When done, click Next. The New Timer Recording—Set Stop Time And Recording Mode pops up (Figure 13-10). On this screen, enter the recording stop time. Set the time between 1:00 to 12:59 A.M. and 1:00 to 12:59 P.M. To change the recording stop time, check the Control Stop Time button and set how much of an extension you want. For example, when you record a movie after a baseball game starring your beloved San Francisco Giants, you can extend the recording stop time of the movie in case the baseball game goes into extra innings.

Next, select a recording mode, similar to how you do it when recording on your trusty old VCR. Choices are SP (Standard Play), HQ (High Quality), or LP (Long Play). Naturally, the HQ choice has the best image quality, but it also eats up more hard drive space.

When you're selecting the recording mode, if the amount of used disk space exceeds the free disk space, the Next and Done buttons on this window are disabled,

13

FIGURE 13-10 Setting the program stop time and recording method

and you can't set up the timer for recording. If that's the case, it might be time to start deleting, moving, or burning some of your recorded video files. Click Done to complete the timer recording setup.

 *You can set the recording time length to up to 12 hours. You just need the necessary disk space.*

Edit the Clips Stored on Your Hard Drive

If you want to edit out and save just a portion of a TV show, sporting event, or movie you've recorded on your hard drive, you can use Sony's DVgate Plus software, discussed in detail in Chapter 11. To open DVgate Plus, first open Giga Pocket Explorer, as described previously. Select the clip you want to edit by clicking it once, and an icon of a film strip with scissors cutting through it becomes visible at the top of the Giga Pocket Explorer window. Click the icon to open DVgate Plus. Once there, you'll see a list of clips and TV shows. Highlight the video capsule you want to edit, then click the Edit Clip button, which opens a separate Edit Movie Clips window. From there, go to Chapter 11 and follow the instructions in the section "Use DVgate Plus to Edit and Export Video."

Burn Recorded Shows to DVD

Click to DVD is a versatile Sony software package that lets you burn TV shows
(or your camcorder movies; see Chapter 11) recorded by Giga Pocket onto DVD.
When you send a video capsule to Click to DVD (launchable from an icon in Giga
Pocket Explorer), chapters will be created automatically to divide the video tracks
based on bookmarks. A high-quality DVD with a moving thumbnail menu and editable
chapter titles is quickly produced. In addition, multitrack broadcasts are supported,
so bilingual shows can be burned on a DVD. During playback, sound channels can
be switched using a remote control for enhanced viewing. For all the skinny on using
Click to DVD, see Chapter 11.

Now that you've learned how to record TV shows to your VAIO (if you have the
right machine), it's time to take a well-deserved break and play some games, whether
your opponent is your computer or other players in an online multiplayer game.

13

Chapter 14

Would You Like to Play a Game?

How to...

- Play on a VAIO PC vs. a VAIO notebook
- Play the games included with Windows XP
- Learn about other cool games

Before I start this chapter, I should say that I'm not a big gamer. Oh sure, I hit some high scores on Centipede in 1982 at the pizza parlor, and yeah, my seven-year-old son is teaching me GameBoy *and* the Bedrock Bowling PC game (yabba dabba doo!). But I'm not one of those guys who lives for the next first-person shooter game or gets goosebumps at the mere mention of Unreal Tournament. I've never been to a LAN party, where hundreds of (or even just a few) people gather together with their computers and all play the same game nonstop. And I've never played an online multiplayer game.

On the other hand, I know tons of people like that, including the game-crazed editors at CNET's Gamespot, who work in the same building with me. And gaming is obviously a huge market. So I'd be remiss if I didn't offer you at least the basics on gaming with your VAIO. I'll briefly get you started with some things you should know about playing games on a VAIO PC or notebook. Then I'll introduce you to the games that ship with your VAIO, as well as some of the more popular titles you can pick up on your own.

Play on a VAIO PC vs. a VAIO Notebook

To play most PC games, you don't need anything but a keyboard and screen so you might think playing games on a VAIO PC isn't that different from playing them on a Sony laptop. But there are a few differences that may irk you, especially if you become more and more addicted to games.

One thing to keep in mind is that *notebook components are generally slower than PC parts.* You already know from reading Chapter 2 that almost everything in a laptop, including the processor, memory, and hard drive, lags behind the corresponding components in a PC. When working on a Word document, you probably wouldn't notice a performance difference. However, getting your system to reproduce all of a game's intricate graphics that continuously change with the blink of an eye takes a lot of speed.

Another factor affecting play is that PC screens and keyboards are usually larger than those in laptops. It's not impossible to play a game using the diminutive keyboard and display of an ultralight laptop like the VAIO TR Series, but if you've

Did you know?

Lots of Web Sites Offer Information on Games

Computer gamers are just as devoted to their craft as Trekkies are to *Star Trek*. Most of them converge on various web sites that offer news, reviews, downloads, feature stories, and plenty of other stuff all related to gaming. Some of the ones you should check out include

- http://www.gamespot.com
- http://www.gamespy.com
- http://www.ign.com
- http://www.1up.com

ever tried it, I'm guessing you were less than thrilled. Having or lacking the comfort of a full-sized keyboard and the brilliance of a big screen can make or break your gaming experience.

Audio is key in many games, especially those that include explosions, crashes, or music. The bigger and better your speakers, the better your sound (duh). So remember that *many PCs come with external speakers and even subwoofers, while notebooks rely on their small, built-in speakers.* This translates to overall respectable audio from PCs and entirely underwhelming sound from notebooks. If you're hell-bent on playing games with your notebook, you might want to invest in a set of external speakers that you can plug into one of your laptop's audio jacks.

TIP *If your VAIO has one of the S/PDIF ports we discussed in Chapter 2, you can plug in cool digital speakers.*

14

Play the Games Included with Windows XP

You know by now that Windows XP lets you both work and play with your VAIO. As part of the latter activities, the operating system includes a handful of very simple games, most of which you've probably played before in card or board form. These titles might seem too easy at first, but they're actually a great way to get started down the road to becoming a serious gamer.

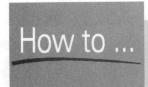

How to ... Soup-Up Your System for Game Play

Even if you already bought your VAIO, there are some things you can do post-purchase to optimize your game play.

- **Add memory**   Like any other software application, games need memory to run on your computer. The more memory you have to open and run those games, the faster they'll work on your system.

- **Install a new graphics card in your PC**   As you know from Chapter 2, your VAIO's graphics card handles most of the image-rendering tasks you throw at your computer. As you also learned in that same chapter, you can't swap out a notebook's graphic card, although that option is slowly making its way into the laptop arena. But exchanging the graphics card in most PCs is fairly simple. If you're at all serious about gaming, you'll want to get the fastest card with the most video RAM available. Today, that amounts to either the 256MB ATI Radeon 9800XT or the 256MB Nvidia GeForce FX5900.

- **Upgrade your hard drive**   This is an option for both PCs and notebooks, though a faster hard drive is not going to give you the performance jump of more memory or a new graphics card. You should also weigh whether transferring all of your data to a new hard drive is worth that small bump in speed.

To get to all of the games in Windows XP, follow this path: Start | All Programs | Games.

Single-Player Games

A number of the preloaded games on your VAIO are single-player games, where it's just you against yourself or your VAIO. You use various mouse and keyboard maneuvers to play each game. The quick-list includes

- **Hearts**   The vintage card game comes to life on the computer screen (see Figure 14-1).

- **Solitaire**   Another oldie-but-goodie goes electronic.

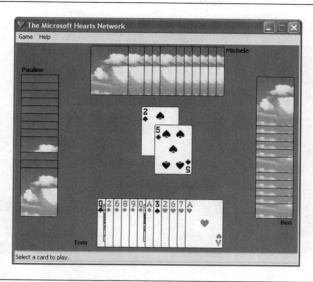

| FIGURE 14-1 | The version of Hearts in Windows XP lets you type in your own name while playing against three other fictitious players that are all controlled by your computer. |

- ■ **Pinball**   This game speaks for itself.

- ■ **Minesweeper**   An electronic type of Battleship, where you click inside cells while trying to avoid hidden mines.

A couple of these games, like Pinball, get you comfortable with the concept of adjusting keyboard settings to fit your preferences. For example, Pinball's Player Controls window (see Figure 14-2) allows you to choose which keys you want to use as your left and right flippers, plunger, and more.

Multiplayer Internet Games

Single-player games make up about half of Windows XP's games selection. The other half is comprised of multiplayer Internet games. Where do you find those players? On the Net, of course. First, here are the titles, all of which are prefaced by the word "Internet":

- ■ **Hearts**   This time, you play with real people over the Internet.

- ■ **Checkers**   Just like the common board game but with a random player you meet on the Web.

14

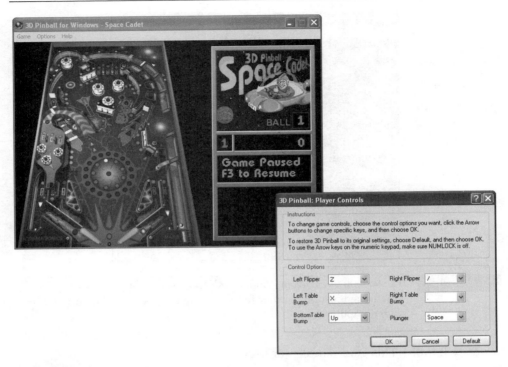

FIGURE 14-2   In the Player Controls window, you can determine which keys control specific parts of the Pinball machine.

- **Backgammon**   Ditto.

- **Reversi**   An online version of the board game Othello, Reversi involves booting your opponent's stones off of a chess-like board.

> NOTE   *Obviously, you must be connected to the Web before you can play any multiplayer Internet games.*

Making an online connection with another player is easy. Once you launch the game, a window will appear that explains how you are about to make yourself available to play with another person who, like yourself, is waiting to play as well. Click the Play button, and Windows XP takes a couple seconds to search for your match. When it finds another player, the game window appears, such as the Backgammon window in Figure 14-3. Then you're ready to begin.

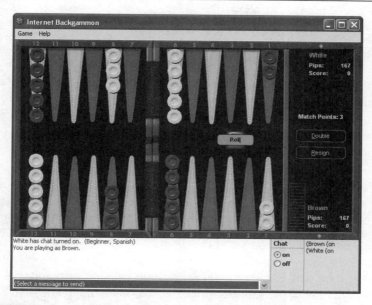

FIGURE 14-3   In this game of Internet Backgammon, I hooked up with a Spanish player from across the Atlantic.

Learn About Other Cool Games

There are certainly a lot more computer games than the handful of titles that come preloaded on your VAIO. They span all sorts of subject matter, from World War II to everyday-life scenarios. But no matter what their subject, most of them have similarities in the ways they're played and their overall objectives.

The Three Main Genres in Computer Gaming

While there are a few exceptions, nearly all computer games fall into one of three specific gaming genres: first-person shooter, real-time strategy, and role-playing games. Keep reading to get acquainted with the three, as well as a few of today's most popular games in each one.

First-Person Shooter

The name of the first-person shooter genre says a lot about the games that fall within it. First-person shooter titles typically put you behind the action, which usually means, a gun. You then play against your computer, or another player on a different computer. First-person shooters often allow you to pause the game and pick it back up where

14

How to ... Make Your VAIO into an Arcade Machine

If you grow increasingly hardcore about gaming, you'll probably find that playing with your keyboard just isn't cutting it. Plenty of peripheral manufacturers are waiting to come to your aid with add-ons to enhance your gaming experience. Most of these components connect to your VAIO's USB 2.0 port, making them easy to just plug and unplug at will.

- **Joysticks**   Looks a lot like the one for your old Atari—only much more ornate. They make some games, like Microsoft's Flight Simulator, seem more authentic by giving you the feeling you're behind real controls.

- **Game pads**   These are small devices you hold between your hands, and then use your thumbs to press the buttons and other controls on the top of the pad. Some of them even come with *force feedback,* where the pad vibrates as a result of things that happen in the game, like gunfire.

- **Wheels and pedals**   These are what you'd expect, and come in handy for driving games.

you left off. The large majority of games in this genre are about war. Kids (and kids-at-heart) these days are crazy about a few particular first-person shooters.

Call of Duty   The bleak battlefields of World War II come to life again in Call of Duty. You play this game by sitting behind the barrel of a gun (Figure 14-4) and shooting your opponents until you finish a mission and advance to the next round—or become eliminated yourself. The game provides you with all sorts of options, from the type of gun you use to the nationality you choose to be. You can also play against either the computer or other gamers online.

Battlefield 1942   You probably can guess by its name that Battlefield 1942 is also about World War II. Highlights in this game include the ability to drive tanks and parachute from planes. Like Call of Duty, you can play Battlefield 1942 against either your VAIO or additional online players.

Unreal Tournament   Unreal Tournament is another single or multiplayer combat game, but this time, the action takes place in outer space, and not all of the characters are human, as you can see in Figure 14-5. Still, the object remains to *frag,* or kill, your opponents in various settings.

FIGURE 14-4 Call of Duty is currently one of the most sought-after first-person shooter games.

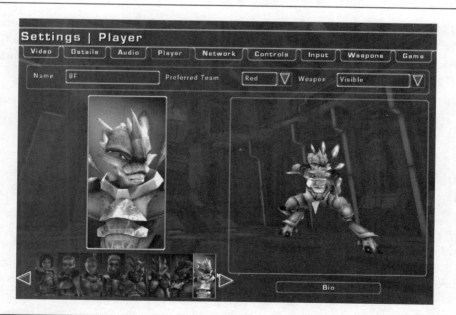

14

FIGURE 14-5 The characters in Unreal Tournament range from heavily clad humans to alien beings.

 *You'll often see several different versions of a game series. For example, since the original Unreal Tournament was released in 1999, Unreal Tournaments 2003 and 2004 have subsequently become available. New versions can vary significantly from their predecessors, so be sure to read reviews of each version before buying to ensure you're getting the features you want.*

Real-Time Strategy

Real-time strategy games are similar to the Internet games in Windows XP that we just discussed. You play these games against one or more opponents that you meet on the Web, or friends who are on your network. Unlike first-person shooters, you can't just pause your game and expect to resume it at the same point later. While you've been away, the other opponents in the game may have continued playing. So you can reenter a gaming world that looks quite different from the one you left. The subject matter of real-time strategy games often deals with *Iliad*-and-*Odyssey*-style mythology. The current rage in real-time strategy games revolves around a few key titles.

Warcraft III: Frozen Throne   Warcraft III: Frozen Throne involves orcs, night elves, and humans, among others. The goal of the story is to wrest the world's forests from the clutches of corrupt forest creatures. This version continues the saga of the original Warcraft that was released in the late 1990s.

Age of Mythology   Age of Mythology pits cavalry, archers, minotaurs, trolls, and additional characters, like the ones in Figure 14-6, against each other. The action takes place in your choice of either the ancient Greek, Egyptian, or Norse civilizations.

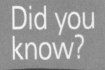

The Sims Lets You Manipulate Minds

OK, so I stretched the truth a little in the title to this box. The Sims may not let you control the thoughts of the average person walking down the street, but it does allow you to manipulate the minds of its virtual characters. The name of this incredibly popular game, which defies classification in one of the three main genres, is short for *simulation*—and that's just what it's about. You create simulated people from the ground up, choosing everything from their personality types to their jobs. Then you tell them what to do, whether it be talk to other characters, buy stuff, cook meals, or perform other activities. Your sims then grow and change based on their actions.

FIGURE 14-6   Ancient civilizations and mythical characters set the stage for Age of Mythology.

Role-Playing Games

If you see a game described as an *RPG,* you know it's a role-playing game. Titles in this genre involve the creation and evolution of specific characters that partake in storylines. As the characters progress through the story, they generally become stronger and faster, gaining enhanced abilities such as the power to cast spells. Ever played Dungeons & Dragons? RPGs are like D&D, only on the computer. There are two types of RPGs: regular RPGs, in which you play against your computer, and multiplayer RPGs, where you play online with other people. RPG fans are currently buzzing about the following games.

Star Wars: Knights of the Old Republic   Star Wars: Knights of the Old Republic starts out hundreds of years before Episode I. It includes several characters, such as the one in Figure 14-7, whom you may recognize from one of the films. Your job throughout the game is to strategize and fight your way through conflicts with opponents. You have various weapons and even Jedi powers at your disposal.

14

FIGURE 14-7   Yoda, Jabba the Hut, and other characters from the *Star Wars* series appear in the RPG Star Wars: Knights of the Old Republic.

EverQuest   EverQuest is another RPG that takes place in a fantasy world containing the usual suspects: monsters, elves, dwarves…you get the picture. Again, the task in front of you is to transcend a host of obstacles in order to advance to the next level in the story.

That about wraps up the discussion we started in Chapter 3 detailing all of the different things you can do with your VAIO PC or notebook. Although I'm hoping you didn't, chances are you ran into a few malfunctions along the way. The last two chapters of this book will help you figure out how to deal with those problems and keep your VAIO running smoothly.

Part IV

Upgrading, Maintaining, and Troubleshooting Your VAIO

Chapter 15

Upgrading and Maintaining Your VAIO

How to...

- Determine what kind of warranty you need

- Beware of Sony's warranty limitations

- Keep your hardware fit

- Clean your computer, screen, and mouse

- Clean up a disk

- Defragment your hard drive

Whether you're new to computers or an old hand, you're going to run into some problems now and again. Computers just aren't as smart as we'd like them to be, and you should be prepared for some frustrating experiences. You should also know how to keep your hardware clean.

What you'll find in this chapter is a backgrounder on computer warranties, including general terms and Sony's many warranty options and limitations. I also give you a primer on how to keep the dust out of your machine, the gunk off your screen, and your hard drive in top shape.

Determine What Kind of Warranty You Need

Because I'm a technology journalist at a popular online site, CNET.com, people are always e-mailing me questions, ranging from "What's the meaning of life?" to the almost-as-vexing "Should I get the extended warranty?" And, of course, there's the eternal "Why the hell haven't you covered (insert obscure notebook here)!" Regarding the warranty conundrum, there are as many opinions as there are coverage plans and warranty-extension options. Some consumer groups say that an extended warranty is not cost-effective. They argue that if your VAIO works in the first hour after you set it up—and this is especially true with VAIO PCs—that the computer will probably work for years to come (very few moving parts reside in your PC to wear out, unlike a car). Plus, some extended-warranty plans from tiny, practically unknown companies seem like a rip-off.

Ask Yourself These Warranty Questions

As for me, I see more gray areas in the warranty wars. Before I answer the extended-warranty question, I always ask the reader a couple of questions, starting with: How will you use your VAIO? If your system sits on the desk in your office, never moves, has only one or two users, is used for basic tasks like office work, e-mailing, and Web surfing, and you don't pound on it for eight hours (or more) a day, you might be able to get by with one year. But if you constantly subject your VAIO notebook to the rigors of the road, bang it around in your backpack or briefcase, drink coffee over it in a Monday morning haze, take it to meetings, load tons of software, or plan to burn CDs or DVDs, then I recommend you get an extended warranty, if possible.

There are other factors to consider as well. Whether to get an extended warranty also depends on how tech savvy you are. In general, the more experienced you are, the less important a long warranty is. You may not need to pay extra for an extended warranty unless you know *nothing* about computers or you bought an extremely expensive system and you don't want to void your warranty by monkeying with it yourself.

Finally, when I answer the extended-warranty question, I always mix in a little personal experience. Just about every notebook I've used for more than a year or two develops some sort of problem with either the hardware or software. I can usually fix it, or sometimes the tech whizzes in CNET Labs in San Francisco are summoned for triage. But sometimes we can't work magic, and it must go back to the company or to an authorized repair center. My rule of thumb? Just about 100 percent of all heavily used notebooks will have problems at some point.

Warranty Basics

Here are some terms to remember when buying your warranty. These terms apply whether you're buying Sony's standard one-year warranty, Sony's three-year warranty that you can upgrade to with most VAIOs for about $200, or a plan from another company.

- **Warranty** A warranty is a company's guarantee that the product you've bought is in working order and doesn't have any known problems. It also guarantees that the maker of the product will repair or replace defective parts, without charge, within a specified time. Often, a vendor will attach some conditions to this policy to protect against paying to repair a defect that you, the user, have inflicted.

- **Unlimited warranty** An unlimited warranty guarantees free replacement or repair of *any* defective parts, usually within a specified period of time (such as one, two, or three years or, possibly, the lifetime of the product).

- **Limited warranty**   A limited warranty replaces only some, not all, defective parts within a specific period of time. Parts that are subject to free repair should be spelled out in a warranty agreement, which should be available on a vendor's web site.

> **NOTE**   *Limited warranties may also restrict repairs, depending on how the damage was caused.*

- **Customer support**   Service that computer and software manufacturers, and third-party service companies, offer to customers, either on the phone or in person.

- **Mail-in or return-to-depot service**   The manufacturer will repair your equipment if you mail it in. Typical turnaround time is about four business days. In some service plans, the manufacturer charges you for shipping expenses.

- **Carry-in service**   The manufacturer will repair your equipment, but you must deliver it to a local service site. This is sometimes called *depot service.*

- **Onsite service**   A repair person will come to your site to fix problems. Most onsite contracts guarantee that the service will be rendered within a fixed number of hours from when you report a problem.

- **Hotlines**   Many software manufacturers provide a phone number you can call for advice and trouble-shooting. Often, the number is toll-free. The quality of this type of support varies considerably from one company to another, but the best phone support plans let you call in 24/7.

- **Bulletin board system**   Some companies maintain electronic bulletin boards, also called forums, staffed by service engineers. If you can get online, you can report a problem to the bulletin board and a technician will respond. This can be convenient because bulletin boards are usually open 24 hours a day. Also, bulletin boards enable you to download software updates that correct known bugs.

> **TIP**   *Customer support is also called* technical support.

Beware Sony's Warranty Limitations

There are some limitations to Sony's warranty coverage that you should know about. Most parts of Sony's technical support are strong, including manuals, standard warranties, extended warranties, online support, software downloads, online tutorials, and an online service locator (to help you find a local repair center). However, you should be aware of the following limitations:

- Onsite service is not provided as a standard condition of the limited warranty for any VAIO. However, onsite service is provided, at Sony's discretion, on certain VAIO desktops. Additionally, you can upgrade to onsite service through some of Sony's extended warranties. Keep in mind that if you can't get onsite service, you must either carry the product into an authorized repair shop, pay to ship the product to the nearest facility for service, or call in a repairman that you pay for.

- Sony technical support via the phone is available for free, 24/7 for the life of the warranty, after which you'll pay $19.95 per service incident.

- If you buy your VAIO notebook online at www.sonystyle.com, there's a chance you'll only get a one-year limited warranty, with no three-year option. Why? It's complicated, but the gist is that Sony only offers warranty extensions when doing online purchasing of *configure-to-order* (CTO) models. However, Sony offers a range of point-of-sale extended warranty options for all VAIOs when purchased via the phone, and Sony is planning to add more warranty expansion options when buying online. In addition, Sony offers a full range of aftermarket extended warranty options as well on all VAIOs. You can also consider an extended warranty from a brick-and-mortar retailer like Best Buy. (See the Did you know? sidebar, "Third-Party Warranties," later in this chapter.)

NOTE   *Companies like Sony occasionally change their warranties. They adjust what they cover, change prices, or change the length of service. So keep in mind that the warranty information in this chapter might change soon, or Sony may have made adjustments before this book even hits the shelves.*

15

Keep Your Hardware Fit

You want to avoid sending your VAIO to the shop for repairs, right? Then follow your mother's advice and keep it clean, both on the inside and out. Most VAIOs have fans, which, in addition to keeping your system cool, also suck in dust from your room and deposit it on the sensitive electrical components inside your computer. Plus, the static electricity that builds up in the monitor, printer, and other devices is like a dust magnet, gathering all those tiny particles that the system unit misses.

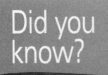

Third-Party Warranties

As I mentioned, you may get a limited warranty with your VAIO when buying online, so explore your options. If you buy the notebook at a retail store, like Best Buy, Fry's, or CompUSA, those stores may offer their own extended warranties, separate from what Sony offers. The terms and costs vary, as well as what the stores cover, so carefully go over the third-party warranty before you buy it.

If you don't clean this dust and gunk from your computer regularly, it builds up and can cause problems. Your mouse pointer might skip around on the screen, you might get disk errors, or you might have problems with other parts of your system. In this section, you'll learn how to keep your computer clean.

Cleaning Products

Before you start cleaning, turn off your computer and any attached devices, and round up the cleaning products you need. You could always buy a special toolkit designed specifically for maintaining computers, but you would end up spending more than necessary. The following list helps you assemble your own computer cleaning toolkit using items found in your home, or at the local computer store:

- **Computer vacuum**   Yes, there are vacuum cleaners especially designed for computers.

- **Screwdriver for taking the cover off your system**   If you don't feel comfortable taking off your PC's cover, take the system to a qualified technician for an annual cleaning.

- **Can of compressed air**   You can get this at computer or electronic stores.

- **Rubbing alcohol**   For cleaning your screen and other surfaces.

- **Soft brush**   A clean paintbrush with soft bristles will work. Use the brush to loosen any dirt that the vacuum won't pick up.

- **Toothpicks**   For mouse cleaning.

- **Q-Tips and cotton swabs**   Essential for swabbing dust and gunk out of tight places.

- **Paper towels and clean rags**   To wipe the smudges off your monitor and elsewhere.

- **Distilled water**   You can buy special wipes for your monitor, but paper towels and water will do the trick just as well. Or use rubbing alcohol and cotton swabs for the tough jobs.

Vacuum and Dust Your VAIO

Work from the top down and from the outside in. Start with your PC's monitor or the display on your notebook. Vacuum your printers, speakers, and other devices. If the dust is stuck to a device, wipe it off with a damp (not soaking wet) paper towel.

Make sure you vacuum all the ventilation holes, including the CD-ROM drive, power button, open drive bays, and so on. Vacuum the open CD-ROM tray very gently. If you have a VAIO PC and want to dust the inside of the case, be aware of the following precautions:

- Use only a vacuum designed for computers or use a can of compressed air to blow out the dust. Use short bursts to avoid condensation. Don't use a Dust Buster or your regular vacuum. These can suck components off of your circuit boards and emit enough static electricity to fry a component. A computer vacuum is grounded and gentler on components.

- Touch a metal part of the case to discharge any static electricity from your body, and keep your finger away from the circuit boards, cables, and any other objects inside the case.

Take the cover off the system unit and vacuum any dusty areas. Dust tends to gather around the fan, ventilation holes, and disk drives. Try to vacuum the fan blades, but if you can't, gently wipe them with a Q-Tip. Some fans have a filter where the fan is mounted. If you're really tech savvy, remove the fan and clean the filter.

15

Clean Your Screen

Screen cleaning is near and dear to my heart. Several years ago, my son, Paul, scribbled on my notebook's display with a big black felt tip pen. After consulting a couple experts, I cleaned it with a combination of rubbing alcohol, regular alcohol (for me), and cotton balls. It worked like a charm. Paul and I were on speaking terms again in a couple hours.

 *Don't try to clean the inside of a conventional monitor (CRT) unless you are an experienced technician. The picture tube retains a high voltage even after the power is shut off.*

But before you start swabbing your grimy screen, check the documentation to see if using window cleaner or rubbing alcohol is OK; the screen might have an antiglare coating that can be damaged by alcohol. If it's not OK, use the distilled water. If you can use window cleaner, spray it on the rag or paper towel, not on the screen—you don't want moisture to seep in. Wipe gently.

Rescue a Drowning Keyboard

Have you looked at your keyboard lately? Chances are that dirt, dust, and grime have been building up for quite some time. If you eat lunch or snack while you work, the situation is even worse. Before you decide to buy a new keyboard or quarantine your desk, clean your keyboard. The easiest way to get the major crumbs out is to turn it upside down and shake it gently. Repeat two or three times to get any particles that fall behind the backs of the keys when you flip it over. If you don't like that idea, get your can of compressed air and blow between the keys.

NOTE *Rubbing alcohol can be a great cleaning solution for most electronic devices because it cleans well and dries fast. Use it for your keyboard, plastics, and most glass surfaces (excluding some monitors).*

If you've just dumped coffee on your keyboard, a more thorough cleaning is obviously in the offing. Here's what to do:

1. Before you clean your keyboard, turn your computer off. Next, write down the locations of the keys (or take a digital photo or a Polaroid shot if you still have one of those cameras) so you can put them back in the right places.

2. Use a thin screwdriver or small knife to gently pry up the keycaps. Don't try to remove the spacebar, SHIFT key, ENTER key, or any other oversize keys. They can be difficult to put back in place.

3. If liquid is present, sop it up with a paper towel. Use compressed air to remove dust, crumbs, paper clips, and other loose materials. If you find built-up muck and mire, use a mild household cleaner on a cotton swab to clean it up.

Did you know?

The Best Mouse-Cleaning Tip

Get rid of your old mechanical mouse and its grunge-catching little ball. Buy an optical mouse. As long as your desk isn't made of glass or is a mirror, the tiny CMOS sensor in the base of the mouse picks up reflected light from a built-in LED light. The mouse glides. If you have it on the right surface, it pretty much never stops, jerks, stutters, or annoys you like a mechanical mouse. (Make sure though that you keep your desk surface or mouse pad clean. A piece of lint or hair can cause your pointer to skip.) An optical mouse won't drain your wallet, either, with some models under $20.

4. Gently but firmly press each keycap back in place, following the layout in your drawing or picture.

5. If some of the keys are still sticky, clean around them with a cotton swab dipped in rubbing alcohol.

Clean Your Mouse

Standard mechanical mice (as opposed to optical or wireless mice) almost always need cleaning. You can tell when they start working very slowly or just quit altogether. The easiest way to clean a mechanical mouse is to remove the mouse ball to get at the X and Y rollers. You do that by flipping the critter over and pushing the small cover around in a circle with your thumbs. With the cover off, turn the mouse over and plop the rubber ball into your free hand.

A careful inspection of the small rollers usually reveals stuck-on gunk. This stuff can be removed using a toothpick (or your fingernail) to help free the particles, and a Q-Tip dampened with rubbing alcohol. The ball can also be cleaned with a damp rag. Don't use rubbing alcohol on the ball, because it can dry out the rubber and make it brittle.

Clean Up a Disk

Maintaining your VAIO doesn't stop at keeping it clean and shiny. Over time, your hard disk will accumulate temporary files, stale components, recycled junk, and space-wasters that you should remove. Use Disk Cleanup to reclaim disk space

15

if you're running out of room. To remove unneeded files with Disk Cleanup, follow these steps:

1. Choose Start | All Programs | Accessories | System Tools | Disk Cleanup, and then select a drive (if you have more than one). Click OK.

2. Alternatively, right-click a drive icon in My Computer, and then choose Properties | General Tab | Disk Cleanup.

3. Or, for those comfortable using the Run command, choose Start | Run, type **cleanmgr,** press ENTER, select a drive, and then click OK.

4. A window briefly appears (or it might be there for a couple minutes) telling you that "Disk Cleanup is calculating how much space you will be able to free on (C:). This may take a few minutes to complete." (See Figure 15-1.)

5. That small window closes and is replaced by the Disk Cleanup dialog box. Check the boxes of the files that you want to delete (Figure 15-2). The right column shows how much space you can make available. The text below the list box describes the selection options.

6. The More Options tab contains three other cleanup tools that let you remove optional Windows components, and all but your most recent System Restore restore points. (See Chapter 16 for an explanation of the handy System Restore feature.)

7. Avoid deleting Downloaded Program Files, which are often useful add-ins.

8. When you're done with the Files To Delete list, click OK.

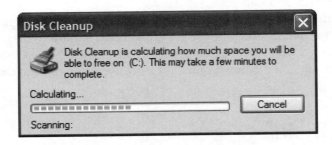

FIGURE 15-1 This small window appears as the Disk Cleanup utility starts to work.

FIGURE 15-2 Disk Cleanup searches your hard drive and then shows you temporary files, Internet cache files, and unnecessary program files that you can delete safely.

NOTE *The Temporary Files option in the Disk Cleanup dialog box deletes only temporary files more than a week old, so the right column may show 0KB even if your temporary folder contains many files. To clean out this folder manually, close all windows and programs, choose Start | Run, type %temp%, and press ENTER. Then, delete the files in the folder window that appears.*

Defragment Your Drive

When a file grows, it won't fit back into its original hard disk location, which means that bits and pieces of each file are scattered throughout the disk. This doesn't prevent Windows from accessing the data, but it can slow down access as your disk drive's read-write heads have to jump all over the disk to reassemble the data. Disk Defragmenter consolidates fragmented files, making both files and free space contiguous. Large blocks of available space make it less likely that new files will be fragmented. This is a great program to run once a month or so, but it takes a while to defrag a disk, so it's best to use it when you're about to take a break.

15

Did you know?

Don't Let Your Hard Drive Fill Up

It's a good idea to make sure your hard drive does not fill up. Every once in a while, take a run through your files and delete all unnecessary files and folders. Empty your Recycle Bin frequently. To check how full your hard drive is, double-click the My Computer icon, either from your Windows desktop or from the Start menu. Right-click the icon for your hard drive (usually C or D) and select Properties. To safely and thoroughly remove old applications that you never run any more, use the Add/Remove Programs feature. (See Chapter 3 for tips on removing programs.) If you still can't keep your hard drive from filling up, consider asking your service shop to install an additional hard drive, hook up an external hard drive, or replace the one you have with a bigger drive. Some notebooks let you put a second hard drive into the swappable media bay on the side.

NOTE　*Don't defragment your hard drive unless you have your computer attached to a reliable power source. If you are defragging and the power goes out, there is a slight risk that you may lose the file that was being relocated at the time of the power outage.*

When you're ready to defrag your disk, here's what you do.

1. Exit all programs. Choose Start | All Programs | Accessories | System Tools | Disk Defragmenter

2. Click a drive to defragment.

3. Click Analyze. The program analyzes the disk and makes a recommendation (Figure 15-3).

4. Click View Report to get details on the amount of fragmentation on your disk, along with a bunch of other information (see Figure 15-4).

5. Click Defragment to start defragmentation (see Figure 15-5). Colored graphs and the status bar display the defrag process.

6. When defragmentation completes, click close in the dialog box that appears.

7. Choose File | Exit, or defrag other disks as necessary.

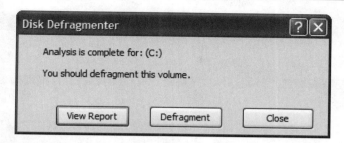

FIGURE 15-3 Defragging can take a long time. Don't bother for drives that are only slightly fragmented.

So, how often should you defragment your drives? The rule of thumb is based on how often you use your VAIO. If you're a typical home user, you should run the Disk Defragmenter utility about once every two to three months. If you use your PC every day, all day, and you use lots of program and files, you should defrag your drives once a month. Doing this will help keep your file system in peak operating condition.

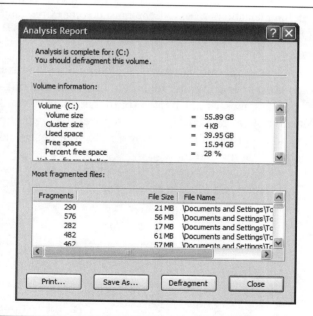

15

FIGURE 15-4 When you click View Report on the previous Disk Defragmenter window, you see a list of fragmented files and the number of pieces they're in.

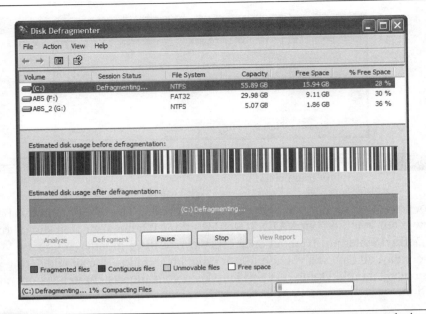

FIGURE 15-5 For best results, don't do anything else on your computer during the defragmentation process. If you must do other work on the system, click Pause.

Now that you've learned about warranties, including Sony's warranty limitations, and learned how to keep your computer clean on the inside and out, it's time to go over the troubleshooting checklist in Chapter 16. In that chapter, you'll learn the sad story of data loss and how to prevent it, how to recover files, what to do when your VAIO is stuck, how to restore your system, how to use your emergency startup disk, how to get in touch with Sony, and more.

Chapter 16

Troubleshooting Checklist

How to...

- Understand your backup options
- Save your work in several places
- What to do when your VAIO is stuck
- Fix a stuck program
- Enter Safe Mode
- Use System Restore
- Reach out for help

Sooner or later, most of us experience the dreaded *hard-drive crash* or other problems that cause the loss of some data or even the loss of the ability to start Windows. If it hasn't happened to you, then you've probably heard some of these sad "my dog ate my homework" types of crash stories. This is true even with Windows XP Home or Pro, two of the more stable Windows products ever. Backing up your VAIO is a necessity if you want to recover from such a problem without tearing your hair out. Backups also protect you against accidental deletions and let you archive data on remote storage devices.

This chapter introduces the major forms of backup available for your VAIO. I've also provided some tips on which type of backup to use when, some steps to take to protect yourself from disaster when and if it strikes your system, and how to reach out for technical help. I hope you're never forced to rely on your backups to recover from a disaster but, in case you do, the information in this chapter should maximize your chances of recovering without too much hassle.

Understand Your VAIO's Backup Options

When it comes to backing up your VAIO, you have two main options: regular backups and system restores. Regular backups are what you probably think of when you consider backing up your data. They involve creating copies of your personal data, pictures, movies, files, and so on, and then storing that data somewhere other than your hard drive so you can retrieve the stuff later.

> **TIP** *The first rule for protecting your work is to use Save frequently. Hitting CTRL-S is my favorite way of saving a file I've been working on. For more information on how and where to save a file, see Chapter 3.*

System restores, on the other hand, take a snapshot of the system files and settings on a regular basis from time to time (you can set the schedule if you want, but the standard setting is fine). When you run System Restore, it turns back the clock, in effect, to a configuration that was working properly. The rest of this chapter explains the differences in backup methods, and shows you how and when to use them.

Use Backup to Protect Your Data

Windows XP's Backup program lets you back up an entire hard disk or specific files and folders periodically. There are numerous places to save a copy of your data, including a second hard drive, a shared network folder, a storage device like an external USB hard drive or *keychain drive,* a blank CD or DVD, a Zip drive, a floppy drive, or even a big *tape drive* system used mostly in corporations. Remember that the copies of your data need to be on a device other than your hard drive. Also, never back up to a different partition on the same physical hard drive, because if the drive fails, all partitions go with it. (See Chapter 10 for more on hard drive partitions.) The Backup Or Restore Wizard walks you through the process of backing up your files or restoring backed-up files when disaster strikes.

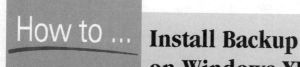

How to ... Install Backup on Windows XP Home Edition

The Backup feature is installed by default on Windows XP Pro edition computers but not on XP Home edition systems. To install Backup on a Home edition computer, follow these steps:

1. Insert the Windows XP Home CD.

2. When the Welcome screen appears, click Exit.

3. Choose Start | My Computer.

4. In the My Computer Window, right-click the CD drive icon, and then choose Explorer.

5. In the Explorer window, navigate to the folder \VALUEADD\NTBACKUP, and then double-click NTBACKUP.MSI.

6. Click Finish when the wizard completes the installation.

If you store your files on a network server at work, you shouldn't have to back up your work, in theory. Your network administrator does it for you. But if you're worried about the state of your network servers, or the quality of your Information Technology staff, then continue to make backups on your own.

As its name implies, the Backup Or Restore Wizard (shown in Figure 16-1) can either back up files and settings, or restore them. When using the wizard to back up your hard disk, you have the option to back up just your own documents and settings, the documents and settings of everyone who uses the computer, all the information on the computer, or the specific items you choose. To back up files:

1. Exit all programs (because Backup can't back up open files).

2. Choose Start | All Programs | Accessories | System Tools | Backup. The Backup Or Restore Wizard starts. (If you have Windows XP Home, read the Did You Know? box titled "Install Backup on Windows XP Home Edition.")

3. Click Next to skip the Welcome page.

4. Select Back Up Files And Settings, and then click Next.

5. Specify the items to back up, and then click Next.

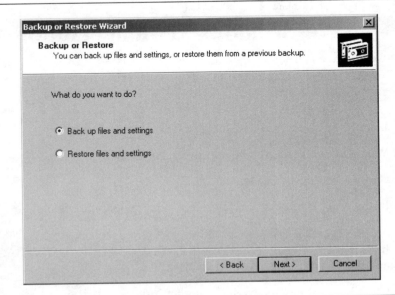

FIGURE 16-1   The Backup Or Restore Wizard's opening window

6. Specify a location and name for the backup, and then click Next. Unless you have an XP-compatible tape drive, the only Backup Type option is File.

7. Click Finish to begin the backup immediately, or click Advanced to choose the additional options.

8. Work your way through the rest of the wizard, selecting the desired options (described in each window).

9. On the last page, review your settings, and then click Finish to start the backup. The process takes minutes or hours, depending on its size and type.

10. Click Close in the Backup Progress dialog box when the backup completes. Backup creates a .bkf file, using the name and location you chose in step 6.

Backups can take some time, so while it's in progress, Windows displays the Backup Progress dialog box. Along with vital information like the name of the backup file it's working on, the dialog box also shows the estimated time remaining before the backup is complete. To restore information you've previously backed up, start the Backup Or Restore Wizard, tell it you want to restore data, and then let it help you select and restore the information.

TIP *If you really want to be thorough in your backup mission, take your home computer's backup files with you to work and bring your work's backup files home. If a disaster hits, such as a fire, you'll be able to restore your data because the backups will not be destroyed.*

Use a Program's Auto-Backup Features

Many software programs now have options you can set to automatically back up your files. To find out if a particular program supports this feature, read its manual or look through its Help file.

Microsoft Word is a great example. Figure 16-2 shows Word's Save options (choose Options from the Word Tools menu and click the Save tab to open this dialog box).

Of particular importance is the Save AutoRecovery Info Every__Minutes option. If you set this to 5, as in Figure 16-2, your work will be automatically saved every 5 minutes, even if you forget to do it. If Word or Windows crashes (appears frozen for an extended period of time) or some other problem crops up, you can just reboot and run Word again. The file should be opened automatically by Word, with the text "(recovered)" after the filename in the title bar. At that point, you need to make sure to save the file again, just like it's a new document.

16

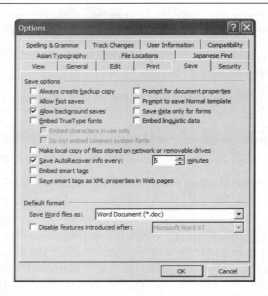

FIGURE 16-2 **FIGURE 16-2**   These are the auto-backup options in Microsoft Word.

Another important setting is Always Create Backup Copy. With this option turned on, when you open an existing document, a copy of it is made. For instance, if you're working on a file called Chapter 16, then the backup copy is called Backup of Chapter 16 and is stored in the same folder as the original. Each new backup replaces the previous backup. This way, if something happens to the original, you can go back to the previous version of it.

When Your VAIO Won't Shut Down and Other Woes

Some computers can have difficulty powering down under software control. Actually, they almost power down but just don't make it all the way. You'll end up staring at a screen that reminds you to wait until you're told it's OK to shut down, or a message that says Windows is shutting down, but that's it. Suppose that you've gone through the standard procedure to shut down (clicked Start, then Shut Down), and then waited and waited, but the PC doesn't shut down or show you the message telling you it's OK to turn off your computer now. In this case, you should just go ahead and turn it off, using the power switch. This might require pressing the power button for more than four seconds.

When Your VAIO Laptop Won't Reboot

When a laptop locks up, pressing CTRL-ALT-DEL sometimes won't restart it. It's even possible that holding down the power switch for four seconds won't shut it off, and banging it on the desk should be left to the professionals. The solution is to remove all sources of power.

1. Unplug the AC power supply.

2. Remove any removable batteries.

3. Wait a few seconds and reinsert the battery.

4. Plug in the AC power cord if the batteries are depleted.

5. Restart the computer.

Startup Problems

Whether it's because you've just installed a new software program or a new piece of hardware, or because of some damage to the operating system files or hard disk, your VAIO might not be able to start up. You try to start it and it just hangs. Here are some things to keep in mind:

- Because normal booting can take up to a minute or more, don't assume there's really a problem unless there is absolutely no activity on the screen. Sometimes, the only movement you'll see is in the little blue, cloud-like bar at the screen's bottom.

- Check that the power is connected, the monitor is on, the brightness isn't turned down, the monitor cable is secure, and that there's no floppy disk inserted in the floppy drive, if you have one. The computer could actually be booting, but if the monitor is off, you'll never know it.

- If the problem persists, press the reset switch or turn the computer off, wait a few seconds, and turn it on again. Let it try to boot a second time. Windows is pretty good at repairing itself. It notes when a bootup has been unsuccessful, and will try to boot one way or another. It may take some time, grinding away on the hard disk for a few minutes.

What can you do if your VAIO still won't start up? There's still hope. You can try Safe Mode and System Restore. If they don't work, you can use your emergency repair disk to start your computer.

When a Program Won't Run

If you try to run a software program using a shortcut icon, the icon might be pointing to the wrong program. Right-click the shortcut, choose Properties, and check the entry in the Target text box (see Figure 16-3). This displays the path to the program's folder followed by the name of the program file that launches it. If the text box is blank or points to the wrong file, click the Find Target button and use the resulting dialog box to change to the program's folder and choose the right program file.

If the application starts immediately and closes, you might not have sufficient memory or disk space on your VAIO. Right-click the My Computer icon (either on the Desktop or in the Start Menu) and click Properties. Click the Advanced tab, choose the Settings button under the Performance section, Advanced tab (see Figure 16-4). Check the amount of *Virtual Memory* you have. Make sure you have at least 30MB of free space on the disk that Windows is using for virtual memory. If you have any less, you have to clear some files from your hard disk.

If the program still won't run, try reinstalling it. If that doesn't work, contact the program manufacturer's tech support to determine the problem and the fix. The application might need special hardware or additional software that is not available on your computer.

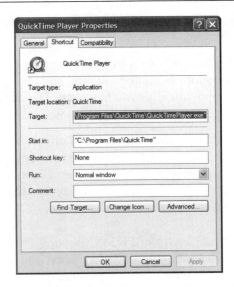

FIGURE 16-3   Showing a shortcut's path

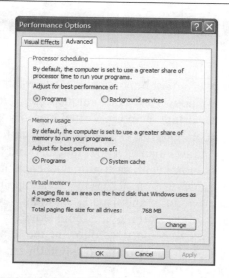

FIGURE 16-4   This window shows you how much virtual memory you have.

Is It Safe?

In certain cases—for instance, if you install a wrong device driver—Windows may start in Safe Mode. In this mode, the words Safe Mode are plastered on all four corners of the screen. It means that Windows has detected some system problems, but in most cases, you can simply restart Windows to have it load the previous driver. If on restarting, the Windows desktop is not visible or you can't use the mouse, restart your computer in Safe Mode by performing the following steps:

1. Click Start, Shut Down, choose Restart, and then click OK.

2. Tap the F8 key every two seconds as the computer boots up. This tells Windows to load a startup menu rather than loading the operating system. (You can try pressing once right when the computer beeps, but you'll have a better chance of bringing up the Startup menu by tapping the F8 key.)

3. Choose Safe Mode and press ENTER.

Windows loads a standard mouse and video drivers in Safe Mode, so you can see what you're doing and use the mouse to point and click. This allows you to install a different or updated driver or change settings back to what they were before you encountered problems. You can also use the System Restore feature to return your VAIO to a known good state, as described in the next section.

16

Did you know?

What Is Virtual Memory?

Running out of memory is almost impossible, despite whatever amount is in your VAIO. That's because Windows uses a technique to prevent memory from ever becoming full. It creates virtual memory. Virtual memory works to augment the physical RAM in your computer by swapping out big chunks of memory to the hard drive. Because Windows manages both memory and hard drive storage, it can keep track of things rather well, swapping data back and forth.

The only problem with virtual memory is that the swapping slows things down. Although it can happen quickly and usually without your noticing it, virtual memory takes over and things start moving more slowly.

You can adjust the virtual memory by following the steps listed in the "When a Program Won't Run" section, although you shouldn't attempt to monkey with this setting unless you're pretty tech savvy.

System Restore

If your VAIO stops running correctly or acts weird after you install something, you can run System Restore. This handy feature of XP returns your computer's configuration to its previous, workable state without harming personal documents, cookies, e-mail, and Favorites. System Restore protects only Windows system files and settings; use Backup (detailed earlier in this chapter) to protect your personal data files and documents. You also can't depend on System Restore to protect you from computer viruses. By the time you discover a virus, it may have spread to other files that System Restore doesn't reach, in which case rolling back to a previous configuration does you no good. Instead, use an antivirus program.

System Restore requires at least 200MB of free disk space. When a drive runs low on space, System Restore turns itself off automatically, losing all that drive's restore points. If you get a "low disk space" warning for a drive, check the drive's status to see whether it's listed as Suspended. System Restore turns itself back on when you free enough disk space.

System Restore runs invisibly in the background, monitoring and taking a snapshot of critical system files and Registry entries. When you run System Restore, you choose a time to revert the system to a *restore point* or *system checkpoint,* and System Restore does the rest. Then you reboot, and your VAIO should be fixed. You can also undo a restoration, in case it made things worse, or you can choose an earlier checkpoint in case the problem wasn't fixed.

You might consider creating your own restore point when you're about to make changes to your VAIO that are risky or might make your computer unstable. Start System Restore, as described in the next section, and choose Create A Restore Point.

Run System Restore

There's a lot of information about this powerful tool in the Windows XP Help file. Just open Help from the Start menu and do a search for System Restore. Click through the links and poke around all the options you have. If you'd rather just run the program, the wizard will walk you through the steps. Here's how:

1. Click Start | All Programs | Accessories | System Tools | System Restore. You'll see the first System Restore window, as shown in Figure 16-5.

2. To fix your VAIO, select Restore My Computer To An Earlier Time and click Next. Now you'll see the window for selecting your restore point.

3. Click a bold date in the calendar. The exact restore point times appear in a box to the right of the calendar, as shown in the example in Figure 16-6. Choose one to send the system back to.

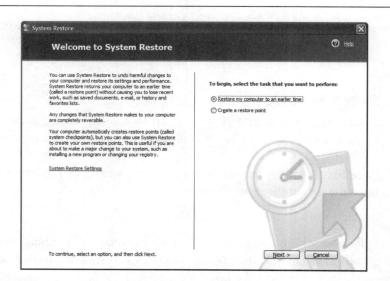

16

System Restore's opening window

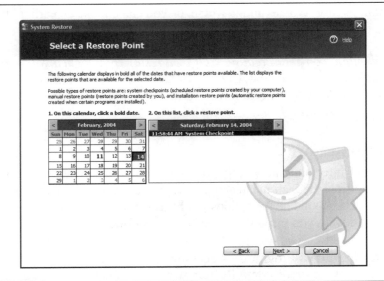

FIGURE 16-6   Choose a restore point on this window.

4. Click Next. System Restore will display a warning about closing files and programs. Make sure you've done what it says and then click Next.

5. Close your files and programs, and then click OK. The system restoration will take place. You'll be told what to do.

 System Restore deletes restore points older than 90 days automatically.

Undo a System Restore

You may find that returning to a previous state isn't what you wanted to do after all. If that happens, you can undo any successful restore by following these steps:

1. Choose Start | All Programs | Accessories | System Tools | System Restore to open the System Restore Window.

2. Click Undo My Last Restoration | Next.

3. You'll again be advised to save all work and close all applications before continuing. When you click Next, Windows will shut down for a while as System Restore undoes the last restoration.

Reach Out for Help

If you've tried and failed to solve a problem with your VAIO but just can't crack the code, it's time to dig a little deeper, either at the VAIO Support Center or on the Internet. And if that doesn't work, it's time to reach out for technical support. If that happens, try not to feel frustrated. Just about everyone who uses a computer needs technical support at some time.

VAIO Support Center

Before you call Sony's technical support line, first try to find the answer yourself. Check the manual. If you can't find the answer, dig around Sony's VAIO Support Center web sites for FAQs (frequently asked questions), online tutorials, online manuals, the knowledge base, downloadable drivers, and more. It's quite possible the answer you seek is already there.

Sony provides shortcuts to its VAIO Support Center. If you have the typical VAIO desktop, you have an icon on it that says Help And Support. Click that, and you get to a helpful screen (Figure 16-7) that lists numerous support options and shortcuts to useful programs, with headings like: "Connect to the VAIO Support Center for the latest software updates and FAQs," "Browse VAIO Software Tutorials for the most common support issues," "Get support, or find information in Windows XP newsgroups," and "Add/Remove Programs to customize your VAIO computer."

FIGURE 16-7   From your desktop, you can connect to Sony's helpful VAIO Support Center.

16

In addition to the Help And Support icon on your desktop, the default home page you'll see when you open your browser will likely be www.vaio.net. That site also offers support links and links to important updates.

Phone Support

If you can't fix your problem by scouring Sony's web sites, you may need to call Sony's technical support. (In the U.S., start with this number: 1-888-4SONYPC.) If you do call, keep in mind these tips:

- Only diehard Musak lovers like me enjoy being put on hold, so try calling tech support during slower periods. Support centers are generally busiest at the start of a business day and when users get home from work at 5 P.M. or so. Try making your call during off-peak hours.

- Be at the computer when you call tech support. The technician probably can't help you if you're on a cell phone miles from the troublesome VAIO.

- If your problem generated an error message, be ready to recite it chapter and verse to the technician and let him or her know what you were doing when it appeared. If possible, see if you can reproduce the problem before you call.

- Try not to call from the same phone line the computer uses to dial into the Internet, especially if the problem is related to your modem or Internet connection. The technician may also ask you to download a file while you're on the line so use a second line or cell phone if necessary.

- Don't budge until you've received a satisfactory answer. Don't be afraid to ask the technician to wait while you reboot your VAIO to test a fix. If you're not getting anywhere with a support technician, ask to speak to someone who knows more about your product or with your technician's supervisor.

- If your problem can't be solved quickly, you may end up talking to two or more technicians. Write down names, titles, and phone extensions of all the reps you talk to and jot notes about what happened during the call.

- Don't call when you're mad, and try to be polite. Your rep may be sitting in a cubicle answering call after call from frustrated users. A friendly tone will go a long way.

TIP *If your VAIO seems sluggish or you just want to find out if it's running at peak performance, have your system evaluated online. Several companies on the Internet have free utilities that can inspect your computer and recommend upgrades to boost performance. One of these evaluation sites is PC Pitstop, at www.pcpitstop.com.*

Alternate Tech Support Resources

There are plenty of reasons to look beyond Sony for technical help. You may have exceeded the free support period, you may be a fix-it type who likes to do it yourself, or you may need help to fix a software program you downloaded from the Internet. Luckily, there are plenty of other resources you can turn to.

VAIO Village Online Support Group

The VAIO Village online support group has a vibrant message board (at http://pub173. ezboard.com/bunofficialsony) and more than 6700 members at this writing, making it one of the best sources to find VAIO tech support tips and tricks. You can browse through the many subgroups and threads, or go through a quick and simple registration process if you want to post messages. If you have any problems using the message boards, contact Steve Alimonti (steve1a@hotmail.com). Steve has been involved with VAIO Village for years, after Sony's attempts at running and maintaining Club VAIO did not go smoothly. (See Steve's Voices from the Community sidebar in Chapter 3.)

Newsgroups

I covered the vast and dangerous territory of Newsgroups (also called Usenet) in Chapter 7. Among the many thousands of newsgroups are hundreds of groups devoted to fixing (or complaining about) just about every piece of hardware or software program you can think of. One of the best ways to drill down into newsgroups is to use Google's Advanced Groups Search (www.google.com/advanced_group_ search?hl=en). Once there, you can experiment with what search terms and what time periods work best in finding your answers. You can post a question in a newsgroup if you feel comfortable doing that, or just read "threads" of messages on your problem (most likely).

Google Answers

If you need more structure than a random Newsgroup search might get you, then Google's personalized answer service (www.answers.google.com/anwers) may help. You can ask the panel of experts about anything from computers to movies and all points in between. Computer categories include Hardware, Security, and Wireless and Mobile. When you pose a question via the online form, you specify what you're willing to pay for the answer (as little as $2.50). If a researcher can answer your question and thinks your price is fair, you'll get an e-mail notification. Many questions are answered in a couple of hours. You can also search past questions and answers.

16

Tech Support Guy

For free support, check out Tech Support Guy (www.techsupportguy.com). But it's not really just one guy: it's a gaggle of experts who can answer questions about computers, networking, applications, and more via the site's message boards.

Library or Bookstore

Computer books contain tons of help.

A Hired Gun

You can also hire a local computer technician. Look for one with a good track record and try to get a recommendation from someone you know. Find out how much he or she charges first, so you don't get stuck with a huge bill.

Index

INTERNATIONAL CONTACT INFORMATION

AUSTRALIA
McGraw-Hill Book Company
Australia Pty. Ltd.
TEL +61-2-9900-1800
FAX +61-2-9878-8881
http://www.mcgraw-hill.com.au
books-it_sydney@mcgraw-hill.com

CANADA
McGraw-Hill Ryerson Ltd.
TEL +905-430-5000
FAX +905-430-5020
http://www.mcgraw-hill.ca

GREECE, MIDDLE EAST, & AFRICA
(Excluding South Africa)
McGraw-Hill Hellas
TEL +30-210-6560-990
TEL +30-210-6560-993
TEL +30-210-6560-994
FAX +30-210-6545-525

MEXICO (Also serving Latin America)
McGraw-Hill Interamericana Editores
S.A. de C.V.
TEL +525-1500-5108
FAX +525-117-1589
http://www.mcgraw-hill.com.mx
carlos_ruiz@mcgraw-hill.com

SINGAPORE (Serving Asia)
McGraw-Hill Book Company
TEL +65-6863-1580
FAX +65-6862-3354
http://www.mcgraw-hill.com.sg
mghasia@mcgraw-hill.com

SOUTH AFRICA
McGraw-Hill South Africa
TEL +27-11-622-7512
FAX +27-11-622-9045
robyn_swanepoel@mcgraw-hill.com

SPAIN
McGraw-Hill/
Interamericana de España, S.A.U.
TEL +34-91-180-3000
FAX +34-91-372-8513
http://www.mcgraw-hill.es
professional@mcgraw-hill.es

UNITED KINGDOM, NORTHERN,
EASTERN, & CENTRAL EUROPE
McGraw-Hill Education Europe
TEL +44-1-628-502500
FAX +44-1-628-770224
http://www.mcgraw-hill.co.uk
emea_queries@mcgraw-hill.com

ALL OTHER INQUIRIES Contact:
McGraw-Hill/Osborne
TEL +1-510-420-7700
FAX +1-510-420-7703
http://www.osborne.com
omg_international@mcgraw-hill.com

Know How

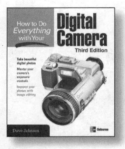

How to Do Everything with Your Digital Camera

Third Edition
ISBN: 0-07-223081-9

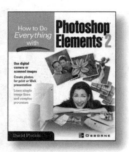

How to Do Everything with Photoshop Elements 2

ISBN: 0-07-222638-2

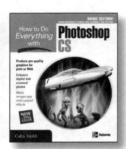

How to Do Everything with Photoshop CS

ISBN: 0-07-223143-2
4-color

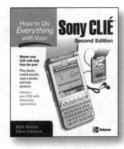

How to Do Everything with Your Sony CLIÉ

Second Edition
ISBN: 0-07-223074-6

How to Do Everything with Macromedia Contribute

0-07-222892-X

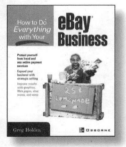

How to Do Everything with Your eBay Business

0-07-222948-9

How to Do Everything with Illustrator CS

ISBN: 0-07-223092-4
4-color

How to Do Everything with Your iPod

ISBN: 0-07-222700-1

How to Do Everything with Your iMac,

Third Edition
ISBN: 0-07-213172-1

How to Do Everything with Your iPAQ Pocket PC

Second Edition
ISBN: 0-07-222950-0